Emi shook her head. "Okay, then why don't you tell me what happened that day she left?"

"I don't know."

"You're the last person to see her. And I know you did something to her."

"You talk crazy. I love Ann."

"How can you say you love her, and then accuse her of those awful things you just said?"

"Well," John snorted, "you can love a person and still say the truth about them."

"You're sick," Emi hissed.

"When Ann comes back—"

Emi interrupted with an incredulous laugh. "You know that Ann can't come back. You killed her!"

Ignoring the dramatic indictment, John continued. "When Ann comes back and wants the kids, will you help me out?"

This sudden swerve from all logic or reality struck Emi like a scene from *Jerry Springer*. "You're crazy and you're sick. How can you sleep at night, knowing what you did?"

His face blank again, John replied, "I sleep good at night because I did nothing to Ann."

"Well, I have a terrible time sleeping," said Emi, "because worrying and thinking about Ann keeps me awake. How can you be so apathetic with your wife missing? Aren't you worried that something might have happened to her?"

"No. She's the one who left and she can come back at any time. It's up to her. She's the one who left."

"I think you are the one who got rid of her."

Also by Don Lasseter:

YOU'LL NEVER FIND MY BODY

DON LASSETER
WITH RONALD E. BOWERS

PINNACLE BOOKS
Kensington Publishing Corp.
http://www.kensingtonbooks.com

Some names have been changed to protect the privacy of individuals connected to this story.

364.1523
LAS

PINNACLE BOOKS are published by

Kensington Publishing Corp.
850 Third Avenue
New York, NY 10022

All Kensington Titles, Imprints, and Distributed Lines are available at special quantity discounts for bulk purchases for sales promotions, premiums, fund-raising, and educational or institutional use. Special book excerpts or customized printings can also be created to fit specific needs. For details, write or phone the office of the Kensington special sales manager: Kensington Publishing Corp., 850 Third Avenue, New York, NY 10022, attn: Special Sales Department, Phone: 1-800-221-2647.

Pinnacle and the P logo Reg. U.S. Pat. & TM Off.

ISBN-13: 978-0-7860-1928-1
ISBN-10: 0-7860-1928-X

First Printing: January 2009

10 9 8 7 6 5 4 3 2 1

Printed in the United States of America

FOREWORD

On a summer day in 2007, I listened all morning to defense testimony at the murder trial of John Racz while scribbling notes as fast as possible. The noon break came as a welcome relief. Even though searing August temperatures outside in San Fernando, California, broke the century mark, I chose to walk downtown, buy film, and snap some pictures of the courthouse.

What I had heard so far made me wonder if the prosecution had any chance at all of convicting Racz. No forensic evidence had been introduced; no witnesses to the alleged killing had testified; no fingerprints, fibers, DNA, or anything else traditionally expected had made an appearance. Remarkably, investigators had never even found the purported victim's body! Beth Silverman, the attractive deputy district attorney (DDA), and her assistant had relied primarily on what appeared to be inconsistent statements made by the defendant over a period of sixteen years since his wife had vanished.

They hadn't shown the jury any concrete proof of Ann Racz's death, much less that she had been murdered by her husband, an elegantly composed man with "movie star" good looks. His full, perfectly groomed silver-white hair, finely chiseled and tanned profile, six-two height, and proportioned body brought to mind a handsome middle-aged CEO or politician.

Upon reentering the courthouse through tight security, and wiping perspiration from my forehead, I stepped into one of three elevators. Two men shared it with me. I immediately recognized John Racz, in his light tan suit, and one of the investigators on his defense team.

Ordinarily, murder defendants are in tight custody during a trial, but John Racz had posted a million-dollar bail, which made him eligible to walk about freely and return each night to his upscale Valencia home in the foothills, about ten miles north of San Fernando. This former schoolteacher and twelve-year veteran of the Los Angeles County Sheriff's Department (LASD) certainly didn't fit any preconceived notion of what a cold-blooded killer might look like.

The private eye turned toward me and asked, "Excuse me, are you a doctor?"

"No," I replied, "but in this heat, I feel like I need one."

He apologized for asking, and explained that he expected the arrival of an expert witness, a professor of astronomy, and thought I might have been that person.

Pausing momentarily to consider my next words, I said, "No, I'm not the doctor, but I think I should tell you what I am doing here. My name is Don Lasseter, and I'm probably going to write a book about this case. Of course, I recognize you, John." I handed each of them one of my business cards. Racz asked about other books I had written, and I explained that most of my work focused on true crime. At that moment, the elevator opened to disgorge us on the third floor. We parted company in the hallway.

That afternoon, when Judge Ronald Coen announced a fifteen-minute break, I remained seated in the gallery, concentrating on my notebook. I felt something touch my shoulder. Startled, I turned to see who had made the contact, and felt a rush of surprise when Racz stood there, extending his right hand. Spontaneously I gripped it in a friendly handshake. It felt a bit strange. Over the years, I have attended numerous murder trials, and never had yet shaken hands with a defendant. Racz wore a pleasant expression, saying simply, "Good luck with the book." He smiled, then left the courtroom with one of his lawyers.

I realized that this story would be a sharp departure from many of my other books. And I wondered again just how jurors would handle the paucity of hard evidence. Would sympathy for this man play any role? Could anyone be convinced beyond a reasonable doubt that he had killed his wife—mother of their son and two daughters—even though her body had never been found?

As it turned out, this tale of deception, infidelity, betrayal, raw conflicts, and torn loyalties would lead me through avenues of jaw-dropping surprises and mind-rattling emotions.

It all began one sunny morning in 1991.

Some dates are charged with energy, power, drama, and death, making them spring from the calendar like a bolt of lightning.

One of those days is etched forever in an epic poem by Henry Wadsworth Longfellow. It states:

On the eighteenth of April, in Seventy-five;
Hardly a man is now alive
who remembers that famous day and year.

The poet makes certain, in "Paul Revere's Ride," that readers in subsequent generations would always remember how a little-known silversmith rode through every Middlesex village and farm to warn that the British were coming, and the American Revolution would begin.

On another April 18, in 1906, tragedy rattled California when a massive earthquake and fire destroyed most of San Francisco, taking approximately three thousand lives.

One of the most dramatic events of World War II occurred on April 18, 1942, when Lieutenant Colonel James "Jimmy" Doolittle led sixteen bombers, carrying eighty men, from the deck of an aircraft carrier to bomb the city of Tokyo, Japan. Nearly out of fuel, the warplanes headed for China, where all crashed except one, which made it to Russia. Three men died baling out or in the wreckage. Japanese soldiers captured eight of the downed airmen, executed three of them, and starved another one to death. Albert Einstein died on April 18 in 1955, and ten years earlier, famed WWII correspondent Ernie Pyle's life ended with the staccato rattle of Japanese machine-gun fire on a Pacific Island.

If that particular date has foreshadowed tragedy and death throughout the ages, it happened again.

On the eighteenth of April, in 1991, not far from a Southern California amusement park called Magic Mountain, a Hawaiian-born Japanese-American, Ann Racz, put into motion a plan that would light a fuse. It burned for sixteen years, and finally exploded in the late summer of 2007.

—Don Lasseter, 2008

CHAPTER 1

MOVING DAY

Ann Mineko Racz tiptoed into her daughter's room before dawn, careful to avoid making any sound. She sat near the sleeping girl's pillow and gently touched her shoulder. As soon as the fourteen-year-old stirred, yawned, and looked up, Ann held a shushing finger to her lips and whispered, "Today is the day. We are moving and you mustn't tell anyone where we are going, especially your dad."

Joann Racz frowned and rubbed the drowsiness from her soft brown eyes. She saw the fear in her mother's expression.

Trying to cover her trembling, Ann said, "He's already gone to work, and the moving truck will be here shortly. I didn't want to tell your brother or sister yet, because I don't want them to know about what's happening until later today. I'm scared to death that your father's going to hurt me." Almost as an afterthought, she added, "I will take all three of you to school, pick you up this afternoon, and take you to our new place."

Ann had given Joann some advance warning of her intentions

a month earlier with a brief mention of the unsettling plans, but at the time it didn't seem real to the teenager.

The first time Ann brought up the idea, in March, she had tried to make her daughter understand the reasoning for plans to move, but she hadn't been entirely convincing. Years later, Joann would recall it: "My mom had told me a couple of things beforehand that kind of made me feel like she was scared. She comes in my room that morning too, sits on the bed, and says . . . 'We're going to move soon,' and 'If you have anything important you want to keep with you, let me know what it is.' I kind of took it that maybe she was interested in what was important to me, like what would I grab if there was an emergency. Like a fire or something. I thought, 'Well, my blanket.' She had knitted a blanket for me, and I realized that if I had to take only one thing, it would be that. And then I realized she was concerned about something. 'We are moving. Don't tell anybody. Don't tell your friends, don't talk about it with Glenn and Kate. Don't tell Dad, and don't tell your teacher. Nobody.' And I kept that secret. I didn't feel like it was a life-and-death situation at that time. I just wasn't able to see all that adult stuff going on, you know.

"I just thought, 'Oh, it's adults fighting, like getting slapped across the face. Pushed against the wall or something.' That's the extent I thought she meant. Her telling me that is still one hundred percent clear in my mind and I never forgot it. And I never really looked down on my dad, like he would hurt my mom. I didn't take it seriously. I understand that she may have meant that my dad said he was going to kill her if she leaves. So, in April, she said that 'Today's the day, we are leaving, we'll get your blanket and some other things. I'll pick you up from school, and we'll go over to the new place.' She didn't tell me more, or give me a schedule. It was like we've had an important talk and that's it. I did not tell anybody."

Even though the anxious forty-two-year-old mother instructed Joann not to reveal the plans to anyone, several of

Ann's intimate friends knew of the impending breakup. They knew of Ann's fear, dissatisfaction with the nineteen-year marriage, her husband's demanding sexual habits, and his odd parsimony. Some of her close confidantes even knew of the "other" man in whom Ann saw a soul mate.

Earlier on that Thursday morning, April 18, 1991, John Racz left the house in Valencia for his predawn journey to Compton, more than forty miles away, where he taught elementary school. To wait until sunrise would add at least an hour to the journey through jerk-and-go traffic along five jammed freeways. It was easier to navigate through darkness, following an endless red stream of taillights flowing against the oncoming torrent of bright headlights.

The early-morning departure by Ann's husband created a perfect window of opportunity for moving out of their home on that day. The timing, she prayed, would allow her to avoid his wrath. First she had to take Joann, Glenn, age eleven, and Katelin, age seven, to school.

Escorting the kids into their respective classes, Ann stopped for a brief conference with each teacher to advise them that her children would have a new address. This completed, she returned home and stopped next to a white moving van parked down the block. She glanced at her watch, noted that it was eight-twenty, and apologized for being late.

Both men in the cab had been informed the previous day to wait for Ann's signal before pulling into the driveway of an upscale two-story home near the end of a cul-de-sac on Fortuna Drive. Then, according to their instructions, they needed to perform their task as rapidly as possible. The company owner would later explain, "We was told, when we got there, we just had to move the things that she wanted moved as fast as possible and get out of there. . . . Mrs. Racz, she was very afraid of her spouse coming back while we was moving her out and she didn't want any problems."

The movers followed as she led them through the spacious

house, pointing out the exact items to be loaded. Uneasy about the circumstances, and observing a photo depicting a man wearing the uniform of a deputy sheriff, one of the men asked, "Are you separating or divorcing?"

Ann replied, "We are separating."

"Does your husband know about it?"

"Yes," she answered, "but he doesn't know when." After a slight pause, she added, "I don't want to sound like a bitch, but please get it loaded and get out of here. I need to be out as soon as possible."

Her advance arrangements made it easy for the workers. According to one of Ann's good friends, she carefully planned every detail of the move in advance and made meticulous preparations. Beginning as early as August 1990, Ann surreptitiously placed everything she planned to take with her in the rear of closets and cupboards. These gradual rearrangements of clothing, foodstuffs, cookware, and other essentials would prevent her husband from noticing, and would allow her to grab them quickly for packing on the big day. She acquired boxes and baskets in advance, and stored them out of John Racz's sight, to allow for rapid loading and packing. The majority of items marked for removal were for the children, including clothing, toys, books, a computer, and three mattresses. While the driver and his helper rushed to load the truck, they observed obvious manifestations of Ann's fear. Each time she heard the sound of a vehicle or a car door slamming, she jumped and ran to a window to look outside.

The loading process, including boxes Ann piled into her 1989 white Plymouth Vista minivan, took only about ninety minutes. The truck driver followed Ann's car downhill along the short curve of Fortuna Drive, through a couple of turns, east on Lyons Avenue, and a right turn onto Peachland Avenue. After a trip of less than two miles, they pulled into a sprawling condominium complex, identified by a large sign as Peachland, where Ann had leased a two-bedroom unit. It took about an hour to unload everything. To the movers, Ann appeared visibly relieved and much more relaxed.

Ann paid the men in cash. As part of her meticulous plans to keep any hint of her intentions from John, she had waited until their income tax refund arrived in the mail. After endorsing the check with both of their names, she cashed it and had the money in her purse for payment to the movers. As they departed, she walked across the street to a public telephone located in a medical building. She had chosen not to have a telephone installed in her new residence, fearing that her husband could trace it and discover the address.

A few days earlier, Ann had requested help from two women she trusted unequivocally. One was her niece Katherine "Kathy" Ryan, the daughter of her older sister. The other was a longtime confidante she regarded as her closest friend, Dee Ann Wood.

Kathy had lived with Ann and John for three months in 1988. Their relationship transcended the usual aunt-niece filiation, despite a fourteen-year age gap between them. They talked either in person or by telephone at least weekly and often attended movies together. Ann confided details of her unhappiness to Kathy, allowing the niece an intimate understanding of the fractured marriage. Several aspects of John's behavior bothered Kathy. Among the characteristics she personally observed, or heard about from Ann, Kathy especially deplored his tightfisted control of the family purse strings. Frugality was one thing, she thought, but John's methods were exceptional. She hated the idea that he ordered Ann and the kids not to flush toilets every time they used the bathroom in order to reduce the water bill. And she thought it miserly that he would bundle all of the family trash, toss it in his car, and transport it to bins at supermarkets or behind strip malls to avoid paying for disposal services. Sometimes, Kathy later recalled, John hauled bags of garbage over to the Peachland condominiums and tossed them into the Dumpsters provided for residents.

When Ann told Kathy that she planned to move out and divorce John, it came as no surprise. But she felt a sense of foreboding when Ann confirmed it on Presidents' Day weekend in February 1991. Kathy and her mother, Emiko, along with Ann, had assembled in San Diego to prepare for an upcoming wedding in April, of Kathy's sister, Patty. Ann announced to Kathy and "Emi" that she wanted to file for a divorce right away, but she needed financial assistance. She hoped Emi would see if their mother, Matsue Yoshiyama, could help. The aging woman lived with Emi and her husband in Mesa, Arizona.

Ann had access to her joint bank account with John, plus a few interest-bearing accounts, but didn't dare withdraw money from them because her husband might realize it immediately. She planned to repay her mother after the divorce settlement. Instead of asking for a loan from Matsue, Emi wrote a check to her for $1,500.

Another important revelation came from Ann during the San Diego meeting with her family. She told Emi and Kathy about a male friend named Bob Russell, who lived near San Francisco. She had known him when they both attended Morningside High School in Inglewood, where they graduated in 1966. The friendship had rekindled, she said, and they had been corresponding for some time. While it mildly surprised both Kathy and her mother, they were not shocked. In their opinions, Ann had been deprived of warmth and affection for too long, and if this old high-school pal could provide her with emotional comfort, then it was probably for the best. A few times within the following weeks, Ann called Bob from Kathy's home. Emi and Kathy didn't learn until much later that the spark of friendship with this man had flared into a major bonfire of love.

In early March, Ann asked Kathy's permission to name her as a reference in the application to lease a condominium at Peachland. She also wanted to use Kathy's home address in obtaining a credit card so that nothing would be sent to the residence on Fortuna Drive. Kathy had no objections at all.

Knowing full well how fracturing the marriage would impact her children, Ann took careful steps to ease the way. To prevent the trauma from undermining Glenn's and Katelin's performances in school, Ann consulted with both of their teachers. At Wiley Canyon Elementary School, Ms. Dorrie Dean's second-grade class included Katelin Racz. Dean and Ann were certainly not strangers, since the mother not only participated in Parent-Teacher Association (PTA) functions and regularly volunteered to assist with school projects, but she also visited the classroom every other week to maintain personal involvement in her daughter's work. At a March 16 parent-teacher conference, Ann discussed Katelin's academic progress, then turned to a personal matter. She told Dean that she planned to leave her husband and take the children with her, but she wasn't yet financially prepared. The kids, she said, didn't yet know about it, nor did her husband. As soon as she could, she would let Dean know the facts.

Glenn also attended Wiley Canyon, in Ms. Lois Becker's sixth-grade class. He was an honor student at the top of his class. Ann gave her the same message, that she and her kids had begun the process of moving. "She said there was going to be a traumatic 'upheaval' in her family," and she wanted to be notified of any changes in Glenn's behavior.

Later that same evening, Ann made a confession to her niece Kathy of being "scared to death." The whispered conversation took place at a wedding shower for Kathy's sister. It alarmed Kathy to hear of her aunt's fear; yet she admired Ann's courage in planning to go ahead with the move and the divorce. Hindsight about possibly borrowing money from her mother made her even more grateful to Emi for the loan. The elderly woman might have inadvertently said something at Patty's wedding, scheduled for Saturday, April 13, near San

Diego. An innocent slip of the tongue could find its way to John, and all hell would break loose.

Of course, Ann could make the move sooner—at the risk of casting gloom over the wedding, which was unthinkable to Ann. She chose to wait and to hope that nothing leaked to arouse John's suspicion.

As it turned out, the nuptials took place without a hitch. On Friday, Ann left the house with her youngest daughter, Katelin. On her way to San Diego, she dropped a postcard, addressed to Bob Russell, into a mailbox. It contained a cryptic note: *Before leaving for S.D. "D" Day is soon. Will give you day-by-day account just to let you know I'm okay.*

Ann drove south, about 150 miles, for the rehearsal, enabling Katelin to practice her role as a flower girl.

John Racz brought Glenn on Saturday morning. Festive behavior and smiles masked any underlying worries or turmoil. Numerous photos show Ann in a black-belted magenta dress, with a corsage on her left shoulder. Even with prematurely graying hair, at forty-two, she didn't look her age. By all appearances, it was a happy family gathering.

On the following Monday morning, April 15, after John left for work, Ann implemented the first preliminary steps of her plan by hauling a few boxes over to the Peachland condominium. Kathy helped and brought a small "dorm-size" refrigerator from her garage for Ann's use. While they worked, Ann made an unexpected comment to her niece. She said, "I'd better give you Bob's phone number in case anything happens to me."

Dee Ann Wood, a vivacious, well-educated woman, with a sharp sense of humor and a grin that deepened captivating dimples, had met Ann in the early 1980s through their common affiliation with the First Presbyterian Church.

As Ann's best friend, Dee Ann had known for nearly two years about the crumbling marriage. She heard all about John's frugal ways—taking trash to supermarket bins, disallowing toilet flushing, and other cheapskate methods. Some of his tactics amused Dee Ann, like his habit of getting free coffee at a nearby fast-food restaurant. He would carry in a previously used Styrofoam cup bearing the establishment's logo, then brazenly pretend that he had paid as he refilled it. She had also heard that he wouldn't allow his family to use air-conditioning in the home on blistering days, but instead ordered them to lie down on the cool concrete floor in the garage.

Dee Ann wondered if all of these accusations were entirely true. And she knew that Ann could be quite frugal as well. "I think they spent money on food and furniture. At that time, Vista Ridge was the nicest neighborhood in Valencia. And their house was paid for, but it wasn't well furnished. Not shabby, but not well appointed either. Her clothes were neat and clean, and she always looked nice, but she wouldn't spend money on designer clothing. Not from a thrift shop, but not expensive. She sewed some, I think. She and I would shop at Target, or Sears, or whatever. I don't mean that she was extremely cheap, but was frugal. They didn't have fancy cars, like a lot of people in Vista Ridge would drive, but had reliable, well-running cars."

Certainly, the couple had accumulated some money and made good investments, including full ownership of their home, considering that John didn't earn a huge salary as a sheriff's deputy or in teaching, and Ann had left her teaching job soon after they married. Dee Ann attributed their wealth to a mutual ability for setting goals and formulating sound plans to reach them. She also knew that several years earlier they had bought a condominium at Peachland and eventually sold it for a tidy profit.

Despite this financial stability, the edginess between John and Ann grew, and Ann mentioned to her friend the possibility of divorce. Dee Ann later said, "I remember we were in a swimming pool at her homeowner's association. The kids—four, five, or six years old—were splashing around in the water. She and I were talking, and I remember her saying that she was thinking about leaving John."

The two women discussed Ann's growing problems in detail for years. Dee Ann recalled it: "She and I often went to the movies on Thursday nights at the Plaza Theater, which is no longer there. They had double features for seventy-five-cents admission. That was in the eighties. Our husbands were home on Thursday nights to babysit. We'd sneak in cans of pop, inside our purses. And when we came back, we'd sit in one of our driveways, depending on who drove, until three in the morning. When we sat out in front of Ann's place, John would sometimes come out, just to see if we were okay. My husband came out a couple of times too when we were at my house, which was only about a mile from hers. We talked a lot. You know, women do that. She told me that she and John were not getting along, and that she was tired of his—she didn't say 'control,' that wasn't the word she used—of his cheapness and making all the decisions."

According to one of Ann's friends who spoke later, another serious and more personal issue undermined the relationship. John made her have sex every night. He demanded that she go to bed at the same time he did and submit to his desires. If she was in the middle of a project, and stayed up to finish, he would order her to wake him when she came to bed so they could have sex. She hated being used like a breeding animal and dreaded the nightly humiliation during the last six months. To avoid his temper, though, she submitted nearly every night. A few times, Ann had confided with a giggle, she didn't wake him, and covered it by saying that she tried, but he was too sound asleep. She hated it. Every single night for the last six months, she didn't want to have sex with him—period—much less every night.

The sexual duties would come to an end with the move,

Ann told her closest friends, but she worried that finances would be tight until the final divorce settlement. Dee Ann later commented, "She wouldn't be able to take the kids to fancy places anymore, Magic Mountain or the movies, and she wanted to make sure they had television for entertainment at home, so she bought a TV and a video recording machine. She was nervous about money. I think she signed a six-month lease, with five hundred dollars down. I went with her for a final walk-through at the lease signing."

The Peachland connection raised in Dee Ann's mind a serious question about her friend's logic in choosing that location. "She kept telling people that she was afraid of John, so this decision was very hard to understand. What are you thinking? The residents park in carports and there is no gated entry. So John could easily drive through anytime looking for her car. I told her she was foolish to move there. I reminded her that they used to own property in the complex, and that he empties his garbage at Peachland. 'No,' she said, 'he won't find me. The rental price is right and it's available.'"

In later recalling it, Dee Ann found a rationalization. "I think she selected Peachland so the kids wouldn't have to change schools." Still, Dee Ann thought, John would surely go searching for her when he arrived home that evening and found that she had moved out. Ann, though, seemed to shrug off the warning and said that she planned to leave her car in a supermarket parking lot on the first night of her absence.

On moving day, April 18, Dee Ann showed up in the early afternoon to help her friend. She later spoke of it: "I was not there that morning. But I know she had everything ready and lined up with lists for the movers. It was mostly heavier things they took, things she couldn't physically handle. She had me come over at about noon. She wanted me to be there after the movers left, but before she had to pick up the kids at two o'clock. So I went to her house on Fortuna Drive and helped her with some boxes she didn't want the movers to take. We loaded things and made trips to the condo."

Ann revealed to Dee Ann that she had left a "Dear John" letter for her husband. "She told me that she wrote it, placed it in an envelope, and put it on the kitchen table for him to find. I didn't read it but saw the envelope on the table, with 'John' printed on it. She was very determined not to talk to him until he had read the letter. She wanted him served with the divorce papers at seven o'clock that night. Not before or after. Her goal, and the scenario in her mind, was that he would find out she had left by reading her letter, and then as he was reading it, the doorbell would ring and he would be served with the divorce papers."

All plans, whether made by generals in war or housewives leaving their husbands, are subject to human failures. Unfortunately, perhaps due to a negligent clerk somewhere, the divorce papers were not served on John Racz until the following evening, April 19.

At the condominium, Ann did her best to make it appear inviting to the children. She and Joann would share one of the two bedrooms and master bath, while Glenn and Katelin shared the other one with a separate bathroom. In midafternoon Ann interrupted her work and left to pick the kids up from their schools. At Hart High School, and at Wiley Canyon Elementary, she chatted with the teachers to let them know that Joann, Glenn, and Katelin would be absent on Friday.

On the way back to the condo, she stopped at a local park to prepare them for the major change in their lives. Joann already knew about the move, having been told by Ann early that morning. But Glenn and Katelin were jolted by the news that they would be living in a different place. Later recalling it, Joann said, "I think she wanted to make sure we all knew that both of our parents loved us, but that my mom wasn't in love with my dad anymore. And she just wanted to probably ease us into knowing about the divorce." For dinner Ann took the three children to a Taco Bell restaurant, where they ran into a church circle member. While they ate, Ann told her about the move and her fears of retaliation by John.

She stopped at a pay phone and called Dee Ann Wood, to request another favor. She asked her friend to drive over to a shopping mall and meet her at the Hughes grocery store. As Ann had mentioned earlier, she wanted to leave her car there so John couldn't find it in the Peachland carports.

Within minutes Dee Ann pulled into the parking lot and spotted Ann standing outside the market with her three children. They all climbed into the car for the short trip to the condo, where Dee Ann dropped them off, said a few words of encouragement to Ann, and left.

In Joann's retrospective comments, she said, "I don't remember much about the day we moved. Mom woke me up a little earlier than usual and told me that the movers were coming. I know that she picked us up after school and we went straight over to the condo, which I thought was so weird, seeing my stuff in a different place. If she would have asked me for anything, sure I would have done it. But she didn't ask us for any help. Just told us we must behave and take it slow. We went there that night and stayed there, and I recall it being totally different from what we were used to. I shared a bed with Mom, and Glenn and Kate had the other bedroom."

That evening Ann paced nervously and watched television with the kids for a short time. At eight o'clock, she told them to stay put while she went to a public telephone to call their father. She felt certain that the notice of her filing for divorce had been served an hour earlier, as she had specified. Frightened that he might be driving around looking for them, she scanned the block before reluctantly walking across the dark street under a barely visible sliver of moon, which resembled a silver fingernail clipping. After entering a medical center building, she fed coins into a slot and keyed in the familiar home number.

It took two tries to reach John, and Ann instantly found out that her plans were already falling apart. The divorce notice had not been served.

She also made another call from the pay phone that evening, a long-distance connection to the San Francisco Bay Area, which made her heart race.

On Friday morning, Dee Ann Wood drove over to the condominium to pick up Ann and take her to the parking lot, where they had left Ann's white Plymouth minivan. The three kids were still home, since Ann had kept them out of school that day. She didn't want John to pick them up and ask a lot of questions about the move.

Ann told her friend about the phone call to John on Thursday night. He hadn't answered on her first attempt, and it sent her into a panic. Her mind reeled, but she tried to remain in control. Desperate, she dialed the number again, and this time he answered.

Recalling Ann's recitation, Dee Ann described it: "She calls again and reaches him. They talked for a long time. Ann said she was a little bit shocked at his mild reaction. He had read the note she left, but didn't seem as angry as she expected, raising his voice only a couple of times. I warned her not to let her guard down. I said, 'That doesn't necessarily mean he's not furious. He may be just controlling himself to give you confidence so you will go over there. I would keep my distance and not tell him where you are.'"

The telephone conversation, Ann told her friend, was interrupted by the medical center janitor, who announced that he had to close and lock the doors. So she hung up and walked about a block to Peachland School, where she used an outdoor public phone and called John back. His calm demeanor made her feel considerably more comfortable.

To Dee Ann, John's behavior didn't seem consistent with a

man who came home and found that his family had deserted him. Although Ann described his reaction as nonviolent and reasonable, alarms went off in Dee Ann's mind. She suggested, "He's probably camouflaging his anger, so don't abandon your thoughts of protecting yourself."

On the way to the car, parked near the Hughes Market, Ann mentioned that she and the kids planned to spend the weekend doing fun things. Maybe they would go to Six Flags Magic Mountain, the huge theme park offering a variety of thrill rides, only about four miles north of their new residence at Peachland. Or she might take them to Malibu Beach, a one-hour drive through the Santa Monica Mountains. She had already announced to Dee Ann and other friends that she probably would not attend the local church on Sunday, April 21.

Dee Ann dropped her near the minivan, gave Ann a hug, cautioned her again to keep up her guard, and drove away. They would never see each other again.

CHAPTER 2

"How Come We Had To Go?"

Blizzards howled across the mainland United States in January 1949, and some of the coldest temperatures in history froze the population. For the only time in the twentieth century, snow fell in San Diego, Laguna Beach, and Long Beach, California. But across the Pacific, in Hilo, Hawaii, gentle trades winds kept temperatures in the mid-70s most of that month, with little rainfall. Perfect weather ushered in a little girl's birth for the Yoshiyama family on January 17.

Ann Mineko Yoshiyama was the fourth offspring for Matsue and her husband, Jerry. Sons Takeo and Joji had entered the world in 1931 and 1934, and the first daughter, Emiko, came along in 1937, all citizens of the United States by being born in the Territory of Hawaii. Ann's birth came ten years before the islands became a state.

Matsue would later admit that it embarrassed her to be pregnant at the age of forty. She also worried that she would not live to see her youngest child grow up, complete her education, and be married. All of those concerns vanished when the perfect child arrived. The first three siblings glowed with pride at their beautiful, vibrant little sister.

Their grandfather, Umekichi Yoshiyama, as a wiry, slim youth, had emigrated to Hawaii from Japan to work the sugarcane fields and on the fishing boats. His family eventually sent a young woman to be his wife. She produced five sons and two daughters, including Jerry in 1901. Short and muscular, with a full, round face, the youth attended school until his fifteenth birthday, then drifted down to the wharf in Honolulu, where he signed on as a cabin boy aboard a Japanese merchant ship. That decision would eventually have a dramatic impact on his family.

He returned to the big island, Hawaii, and settled in Hilo. There he met and married a diminutive beauty named Matsue. Jerry found a profession in the fishing industry, managing a fleet of boats that came into harbor each morning, and working as an auctioneer of the fresh catch they unloaded. As a first son, he inherited a comfortable two-story house in the outskirts of Hilo. He moved his family into it at about the time of Emiko's birth.

Emi remembered her father affectionately. "I don't know how far he went in school, but he was a very learned man. My father was pretty much Westernized in his living style and traditions, and quite broad-minded. He was bilingual, speaking and writing both Japanese and English very fluently. I remember that when people got married in Hawaii, they would always have a speaker, and my father often did this because he spoke both languages perfectly. I guess we lived a middle-class lifestyle."

Emi's brother, Joji Yoshiyama, recalled the strong familial bonds in their home. "My widower grandfather lived with us until he passed away. My mom loved flowers, and she raised a lot of them in our yard, especially orchids."

The family prospered, never having suffered the effects

of the Great Depression, which impoverished farmers and workers in the contiguous states. Jerry worked steadily and his children entered good schools in Hilo. By late 1941, Takeo and Joji were in elementary classes and Emi had started kindergarten. That all came to a grinding halt when the clouds of war burst.

A shock wave spread across the Hawaiian Islands, and the world, on December 7, 1941, when Japanese planes bombed the American naval fleet at Pearl Harbor. A U.S. declaration of war immediately followed. In Washington, D.C., military officials pondered the implications involving people of Japanese ancestry living in the United States, particularly those in California, Oregon, and Washington. President Franklin D. Roosevelt signed Executive Order 9066 on February 14, 1942, authorizing establishment of geographic zones from which "any or all persons may be excluded." Ostensibly to identify people who might represent a danger to the country and its military operations, the order zeroed in primarily on ethnic Japanese. Some 120,000 of them were sent to internment camps. It remains one of the most controversial events in U.S. history.

Regarding residents of Hawaii, a big problem arose. The total population of the Hawaiian Islands at that time numbered about 425,000. More than one-third of them, approximately 158,000, had descended from Japanese origins. At first, top-level discussions hinted at relocating all of them to mainland camps. But wiser heads prevailed after examining the daunting logistics and economic impact on the Hawaiian economy. This ethnic group provided the preponderance of agricultural labor and contributed significantly to other industries. Suddenly it seemed impractical to clear them out in the manner that swept through the western states.

Still, all of the Hawaiian-Japanese couldn't be left in place, so officials made a decision to single out certain individuals based on occupations, religion, background, or any other criteria that might label them as "dangerous."

Jerry Yoshiyama inexplicably fell into this category because he had worked as a teenage cabin boy aboard Japanese merchant vessels. Japanese-American internee records from that time indicate that Jerry had visited Japan twice, staying once for about six months, which may have had some effect. It made no sense to anyone, but military police arrested him, along with about 2,500 others, and took them to Sand Island, a barren plot measuring less than one square mile at the mouth of Honolulu Harbor. Detainees on the island found scant shelter in dirt-floor tents.

Jerry's daughter, Emi, shared her childhood memory of what happened. "My father had two choices. He could stay on Sand Island without his family, or could take his family with him to a relocation camp on the mainland. Several families chose to do that. I wouldn't call Sand Island a relocation camp, it was more like a prison. We always asked, 'How come we had to go?' I had classmates who also were sent to camp. One of them's father was a Buddhist minister. Another classmate had parents who were born in Japan and considered aliens. But we who were born in Hawaii, and were citizens, wondered how come we had to go. It was because my father was on a Japanese merchant ship. Yet, he was very loyal to the United States. We came to California."

According to Joji's recall, they voyaged to California aboard a luxury liner, the *Lurline*. This famous vessel had been carrying wealthy passengers to Hawaii from San Francisco and back since the year of Joji's birth, 1934. During the war, the government used it to transport American troops to Hawaii, and on at least one return voyage, it brought detainees from Hawaii to California. Joji remembered that trip as an exciting adventure.

Upon arrival in Oakland, California, the internees lined up for transportation to "relocation centers." Joji and Takeo believed the family was sent directly to Jerome, Arkansas. Emi recalled being at a racetrack briefly. This is possible, since fairgrounds and tracks throughout the state had been commandeered to process the new internees. Tanforan, on the San Francisco Peninsula at San Bruno, one of the most famous venues for racing horses since 1899, fell into this category, as did Santa Anita in Southern California. In either case, Jerry Yoshiyama, his wife, and three children wound up on a train trip across several states to Arkansas.

Emi recalled three locations where her family spent time. "I think we stayed at a racetrack just a few days. Then they sent us to Jerome, Arkansas. We were there a year and a half. After that, they moved us to Granada camp, which is in Colorado, for another year and a half."

The Jerome Relocation Center, over one hundred miles south of Little Rock, had been constructed on swampy, heavily forested river delta land. More than eight thousand ethnic Japanese, mostly from California and Hawaii, occupied the rudimentary living quarters at Jerome, where they contended with heavy rain, mud, mosquitos, and snakes.

Granada, a tiny, desolate hamlet on Highway 50 in southeastern Colorado, is near the Kansas border amidst miles of prairie called Comanche National Grassland. Beginning in August 1942, more than seven thousand detainees lived in the barracks, surrounded by barbed wire and gun towers. It is also known as the Amache Internment Camp.

Vague images of the life there have remained in Emi's mind. "I don't recall the camps very clearly, but have some recollections of them. I remember eating in the mess halls, like an army camp. I remember seeing snow for the first time in my life. Where we lived, there were potbellied stoves and brick floors. We went to regular school there. I was in the first grade. Most of our teachers were Caucasian from nearby communities. I don't know if they called them government workers or what. Later I had a Japanese teacher who came from Philadelphia."

Joji Yoshiyama remembered it well. "We were first sent to Arkansas. We were in block thirty-nine, which housed people all from Hawaii. After about a year and a half, they shipped us to Amache, Colorado. Most of the people there were from California and we were among the few from Hawaii. In our block, there were only two families from Hawaii, and the rest were from California. But as kids, you make friends. Lots of them. My best friend was a kid my age named Eddy Tanaka. We attended elementary school together there at Amache. Later, after he grew up and went to college, he became the director of Public Welfare for Los Angeles County."

Jerry Yoshiyama and his family endured the camps until the closing months of 1945, after the war ended in September. He, Matsue, and their three children journeyed back to Hilo, Hawaii.

"I remember when we came back from Seattle aboard an old, crowded army transport ship this time, instead of the *Lurline*. We docked in Honolulu on Thanksgiving Day. My parents said something about us being thankful to be back home. My dad was very positive, never looked at things negatively. Then we went over to Hilo," said Joji.

In Emi's memory, she realized an important difference from what happened to mainland internees. "Fortunately, unlike the people who lived on the West Coast and were sent to camps, and lost everything, we didn't suffer that loss." One of Jerry's four brothers had occupied and maintained the old two-story house for them. "My grandfather lived there, and my grandmother died there, soon after I was born. We returned there after the war, and all of our things were still there."

They had a place to live, but no employment, since Jerry's job as a fishing-fleet manager and auctioneer had been given to someone else. Emi remembered hearing her parents talk about it. The former boss, she recalled, had promised to hold the position for Jerry, but failed to keep his word. "So my father had a tough time after that. He took a job with Occidental Life

Insurance Company in Hilo. My mother used to tell me that he was good at it, but too kindhearted and couldn't collect money from people who had a hard time paying."

Jerry's income, while smaller, still provided a comfortable life for his family. By1949, his eldest son, Takeo, graduated from Hilo High School and enrolled in the University of Hawaii. Joji started the tenth grade, and Emi went to the sixth grade in Hilo.

In that same year, on January 17, Matsue gave birth to her fourth baby, Ann Mineko Yoshiyama. She was the only child to be given a middle name. Emi smiled as she recalled it. "I remember my father telling me that I had a new sister. I had always wanted a sister since I already had two brothers. It was great."

The three older siblings watched as their baby sister, Ann, grew, learned to walk, and developed her own personality. Attending college in Honolulu, Takeo saw her only on holidays, family gatherings, and in the summers and even less frequently after joining the U.S. Army. Joji remembered that she was a brave little kid, but sometimes emotional.

Joji earned his diploma from Hilo High School in 1952, when Ann was only three, and he immediately followed his brother into the Army. The military taught him how to repair office equipment, and it gave him the opportunity to spend four years in Europe. He used it wisely for traveling to several countries.

It impressed Emi that little Ann learned early how to write, and expressed herself quite well. By the time she entered school, Ann developed an enduring interest in movies and actors. "I remember three years in a row, on Christmas Eve night, we would watch *Three Godfathers*, with John Wayne, while waiting for midnight so we could open the presents. They always showed it on that night." Ann began writing to popular stars and receiving autographed photos of them. Music also captured the little girl. Joji saw her as a very observant, creative child with a broad range of interests.

Emi spent as much time as she could with her little sister. "I don't recall very much of her first few years, but remember when she started kindergarten. I was just graduating from high school and started the local junior college. I went with my mom to a teachers' conference and decided I wanted to be a teacher. I would help with Ann when she had problems." Emi chuckled when she described the "problem."

"Her kindergarten teacher paid us a visit, and told us that Ann talked too much in class. Maybe it was because she was the youngest one and there was probably some favoritism shown to her, more by my father than my mother," Emi shared.

After completion of school in Hilo, Emi transferred to the University of Hawaii in Honolulu to obtain her teaching credentials. Ann would eventually follow her into the profession.

Takeo and Joji completed their tours of military duty and reentered civilian life. Takeo had earned an engineering degree and moved to the mainland, where he worked for the California Division of Highways. Joji returned from Europe to live with his parents again while attending the University of Hawaii to become a teacher, like his sister Emi. He laughed at one recollection of young Ann during that period. Joji took her for swimming lessons at a fenced-in pool and left. When he returned a little late, he found that the adults in charge had somehow forgotten her. Ann stood all alone inside the fence, with a panicky expression on her face, murmuring in a soft voice, "Help!"

Their shared love of movies helped bond Joji and Ann. He became a big fan of James Dean, and for years afterward, Ann's gift to her brother would consist of books about the enigmatic star who died in a California car crash on September 30, 1955, after making only three major films.

After staying a year in Hilo, Joji transferred to Santa Rosa

Junior College in California, then to Kansas State Teacher's College in Emporia.

Jerry Yoshiyama worked steadily for Occidental Life Insurance Company, but he didn't really enjoy sales. His wife supplemented their income with part-time work at the local movie theater. By 1957, he decided to make a major change.

Occidental offered him an opportunity to take over maintenance of office machines in their Los Angeles headquarters, and he accepted. He moved his wife and youngest daughter to a small but comfortable rental house on St. Elmo Drive, about four miles west of downtown Los Angeles.

They left Emi behind to complete college in Hawaii. Her parents made a trip to watch her graduate in 1958, after which she rejoined them in Los Angeles. As soon as he obtained his degree in Kansas, Joji came too.

While Emi still lived with her family on St. Elmo, bonds with Ann grew, perhaps one of the reasons the little fourth grader set her goal of becoming a teacher. "We were so close to the school, she would wait for the first bell to ring, then run over there. She was always an outgoing kid, never shy. Her best friend was a little girl named Susan Kato, and they remained close for many years. Ann began writing short stories and liked popular music. She, along with my brothers, loved old movies, and were real fans."

Ann performed well in classrooms and progressed into junior high school. She demonstrated extraordinary writing skills, and would eventually express an interest in doing it professionally. Emi and Joji both found jobs as teachers. Married and a father by this time, Takeo continued his work with the California Division of Highways, which became known in 1972 as the California Department of Transportation (Caltrans).

Emi left the Yoshiyama nest in 1962 as the bride of a young man whose given name, Gerard, had been transmogrified to Jerry, the same as Emi's father. Gerard "Jerry" Ryan, bright and articulate, worked at that time as an engineer for LA Airways, a helicopter company offering flights from LAX to Disneyland and Riverside. Emi met him through a girlfriend, and they chose Bastille Day, July 14, 1962, for their wedding. Thirteen-year-old Ann served as a junior bridesmaid.

As a new family member, Jerry Ryan grew fond of Ann. "She wasn't as wild as the typical girls of the sixties, but she was of that generation and liked to have fun. I believe her father was concerned because of the new generation ideals. I think he was fairly conservative, having watched his older kids grow up in Hawaii," he recalled.

Ann attended Los Angeles High School. Gregarious and popular, she easily made friends. One of them, Bob Russell, a quiet, intelligent kid, admired her for many reasons. He saw her as one of the most positive, upbeat people he knew. Her intelligence, articulate language skills, and compassion for other people also impressed Russell. To him, they just "clicked." Their mutual interests led to a few dates and an enduring friendship. No one at that time could predict its ultimate impact on their lives.

In 1964, when Emi and Jerry Ryan had their first child, Patty, the Yoshiyama family relocated once more. From West L.A., they moved to a new home on Christopher Avenue in Inglewood, about three miles east of Los Angeles International Airport. Ann enrolled at Morningside High School, only a dozen blocks north of the new residence, and not far from venerable Hollywood Park racetrack. Joji continued to live with his parents a few more months before finding his own place in nearby Gardena.

CHAPTER 3

KINSHIPS AND CALAMITY

Ann Yoshiyama marched to *Pomp and Circumstance* in June 1966 at Morningside High School, flipped the tassel on her mortarboard hat, and said good-bye to old classmates. She did, though, maintain correspondence with a few of them, including Bob Russell.

At the end of summer, she entered El Camino Community College, about four miles south of their Inglewood home, where she earned an Associate of Arts degree. In 1968, she transferred to California State University, Long Beach, to obtain her Bachelor of Arts, which she did in June 1970.

While attending Long Beach, she dated a young man and brought him to dinner a few times at the home of her sister and brother-in-law. But that match wasn't destined to last. Instead, through him, Ann met someone else, a quiet, introspective man named John Louis Racz, age twenty-four.

Handsome, with full, dark, left-parted hair, brown eyes like her own, a mustache fashionable for that time, solid at nearly two hundred pounds, and towering eleven inches above her five-three height, John Racz made a deep impression on Ann. They found interests in common, including the teaching profession Ann planned to enter. John already held a position teaching the sixth grade at Tibby Elementary School in Compton.

They dated and the relationship grew serious. Ann learned that John had been born in Perth Amboy, New Jersey, and grew up across Raritan Bay in Keyport. He spoke of his one sister, who had moved to Florida, and his parents, who still lived in Keyport. He had attended college in New Jersey, but came to the West Coast to earn a teaching credential at nearby California State University, Dominguez Hills. He seemed to enjoy teaching, but also expressed an interest in law enforcement.

Soon after graduation from Cal State Long Beach, Ann found a job teaching fourth grade at Ramona Elementary School in Hawthorne, the same district where her brother Joji worked.

By the middle of 1972, it didn't surprise Emi and her husband, Jerry, when Ann announced her pending marriage to John Racz. "They got married on July 1, 1972, at a commercial chapel on Gower Street in Hollywood, in the backyard. We lived in Yuma, Arizona, and by that time, I had two daughters, Patty and Kathy. I brought them back to L.A. for the wedding. It was a nice ceremony, and her girlfriend from grade-school days, Susan, was her maid of honor. John's parents traveled from New Jersey to attend," Emi said.

According to Emi, Ann and John had formed a long list of comprehensive plans for their future. Their goals included, at the very top, financial security. Travel took the next priority. And since they had the whole summer off from teaching, they took a driving trip to the East. In Philadelphia they visited Jerry Ryan's newlywed sister, just six months older than Ann. After a stop at his parents' home, they motored leisurely westward across the states. Back in Southern California, Ann and John settled into an apartment in Gardena.

Both John and Ann resumed their jobs as teachers in September. John, though, began thinking of changing his career and took direct aim at entering law enforcement. In 1973, he sat through interviews, took a series of written tests, and passed an intense medical examination to join the Los Angeles County Sheriff's Department. Eighteen weeks of rigorous physical and mental agility training at the Sheriff's Training Academy and Regional Services (STARS) Center followed. He graduated and earned his right to wear the tan uniform and deputy sheriff's badge.

Beginning assignments for new deputies nearly always involve duty at county custodial facilities, more commonly known as jails. Sometimes, when they are still in the academy or immediately after graduation, the novices are given temporary jobs at which their fresh faces give no hint of being a cop. The experience of another rookie is a good example. Bernard Thompson graduated at about the same time John Racz joined LASD. Thompson laughed when he described his first week's activity. He was dispatched to Pirate's Cove at Point Dume, a crescent-shaped stretch of sand north of Malibu Beach. No more than fifty yards long, ensconced at the base of a high cliff and flanked on both sides by projecting rocks, the site was an unofficial nude beach during that era. The fledgling officer was told to wear a bathing suit, lie on the beach, and watch for drug usage, indecent behavior, or any other illegal activity. He said it was not an unpleasant duty. Later he guarded prisoners at the Sybil Brand Institute, a correctional facility for women in the county sheriff's complex, located east of downtown Los Angeles until it closed in 1997. Thompson spoke of having conversations there with Susan Atkins, one of the notorious Charles Manson gang of killers.

John Racz drew duty early in his career guarding prisoners at a correctional facility known then as the Wayside Honor Rancho, originally opened in 1951. The complex would later be expanded and renamed Pitchess Detention Center, in honor of Sheriff Peter J. Pitchess, who served from 1959 to 1982. Located at Castaic in the foothills along I-5, the jail was only about ten miles from Valencia, where John and Ann would eventually invest in a new home.

First, though, Ann gave birth to Joann, on July 14, 1976. The beautiful infant inherited the best features from both of her parents, including liquid brown eyes and a soft mouth, which easily curves into contagious smiles. John and Ann combined their given names to form hers. Joann's earliest memory in her life, she said, flashes back to a time before her third birthday. "I remember looking out the window and seeing my mom and dad's boat. It was at a house in Gardena, and I could hear music in the background. The sun is out and I'm looking at that boat. It kinda feels dreamy, but that's what I remember."

Joann's arrival marked the end of Ann's professional teaching career. The doting parents preferred to give the baby full-time nurturing and not hand her off to a nanny or day care center. John's salary with the LASD would see them through, and with careful management, it would allow a certain amount of savings toward the purchase of a home.

It came in 1978 when they paid a down payment on an up-scale four-bedroom house in the unincorporated community of Valencia, among the foothills of northern Los Angeles County. (Valencia, along with the neighboring towns of Newhall, Saugus, and Canyon Country, would be combined in 1987 into the newly incorporated city of Santa Clarita.) Ann's sister, Emi, and her husband, Jerry Ryan, had moved from Yuma, Arizona, to Valencia, providing additional motivation for John and Ann's relocation to that area.

The new home occupied a large lot in one of most elite subdivisions of Valencia. A man named Charles Westover bought the house two doors away. Music fans knew him better as Del Shannon, a popular singer from the 1960s. His biggest hit,

"Runaway," had peaked in 1961, along with several other Top 40 songs. Shannon's career had rocketed and plummeted, like the roller-coaster rides a few miles away, and he was on his way to a comeback when John and Ann Racz moved into the new home. Ann would befriend Shannon's second wife, Beverly LeAnne Westover.

John's own career with the LASD fared well during assignments in several locations. In South Central Los Angeles, at the Firestone substation, he worked alongside a fellow deputy named John View. Their paths would cross again years later. Both men gradually worked their way up to the position of sergeant. This is not achieved without a great deal of dedication, work, and intelligence.

As a sergeant, Racz earned a coveted appointment as a trainer at the Sheriff's Academy. And with each upward step came raises in pay, certainly to the liking of John Racz. Somewhere along the way, he set the major goal in his life: become a millionaire.

That decision perhaps spawned the seed for John's frugal habits, which would turn from conventional caution in spending to extreme behavior. Emi and Jerry first noticed it during Joann's early childhood. "Ann stopped giving presents to my kids," Emi recalled. "My sister had always been a close aunt to them, but she told me that John said they shouldn't give presents to my kids unless they are going to give presents to nieces and nephews on his side of the family, which they hadn't been doing. I don't think they really knew them that well. My kids grew up with Ann around. And there was another time with the airplane thing. They were planning to fly and they stopped at Grandmas's house on the way to the airport and they put a diaper on Joann. She was already too old for diapers, but they didn't want to pay airfare for her."

Ann no doubt knew of her husband's compulsive monetary ambitions, but John's reticent personality precluded sharing his personal objectives with anyone else. And other disturbing personality characteristics began to emerge.

Emi and Jerry Ryan later recalled his odd behavior. "He was always a loner, even then. When it came time for participation in family events, such as games, he wouldn't play with the adults. Just with the kids. Wouldn't participate in any kind of entertainment. Maybe his mind was on other things or he just didn't feel the need to share thoughts or trivial points with us," stated Jerry.

Image seemed to be all important to John, though. According to Jerry, "If someone took a photo of him and the kids, he would make sure, outwardly, to appear to be a pillar of strength to the family. But I don't know how much he actually applied that in private."

It worried Emi that she never saw much show of affection between John and Ann. "I have to believe that in the beginning there must have been some manifestation of love. I want to believe that. But I never saw it when we got together at holiday parties or such. We seldom socialized as couples. I would get together with Ann and the kids, drive to my mother's house, but as couples, maybe we went out to dinner once or twice during the whole time. John is not a good conversationalist. I don't want to say quiet, it's just that he doesn't talk about things you enjoy."

Other people seemed to be uncomfortable with him as well. Emi recalled that one of her friends said, "You can be friends with that guy if you want, but don't ever ask me to go out with them as a couple."

When it came to participating in games at a family barbecue or birthday celebration, John usually turned his back. And if he did agree to join in, he made everyone else miserable. Emi described it: "Once, when we played volleyball, and needed someone to balance the teams, we asked John. Ann couldn't play, but he said he would. And it was no fun. All he did is complain. I thought he would be pretty good because he's tall, but he wasn't good. He complained that none of us were serious enough about the game. We told him that we were doing it just to have fun. It wasn't a professional tournament, but John wanted to treat it that way. I had a big fight with him in the car that night, on the way home. He told me how we should be more serious about winning, and I wouldn't let him bully me about it. I said it was just for fun because we enjoy exercise and companionship. After that, we didn't do much with them as a couple."

At the very end of 1979, on December 31, a second child arrived for John and Ann Racz. This time she gave birth to a son, Glenn. Like Joann, he also inherited genes that would make him exceptionally good-looking, tall, and bright.

The Yoshiyama family had few occasions at which all of them participated, but one took place in August 1980 when everyone gathered at Mishima's, a Japanese-Polynesian restaurant in Gardena. The joyous event celebrated Jerry and Matsue's fiftieth wedding anniversary.

One year later, the joy turned to profound sorrow. Jerry Yoshiyama suffered a stroke in the spring of 1981, requiring lengthy hospitalization in Inglewood. As he appeared to be recovering, his sons, Takeo and Joji, arranged for modifications in the home on Christopher Avenue to accommodate his rehabilitation. A doctor informed them that he could be released. On the night before his family planned to take him home, August 28, Jerry Yoshiyama passed away in his hospital bed.

Ann sought solace from the mourning by keeping a busy schedule of child rearing and housekeeping. Community activities occupied much of her time as well. She had joined the First Presbyterian Church of Santa Clarita, shortly after its formation, and attended services conducted by Pastor Glen Thorp. Many of her acquaintances, though, belonged to the one hundred-year-old First Presbyterian Church of Newhall, barely outside the border of Valencia. To be with these people, Ann also joined an adjunct group that met regularly in a conference room of that building. There she came to know a woman who would become her best friend, Dee Ann Wood.

"I met Ann through the Newhall Presbyterian Church. I moved there in January 1978 and joined the church. There was also the Presbyterian Church of Santa Clarita, which is gone now. We both attended two different social groups at the Newhall branch. Presbyterians nationwide are known to have a group called the Mariners. In [the] Newhall church, they were the old people. They were fifty or so," Dee Ann recollected, laughing. "Truly, they were in their late forties to mid sixties, and why would we want to hang around with a bunch of *old* people? So we formed a group called the Gathering, people in their twenties, thirties, or maybe early forties. Some had kids, some didn't, but it was young couples. We'd meet monthly, or every other month, maybe go to a movie, dinner, or other things. It was strictly social, not a Bible study group. Not just women, but couples.

"That was one thing. Then, in another way, I probably got to know her better. The church has a group called the Presbyterian Women. Within that are what we call church circles. In our church, they were named after various Bible people. Mary, Martha, Elizabeth, Rachel. The Elizabeth circle is the one to which Ann and I belonged. The purpose is to get better acquainted. You sit in church on Sunday and you don't really have a close acquaintance with them. In this group of maybe a dozen women who met weekly, we would share mutual problems and pray together, that kind of thing. We would have Bible study and snacks. And then there would be business, like planning for a luncheon we would put on. It was mostly young mothers, and child care was provided so we could meet, and at that time, I was in that group. That's how we became friends."

Explaining further, Dee Ann said that meetings usually took place on Tuesday mornings at the church, in a wing off the sanctuary called the Evans Room. For a while, she said, they gathered in individual homes. But when more and more of the women had children, they found it easier to meet at the church.

A kinship developed between Ann Racz and Dee Ann Wood, and it grew stronger with passing months. The two women confided nearly everything to one another. Looking back in time, Dee Ann examined why they were able to do this. "When I talked about my life to Ann, there were no secrets. I'm very open. I have good relationships with people because I don't put on airs. I don't judge them. I don't hold back in telling bad things about myself. And people are kind of drawn to that because they are so used to people hiding their own flaws. If someone is completely open, like I was to Ann and other women, then they feel safe telling me their confidences. Their perception is that I'm not going to judge them, and for the most part, that is true."

Another event bonded them even closer. Midway through 1982, Ann realized she was pregnant again, at age thirty-three. A few months later, Dee Ann found herself in the same condition. Ann gave birth to her second daughter, Katelin, on November 24, 1983. Dee Ann's son, Ian, arrived in April of the next year. They and their husbands posed proudly with their babies the following June at a joint baptism ceremony.

Nothing meant more to Ann than her children. A conscientious mother, she gave them unconditional love, provided for their needs, and took an active role in their education. Joann remembered when her mother tried to explain the facts of life to her. "Mom tried to tell me all about it when I was about twelve. I think she actually used that old cliché about 'the birds and the bees.'" Her memory brought a giggle to Joann's lips. "I didn't quite get it because I had never heard that term before. She started to get into it, and I was a little confused. I don't think Mom was embarrassed in trying to tell me these things, but I remember I was. I didn't know where she was trying to go with it. She was probably trying to do the proper thing. When Katelin was born, it was a caesarean birth. Mom showed me her scar about a year after Kate was born. I was like 'Wow, that's what happens,' like a big deal."

Ann celebrated her thirty-sixth birthday on January 17, 1985. Other than seeds of discontent with the marriage, most elements of Ann's life gave her happiness, especially with her children. She probably didn't even notice an article in the *Los Angeles Times* that morning spelling out the sad end related to a younger woman's life. The headline announced that a defendant had been exonerated after being tried for murdering a twenty-three-year old woman whose body had never been found.

In 1981, Julie Church had disappeared from the Antelope Valley community of Lancaster, about forty miles northeast of Valencia. She had told her supervisor what he could do with a job she hated, walked out, and stopped at a favorite watering hole to have a few drinks. In her celebration, she chatted with a local guy named Steven Jackson, who managed a nearby boardinghouse. After she left the bar with him, she seemed to have vanished off the face of the earth.

A team of LASD detectives, including a top-notch sleuth named Louis Danoff, searched the surrounding canyons and desert for months and found nothing but dead ends. Their hopes soared, though, when a witness came forward and said that Steven Jackson had admitted killing Julie. Detectives convinced the DA to charge Jackson with murder, even though Julie's body hadn't been found.

"No body" cases seldom found their way into courtrooms, since skeptical juries had difficulty sending a defendant to prison for life or to death row without positive proof that the victim wasn't still out there, hiding somewhere. A landmark 1959 case in Los Angeles, though, established that it could be done. A resident of affluent Bel Air, L. Ewing Scott had been convicted of murdering his socialite wife, Evelyn Throsby Scott, even though her body had never been found. One of the southland's most famous attorneys, J. Miller Leavy, the chief of Trials for the DA's office, prosecuted the case. Scott spent the next twenty years in prison.

Based on that precedent, the DA charged Steven Jackson with murder. J. Miller Leavy even came out of retirement to present the evidence against Jackson. Yet, at the end of a trial lasting months, the jury came back with a verdict of not guilty. The crushing defeat would act as a powerful deterrent for trying future bodyless cases.

Even if Ann Racz read the article, it doubtlessly meant very little to her. Nor could she know the role that Detective Louis Danoff would eventually play in her family's life.

By 1985, John Racz had spent twelve years as a deputy sheriff, and had been posted for some time with the Malibu/Hidden Hills station in Agoura, at the western end of Los Angeles County, near I-101. The unit served a blend of residential, rural, mountain, beach, and recreational areas from the valley to the beach. A peculiar thing happened there in September of that year.

In the watch commander's office, a safe contained money seized in drug arrests, along with cash that had been posted for bail. Sometime during a period of about three weeks—no one could be certain exactly when—a thief managed to take three envelopes stuffed with about $6,000. It seemed peculiar that the robber took only that amount, when more than $100,000 inside the safe could have been stolen. Perhaps the perpetrator hoped the theft might not be noticed. In any case, investigators suspected that one of the officers or a civilian employee might have been involved. No one could find evidence to accuse Sergeant John Racz, but a cloud of uncertainty hung over the station.

Dee Ann Wood recalled a bizarre situation when she heard about the incident. "I was sitting with John and Ann in their family room when it came on [the] television news that there had been a robbery at the Malibu sheriff's station. They thought it was probably an inside job. So I kiddingly said, 'Oh, hey, John, where are you guys going on your vacation this year? Are you getting some new furniture too? Ha, Ha.'" Suddenly Dee Ann noticed Ann standing behind her husband, silently waving her hands and mouthing, "No, no." Dee Ann had been joking and Ann's reaction stunned her. She instantly changed the subject. Later, when she left, Ann followed her out to the car.

Quietly Dee Ann asked, "Ann, do you really think John was involved?"

Ann whispered, "I don't know, but it might be a possibility, so don't ever mention it again." After that, everyone carefully avoided bringing the subject up for discussion.

A short time later, that same September, John Racz retired from his position as a sergeant with the Los Angeles County Sheriff's Department, on an alleged disability. He soon returned to teaching in Compton.

Even with a reduced salary, Racz still maintained lofty financial goals. He and Ann both habitually made lists of their objectives. In 1987, one of John's lists itemized short-term activities, which included landscaping and home repair jobs, things he wished to achieve within five years, and several lifetime targets. Under his five-year plan, he listed staying under 195 pounds, moving, and having $500,000. His printed lifetime goals included staying physically fit, world travel, and having $1,000,000 by the year 2000.

The couple had already made good progress in achieving

financial stability. Dee Ann Wood understood how they had accomplished it. "I was always impressed by the amount of money they had, because I knew that neither of them earned huge salaries or were previously wealthy. It came from goal setting, and they did that meticulously. When they got married, they set many goals, and reviewed them every three, six, nine months, and annually—savings goals, trip goals, places they wanted to go, when they wanted to have kids. I'm not certain, but I don't believe they used credit cards very much. They would save the money for a new couch, for example, and put a certain amount of money aside each month until they could pay cash for it. I know they paid off the house on Fortuna Drive early. I believe they had bought a three-bedroom condominium at the Peachland complex, rented it out, then sold it for a nice profit. They probably used that to pay off the home. And, of course, they were frugal in expenditures. The front yard at their house was landscaped because the city requires it, but John refused to spend money to landscape the backyard. That bothered Ann because she wanted to be able to use it, so she could entertain there, or the kids could play, or she and I could just go back there, sit down and have some refreshments together. He just wouldn't do it."

Ann's friends knew of her home-based business, Monday Flowers, but suspected that it made minimal profit. Before dawn each Monday morning, she drove to downtown Los Angeles and bought a variety of fresh flowers at a wholesale market. Back home, she arranged them in vases and made personal deliveries to banks, doctors' offices, and a few other firms. She told acquaintances that it earned her about three hundred dollars a month. They wondered, though, did the business simply give Ann a way to spend time out of John's presence?

Back in 1966, when Ann Yoshiyama graduated from Morningside High School, she made an agreement with her good friend Bob Russell to stay in contact. They kept the bargain for years, corresponding by mail regularly, even after Russell moved to the San Francisco Bay Area. There he became involved with a lover and fathered a child. Meanwhile, Ann met and married John Racz. The letters stopped.

At Christmastime in 1988, Russell wondered about his former school friend, found her address, and sent her a greeting card. She responded, and the exchange of mail started once again. To avoid trouble at home, Ann gave him the post office box number she used for her flower business.

Through their letters over the next twelve months, Ann and Bob discovered they still had a great deal in common. She felt an overpowering urge to see him in person. In January 1990, she told John that she would like to go to San Francisco for the weekend and even mentioned tentative plans to visit her old high-school friend Bob Russell and his four-year-old daughter. Ann asked John if he would mind. After some serious discussion, he assented, since she would be taking their five-year-old daughter, Katelin, with her. Pushing the envelope a little, Ann asked if it would be okay for her and Katelin to stay at Bob's residence. John adamantly vetoed that idea.

The reunion with Bob in Vallejo, across the bay from San Francisco, went well. He and Ann shared old times and caught up on all the events in their lives over the past twenty-four years. They watched their little girls play together. The characteristics that had attracted Bob to Ann so long ago now seemed even more evident. He would later describe it: "She was easygoing, intelligent, articulate, and very outspoken. We got along. She cared about other people and was very conscientious."

After returning home, Ann couldn't shake the warm feelings she had shared with Bob Russell, nor the strong desire to see him again. They exchanged frequent letters with increasing expressions of mutual affection.

* * *

A tragic event on Fortuna Drive in February 1990 temporarily diverted Ann's thoughts of Bob. A gunshot shattered the neighborhood silence two doors away.

Ann had befriended the woman who lived in that home, Beverly LeAnne Westover, usually known as LeAnne. The two of them had often talked about world travel, and had tentatively planned a trip together. It never came about, because on February 8, her husband, Charles, went into the den, stuck the barrel of a .22-caliber rifle in his mouth, and pulled the trigger. It shocked music fans worldwide to learn that Charles Westover, better known as Del Shannon, had committed suicide.

Ironically, just five days earlier, he had given his final public performance at a concert near the site of another tragedy in music history, Clear Lake, Iowa. Shannon sang his greatest hit, "Runaway," at the event named for Buddy Holly. Holly, Richard Valenzuela, and Jiles Perry Richardson had all died in a small plane brought down by icy winter weather in a snow-covered pasture just outside Clearlake on February 3, 1959. Valenzuela recorded under the name Ritchie Valens, and Richardson called himself the Big Bopper.

Always compassionate, Ann Racz consoled her friend, LeAnne. The woman found enough courage to stay in the home she had shared with one of the top musicians of the 1960s and '70s. Since Ann worked as a volunteer, ten hours a week, with the Santa Clarita Presbyterian Church and Pastor Glen Thorp, she encouraged LeAnne to find solace in faith.

With Bob Russell still constantly on her mind, Ann found the perfect excuse to see him again when the PTA to which she belonged scheduled a San Francisco convention that spring. Her announcement to John that she planned to attend angered him and they argued heatedly. She insisted, though, and bought her ticket. This time Ann went alone.

In the foggy city of the Golden Gate, mutual feelings of

warmth between Ann and Bob blossomed over romantic dinners by the bay. They both realized a strong need for each other, and they consummated it by sleeping together for the first time. Ann told Bob of her extreme unhappiness in her marriage, explaining that she no longer loved her husband and felt trapped by him. She attributed it to his "abusive" nature, not physical but psychological.

When Ann returned home, she and Bob continued contact every day, by phone or mail. As the feelings between them morphed into undeniable love, they began to discuss the possibility of spending the rest of their lives together. She would find a way to leave John and come to Bob.

Bob wanted to make certain that their relationship was not the core reason for her wish to divorce her husband. Ann assured Bob that her marriage was already "beyond repair" and that she had started thinking of separation long ago. He made a commitment to wait for her, even if it took years.

That summer, Bob traveled to Valencia, and Ann risked meeting him in a Hampton Inn hotel within a mile of her home. It stood within sight of a McDonald's restaurant, where Ann sometimes bought fast food for her children. Other fast-food restaurants nearby had caused locals to nickname the area "hamburger hill."

Ann's confidante Dee Ann Wood soon learned about the emergence of Bob in her friend's life, but she was not privy to all the details. In her recollections, Dee Ann said, "I never saw any of the letters she got from him. It's funny, because even though we shared a lot of intimate detailed secrets, talking about sex and that kind of stuff, for some reason I didn't feel like that was something I should ask her about."

On November 22, Thanksgiving, Ann drove to San Diego for yet another meeting. Bob took her to meet his parents. The future of love and soul-sharing looked brilliant for them, but they had no way of knowing that it would soon eclipse into the blackest of nights.

CHAPTER 4

A DANGEROUS RIFT

One of the major goals Ann and John Racz had set for themselves involved travel. Trips, though, still required as much thrift as possible. John usually arranged for overnight accommodations through a home exchange system. And he set stringent rules about purchasing souvenirs during visits to other cities. Before taking his family to Paris, he told them that if they wanted T-shirts inscribed with that name, they should buy them at a Target store, not in the actual "City of Lights." Much cheaper that way.

Dee Ann Wood recalled another example that shocked her. "I was taking them to the airport to go to Europe. Glenn had his flute case. I asked why he was taking that to Europe. And he said, 'Oh, Dad said that on the street corners in Paris if you play an instrument, and have the case open on the sidewalk, people will throw money in. That would help pay for the trip.' I said to John 'You've got to be kidding.' When they came back, we were laughing and I asked Glenn if he had made any money. He said, 'Actually, I did.'"

Ann found these measures annoying. Eventually she chose to travel with her aunt Kimiko "Kay" Jewett, rather than with John. In 1989, she journeyed to Russia with Aunt Kay, and in 1990, they traveled to Hawaii and Japan. While shopping in Honolulu, Ann bought a black-and-gold ring for herself. On May 11, she wrote a letter to Bob Russell and told him of her purchase:

> In a few days I should be receiving my Hawaiian wedding ring. When I put that ring on, it will not be, or signify, a wedding band to me. . . . It's just a ring, even though I'll wear it on my left ring finger. In fact, because it will say sweetheart in Hawaiian, and the word is spelled K-U-U-I-P-O, I will think about you every time I feel it or glance at it. I will visualize both of us being together and happy in the future which I strongly believe and affirm . . . so it will be that way in reality.

Ann showed the ring to Dee Ann Wood, who wondered about the risk of wearing it. This choice about another item of jewelry also concerned Dee Ann. A necklace with a sheriff's star had adorned Ann's throat for a long time, but Bob Russell had sent her a gold chain with a sapphire pendant. Ann began wearing it underneath the neckline of her blouse. She repeatedly said how much she loved the gift from Bob. One day she announced to Dee Ann, "I'm going to wear it on the outside and see if John even notices it."

"Oh, Ann," her friend replied, "that's not a good idea. He's not going to take it well."

With a defiance-laced smile, Ann said, "I don't know. Let me see."

A few days later, Dee Ann saw the necklace boldly hanging outside Ann's blouse. "He didn't even notice it," declared Ann.

"I'll bet he did," Dee Ann warned. "He just didn't say anything to you."

But Ann apparently chose to believe that John's power of

observation failed him. She thought he had overlooked her replacement of the sheriff's star with a sapphire.

Speaking of it later, Dee Ann said, "John didn't say anything to her, but I think he is dumb like a fox. I believe he noticed it, and I'll bet he even knew it was from Bob. Where else would it have come from if she didn't buy it? And he would have known about the expenditure in that case."

The perplexing change in her normally cautious behavior didn't make sense at all. Ann also used public telephones to call Bob, gambling that John wouldn't catch her doing it. She even told Dee Ann once, "John drove by, but I don't think he saw me."

Shaking her head in disbelief, Dee Ann said, "Ann, he saw you. He knows." But the advice just seemed to bounce off into thin air.

Even if Dee Ann couldn't rationalize the risks, she did understand Ann's relationship with Bob Russell. "Every marriage has problems. She and I had talked about it for months, and it didn't seem unusual to me that she would be weighing her options. Many women do that. I think as Bob became more a part of the picture, that truly was more of an issue why Ann ultimately decided, 'Yes, I'm going to leave.' I don't think she looked for a boyfriend, but I think once he was in the picture, she liked the fact that he was kind and considerate, as John had been before they got married. And we all like that, before and after we marry. So I don't think she was oblivious to the fact that marriage is a relationship with pitfalls, and a separate relationship doesn't have those problems. She knew that. But I think she saw Bob as a different kind of man than John and decided maybe that was more where her heart would be."

The idea of divorce grew in Ann's mind, and in her usual methodical approach to problems, she began researching it. First she bought a book on the subject and devoured the details of how to get started. She consulted with several friends who had been through the process. At the public library, she researched the legal aspects of it. Ann next examined their finances to analyze how the community property might be divided. Talking about this with Dee Ann, she expressed concern that John might have opened some separate accounts without her knowledge, and wondered how she could discover them, if they existed.

In retrospect, Dee Ann said, "Ann wanted to take only her fair share of what they owned. She truly wasn't the type of person to take more than she deserved. I'm not saying that to make her glorious, but that was just the way she was. She knew she was entitled to half of the estate. She did a lot of investigation to make sure and documented it all."

Near the beginning of March 1991, Ann took the next step. She consulted a divorce lawyer, Larry Baker, and in a series of meetings, she discussed her intentions with him.

The attorney would later express his impressions of Ann Racz. "She was immaculate. That's the first thought that came into my mind." Her clothing and hair were always perfect, said Baker. "She would joke. She was very upbeat about what her future held for her." Ann's meticulous organization also impressed him.

One of the most painful aspects of marriage dissolution is custody of the children. Ann told Baker that she wanted to take Joann, Glenn, and Katelin with her, but she would certainly be willing to let John have them at least one weekend each month, and a fair share of the holidays. She expressed willingness to let him also have a say in matters such as education, their personal welfare, and other important influences on their lives. But she did want to be the primary custodial parent.

Regarding division of assets, the attorney advised that she would need to collect their bank statements, investment documents, W-2 forms, and all other financial reports. Ann understood that California is a community-property state. Baker explained, "That means, essentially, you take all the assets, all the debts, put it in a pie, add it up, and split it down the middle."

In their discussion, Baker detected a sense of apprehension in his client. She seemed fearful of retribution from her husband, not from the divorce itself, but related more to the splitting of their money. She clearly did not want John to know where she would be living.

It did not appear to the lawyer that Ann feared physical violence, even though she made a vague reference to him slamming his fist through a wall once during an argument. Her concerns seemed to stem more from worry about emotional abuse and splitting their assets.

Ann not only talked to Larry Baker and her close confidante, Dee Ann Wood, about the troubled marriage, but she also sought advice from Pastor Glen Thorp, at the Santa Clarita Presbyterian Church. His doctorate degree, combined with nineteen years as a minister and counselor, made him well qualified to help. She told him of deep concerns about her marriage, that she was being suffocated in it, and wanted to look at "other options," including the possibility of moving out.

The understanding pastor listened when Ann asked, "When do I know that a marriage is over? When do I know that it's not worth continuing to work on it?" She revealed that her husband forced her to do things she didn't want to do, even in their sex life. He controlled her, she complained, and if she did anything without his permission, he would get angry. Trembling and holding back tears, Ann said that she had hinted to John about possibly wanting to leave, but he had replied, "I'll come and find you wherever you are, and I'll stop you from leaving." She even spoke of his experience as a lawman, and that he kept guns in the house. She feared that if she tried to get away, he might use a gun to stop her.

Holding back on one personal matter, Ann mentioned a male friend she had seen a couple of times, but said little more about Bob Russell. Hoping to salvage the union, Thorp listened carefully. He perceived Ann's struggle of conflicting senses about who she was as a woman compared to her role as a wife.

Of course, John Racz realized that his marriage to Ann floundered on the edge of serious danger. He spoke to her about it and Ann mentioned that she had been confiding in Pastor Thorp. He decided they should see him together and seek his counseling.

In their initial session, Thorp questioned both of them. John admitted that he might have a controlling type of personality, but he didn't seem to think it a serious problem. Ann, Thorp knew, had no confidence in restoring any feelings of love. She appeared to be on the verge of making the break, but she continued to seek Thorp's counsel. By early April, she told Thorp that she had reached an unequivocal decision.

Still, in his duty as a counselor, Thorp set up another meeting to include both of them for Saturday evening, April 20, 1991.

Judy Carter, who had been a close friend of Ann's for nine years, heard words that indicated no chance of reconciliation. Judy worked as secretary to Pastor Thorp, and Ann helped her one day each week. Their companionship grew even closer through membership in the Elizabeth circle group meetings. Because Judy had gone through a separation herself, Ann asked her about the experience, then spoke of her problems with John. For months the two women shared thoughts and opinions. Judy would later say that Ann revealed an abiding fear of her husband. It surprised Judy when Ann confided that she had actually told John that she didn't love him anymore. And even though John had replied that he wanted to change, and became more like Ann wanted him to be, for her it was too little, too late. Ann definitely wanted to go through with the separation and divorce.

* * *

The decision made, Ann signed papers with the divorce attorney. She asked for her share of community property, including a money market investment exceeding $100,000. She wanted a reasonable split of her husband's retirement, disability, and medical benefits, the home's value, plus a monthly payment for living expenses. This would include:

Rent, $750
Food and household supplies, $400
Utilities, $90
Telephone, $35
Laundry and cleaning, $25
Clothing, $100
Medical and Dental, $25
Education expenses, $45
Entertainment, $60
Automobile expenses, gas, oil, insurance, $250
Incidentals for children, $75
Total, $1,855

In addition, Ann sued for physical custody of the three children. The lawyer advised her to carry on as normally as possible until moving day. Also, he knew about arrangements for the moving van to wait, out of sight, until Ann would give them the sign to begin loading her furniture. He ordered the process server to deliver the papers to John Racz on Thursday evening, after the move.

Ann attended a meeting of the Elizabeth circle group in the Evans Room at church on Tuesday, April 16. Some of the women thought Ann looked upset and worried. One of them, Pamela "Pam" Cottrel had been looking forward to hearing Ann conduct the lesson that day and take her turn reading a Bible chapter aloud. Cottrel later described it: "Ann apologized to us and said that other things had happened in her life and that she didn't have the lesson prepared that day. She had made a major decision in her life to move out and seek a divorce." The announcement bothered Cottrel, a dark-haired science teacher who wore round tortoiseshell-frame glasses and an easy smile. She and Ann had grown close through discussions about their children. Recalling the friendship, Cottrel said, "She was very involved in all of her kids, and felt it was important to supplement the education they received in school." The emotional impact of divorce on children is often substantial, and Pam Cottrel hoped it wouldn't create problems in school for Joann, Glenn, and Katelin.

All of Ann's friends in the Elizabeth circle listened intently to her comments, and a few of them left the session deeply troubled about her safety. For the next two weeks, Pam Cottrel searched the newspapers every day. "I was very nervous about it and afraid that something would happen to her. From the way that she talked about her fears for herself and the children, and about him having guns in the house . . . I was so afraid." When no articles appeared involving Ann Racz, Cottrel breathed more easily.

Ann told Pastor Thorp, on Wednesday afternoon, that she had signed a lease for a place to live and would be moving on the following day. She had to get away, she said, to a safe environment. Ann also admitted that she hadn't yet told John because she knew he would do everything he could to stop her, and maybe harm her.

On the eighteenth of April, in 1991, Ann Racz waited until John left for his job in Compton, then signaled two men in a moving van to begin work. By that night, she and her two children occupied a condominium at Peachland.

John Racz left Marian Anderson Elementary School that day, and stopped for coffee on his way home. Upon arrival, he found his wife and children gone, then discovered a note inside an envelope, telling him of her decision.

Peter Danna, the Compton school principal, received a telephone call later that afternoon. It caught him off guard to hear the quaking voice of Racz. In Danna's words, Racz usually sounded "steadfast, reasonable, and his behavior didn't show a lot of emotion." Racz told Danna that his wife had left him and taken their three children, and that he would need about a week off to take care of the situation.

Then Racz asked three strange questions. First he said, "Do you think I'm the kind of guy who would be violent?"

Danna had never even considered the issue, but in view of Racz's evidently distressed state of mind, the principal answered with a simple "No."

"Do you think I'm a mean person?"

"No."

"Do you think I'm the kind of person who would hurt somebody?"

"No, John."

To Danna, the questions seemed odd, but the request to be absent sounded urgent, so he said, "I understand and will give you the time off to take care of what you need to do." Danna also expressed the hope that Racz could return to work in time to take care of state assessment duties coming up in the middle of May. With that, the brief conversation ended.

A retired neighbor who lived across Fortuna Drive from the Racz home, Donald "Don" Pedersen, knew of John's tight-fisted attitude about money and that he wouldn't allow his family to use the air conditioner when temperatures soared in the typically hot Santa Clarita Valley. Pedersen even observed that John would lie on the cool concrete garage floor to grade school papers. Still, it had amazed Pedersen, on that Thursday morning, when he saw a moving van being directed by Ann. He thought, *My goodness, they are moving and nobody has told me anything.* He would miss the wonderful lemon bars that Ann often baked and brought over to Pedersen and his ill wife. It surprised him even more when John Racz trotted across the street that afternoon and asked Pedersen if he knew anything about where Ann and the children might be. Of course, the flummoxed neighbor had no idea.

Pastor Thorp answered his home phone at about 7:00 P.M. and heard John Racz's voice. Sounding surprised, John explained that Ann had left. Thorp expressed sympathy, and said he would still like to meet with both of them on Saturday, April 20, hoping to forestall any further damage.

Another telephone conversation took place that night, when Ann called John from the public telephone. According to later comments from John, "Ann was crying and saying she didn't want to be married anymore."

CHAPTER 5

HOT SPARKS

After having been dropped off by Dee Ann Wood at the Peachland condominium on Friday morning, April 19, Ann readied her three kids for a day of seclusion from everyone, especially John. She drove them more than forty miles to spend the day at Malibu Beach, being entertained on the way by an FM radio station playing current hits by Crystal Waters and Lisa Stansfield, or oldies from Creedence Clearwater and Fleetwood Mac. In weather still too cool for sunbathing, they were content to walk the surf line, inhale the invigorating salty air, pick up shells, watch screeching seagulls swoop over the crashing waves, and peer at the homes of rich and famous residents.

En route home that afternoon, Ann stopped at a pay phone to call Bob Russell, who thought she sounded "exuberant." She also telephoned a neighbor and longtime friend, Brenda George, at her home across the street on Fortuna Drive. The two women sometimes swapped child care, with Ann watching Brenda's son and daughter, about the same age as Katelin and Glenn. Brenda had noticed the moving van on the previous day, but didn't ask questions, so Ann explained about her decision to move, then begged the woman not to tell John anything. They arranged for Brenda to drop by the condo for a visit.

Still trying to keep the children distracted on Saturday, and prevent John from discovering their new residency at Peachland, Ann delivered Katelin to the Valencia Hills clubhouse for a field trip to San Diego's SeaWorld with her Girl Scout Brownie troop. She took Glenn and Joann to Magic Mountain, where breathtaking thrill rides diverted them for several hours. On the way back to the condo, Ann dropped off Joann to stay overnight with a friend.

A little later, Brenda George arrived for a visit as promised. She thought Ann seemed nervous but resolute in her decision. Ann once again appealed to Brenda for absolute secrecy about her location so that John wouldn't be able to find her.

Kathy Ryan, Emi's daughter, also called on Ann that day, showing up at about four-thirty. She spotted Ann outside, playing catch with her son, Glenn. Inside the condo, Kathy observed that boxes and suitcases still waited to be unpacked. She asked how everything was going, and heard about an incident that day that demonstrated Ann's financial distress. At a Wendy's fast-food restaurant, Ann had placed an order on the outdoor speaker, requesting three burgers, three orders of fries, and three drinks. When the attendant told her the total charge, Ann canceled it and drove out. She circled back around while Glenn figured out the cost of three small burgers, one large order of fries, and a single large drink. Ann stopped again at the speaker and placed the more thrifty request. The incident would have been funny except that it reflected Ann's serious level of worry.

Other than that concern, and fear that John might still discover her new address, Ann appeared happy and excited. Kathy thought she seemed relieved at making the break and optimistic about the future. Ann confessed that she dreaded the appointment that evening with Pastor Thorp. John would be there too. "She did not want to go. She just felt sick to her stomach that she would have to be in the same room with John again," Kathy later stated. At least she wouldn't have to stay too long because she needed to pick up Katelin from the clubhouse a few blocks away when she arrived back from the field trip.

Despite her anxious foreboding, Ann kept the appointment. She and John arrived at Pastor Glen Thorp's office in separate cars. In the meeting, John still expressed shock as he told about her leaving and his being served with divorce papers. He read aloud from a statement he had written, indicating that he would do anything to get Ann back, promising to help more around the house and making a commitment to be less frugal. It ended with an offer: *If it doesn't work out to your satisfaction after one year from today, I will leave in a friendly way.*

Thorp later said, "We tried to find a way for the two of them to continue the sessions, with the idea that Ann would have a safe space, and I would meet with them on a regular basis." He interpreted "safe space" as Ann being able to live where John couldn't find her.

Before leaving, they agreed to assemble again, on the next day, Sunday, April 21, in the late afternoon. Ann said she planned to take the kids to church that morning, but afterward would bring them over to the Fortuna house for a visit prior to the counseling appointment.

Sunday morning dawned clear and bright, a perfect day for a drive to Malibu Beach. Ann made the distance in about an hour and arrived at the Presbyterian church on Malibu Canyon Road with a distant view of the ocean, and not far from the colorful redbrick buildings of Pepperdine University. (The sixty-year-old church burned to the ground in a disastrous 2007 fire that destroyed scores of homes in the area.) After the services, she stopped again at a public telephone to make a few calls. She spoke with her sister, Emi, and her brother Joji to update them on her situation. Next she told Bob Russell about a recent argument with her husband. Russell cheered her up with an invitation to join him at Disneyland on June 2 to celebrate his daughter's fifth birthday. Delighted, Ann said she would love it.

Back in Valencia, she kept her promise to deliver the kids to John at the Fortuna house. Brenda George, Ann's friend and neighbor across the street, noticed her white minivan pull into the driveway, and the brake lights stayed on while John stood next to the driver's window and talked to Ann through a narrow opening.

Ann pulled out and John followed in his own car to keep the appointment with Pastor Thorp. In their session that time, Ann said she had made her decision and was going to stick with it. John once again read from a letter he had written, asking for another chance to reconcile. He said that nothing in his life had altered his feelings more than events of the past few days. He admitted being angry upon finding her gone on Thursday, but he acknowledged his own faults while complimenting Ann as a mother and wife.

Part of the discussion involved prearranged tile work to be done the next day at the Fortuna house. Ann agreed to show up there and pay for her portion of the expenses. They scheduled another meeting for Thursday, April 25. Before deciding to call it a night, Thorp suggested that Ann and John refrain from getting together alone under any circumstances, because sometimes things happen in the heat of the moment.

John departed, and Ann drove Thorp to his home. On the way, he made another plea for her to reconsider and asked her not to do anything rash. Privately he realized that her demeanor reflected noticeable fear. It was the last time the minister ever saw Ann Racz.

For dinner that Sunday evening, John took his three children to a local Chinese restaurant. Ann drove over to the Fortuna house to take the kids, and found a note taped to the door telling her where they had gone to eat. She picked them up from the restaurant at eight o'clock, after they had completed their meal, and took them back to Peachland.

That night John Racz called Thorp to reaffirm his hope that Ann would relent and return to their home. He said he might even consider asking Ann and the kids to move back in on the condition that he would move out in exchange for her giving up the idea of divorce. Thorp, of course, could make no promises.

With the children asleep in the condo, Ann found some private time to write a letter to Bob Russell:

> *Hello Dear Heart and gentle lover,*
>   *When I need a kiss, you kiss me. When I need to be*
> *held, you put your arms around me to embrace me*
> *with so much warmth and affection. You know just*
> *when to do the things I love you to do.*

Ann's expressions of affection continued with a request for Bob to let her know if her love ever became smothering. Their ability to openly communicate pleased her. Both of them, she noted, had learned from life's experiences and she hoped the wisdom they had gained would contribute to warm compatibility for the remainder of their lives. She expressed deep gratitude for his emotional, physical, and mental support, and volunteered that she would do "anything" for him. Never, she said, in her fantasies or imagination, could she have imagined the fulfillment their relationship provided:

> *It overwhelms me beyond my wildest dreams. This is*
> *greater than fiction. Don't worry, our dream will not*
> *end. We will be able to live up to each other's expecta-*
> *tions because we have such a strong bond of love.*

The strength and power of their love, said Ann, would see them through "trials and tribulations." In reference to her husband, Ann mentioned that his demands and control had only diminished her respect for him, and her pastor had made that point during counseling. A major factor in wrecking the marriage had been John's continued reliance on control. Ann looked forward to a life with Bob that involved none of these wrong-headed tactics. She hoped he felt the same.

With her typical bubbly enthusiasm, Ann wrote of the fun she expected to have with Bob, and committed her perpetual, exclusive love to him. In the letter's final paragraph, Ann turned even more personal:

> *I will never have sex with John again. I will not touch him again. You don't know how good that makes me feel. I'm free. I want to celebrate this first victory, my first big step, by making sensuous mad love to you. I want to share my joy with you. I need you so much, but I'll be a good girl and wait for the appropriate opportunity. The next time we get together everybody stand back or you will get hit by some hot sparks because I may get passionate right there where we stand upon our first embrace. Would you be embarrassed? I may forget I'm a lady. I can't wait to stroll down Main Street with you.*
>
> *Until then, or sooner, Ann*

On a morning that would change the lives of many people, April 22, Ann Racz delivered her three children to their schools, without the realization that she would never be able to do it again. After walking Katelin into Ms. Dorrie Dean's second-grade class, Ann handed the teacher a note written on blue paper. It informed Dean that Katelin would no longer take the school bus home to Fortuna Drive, but would instead be picked up by Ann. The mother also made a change in an information card kept on file for each student. Ann entered the name and telephone number of Dee Ann Wood as the person to be contacted in case of emergency or disaster.

Ann also dropped into Glenn's classroom and told Ms. Lois Becker that the move had taken place.

She returned to the condo, did some housekeeping chores and laundry, then drove to the Target store. The VCR machine she had previously purchased there had malfunctioned, so she traded it for a new one, and left the store before one o'clock with the boxed appliance in the rear of her minivan.

Twenty minutes later, Ann cashed in a $13, 242.13 joint certificate of deposit (CD) at the Home Federal Bank. She withdrew the money in the form of a cashier's check for $3,000, another check made out to John Racz for $8,942.13, and $2,000 in cash. Leaving the bank, she headed for the supermarket, where she shopped for groceries.

Inside the Hughes store, Ann purchased milk and ingredients to make the pizza she planned to prepare for dinner. Back in the condo, she placed the milk in the tiny refrigerator Kathy Ryan had given her, then laid a package of Boboli pizza crust on the counter, alongside a jar of red Ragú sauce.

At two-thirty that afternoon, she arrived at the Fortuna house and gave John the cashier's check for $8,942.13 as his lion's share of the CD, along with the separate check for $3,000 to pay her part of the tile work being done in the kitchen, as she had promised. She left immediately.

Within a few minutes, Ann walked into the First Nationwide Bank, and made a deposit in her Monday Flowers account, using the $2,000 in cash she had received at Home Federal.

The next stop took her to Wiley Canyon Elementary School and Hart High School, where she picked up Glenn and Joann. With them in the minivan, Ann drove to the Valencia Hills clubhouse, where Katelin's Brownie troop usually met every Monday. She exited her car and walked toward the entrance, but she noticed an acquaintance hailing her in the parking lot. It was Douglas Krantz, a professional stagehand who drove to a Los Angeles theater most days to work on a production of *Phantom of the Opera*. His daughter was one of Katelin's classmates and a fellow Brownie. Krantz said, "Oh, the girls aren't here today. They have gone on an excursion. They've gone bowling."

Ann said, "Oh, John must have forgotten to tell me," nodded her thanks, returned to the minivan, and drove to the Fortuna house. Missing her youngest daughter didn't bother Ann because she knew that her friend Carol Kuwata, whose child also belonged to the troop, would bring them as soon as the bowling ended. As transportation chairman for the Brownies, Kuwata frequently gave Katelin a ride to her home on Fortuna Drive. The two women also knew each other as fellow soccer moms.

Monday, April 22, 1991, has seared itself forever in Joann Racz's mind. She later recalled getting out of school at about two-thirty, being picked up by her mother, and going over to the home from which they had moved. "We were going to have homemade pizza for dinner that night. But first, my mom told us that she needed to talk to my dad. They were going to have a talk and we were to go in the house and wait."

Don Pedersen, the retired neighbor on the opposite side of Fortuna Drive, had been curious ever since the moving van incident four days earlier, and he kept an eye out to see what might happen next. In the middle of the afternoon on that Monday, he noticed Ann's white minivan pull into the Racz driveway, and stop about halfway into the garage. Pedersen could see Ann in the driver's seat and the kids inside. He watched as John emerged from the house and talked to Ann through the driver's window. Their conversation, Pedersen thought, lasted about twenty minutes, while the children remained seated. Ann's foot apparently never left the brake pedal because Pedersen could see the brake lights illuminated the entire time. At last, Joann and Glenn emerged and scampered into the house. John and Ann continued to talk perhaps twenty more minutes.

According to Joann's recollection, the conversation between

her parents lasted long enough for the kids to get hungry. Even if they went over to the condo right away, it would take some time to prepare the pizza. "So I came out to the garage, said I was hungry, and asked when we were going to eat. Mom said she would go to McDonald's, up on hamburger hill, and bring something back for us."

She left at about four o'clock. It would normally take only a few minutes to reach the McDonald's fast-food restaurant, no more than a mile from the Racz home.

In Pedersen's memory of events, Ann backed out and drove downhill toward the cul-de-sac exit. Still watching, Pedersen observed John retreat and enter the house through the front door.

Inside, John announced to his kids that he was going to McDonald's to get them some food too.

Meanwhile, Ann drove only about three houses away and parked in a driveway, where another resident, Thomas "Tom" Deardorff, stood outside.

Deardorff's daughter and Katelin, the same age, often played together, and Joann sometimes babysat with her. So, like other neighbors, Deardorff had also been surprised when a moving van appeared at the Racz home a few days earlier. It amazed him even more to hear that Ann and the three children had left John and had moved out. Deardorff wondered if Joann still planned to keep an appointment that Monday night to babysit. As he washed one of several cars he restored as a hobby, he spotted Ann leaving and waved her over. Ann pulled partly into his driveway, and Deardorff asked about Joann's availability that night, at about seven-thirty. Ann said, "No problem, she will be there," and commented that she was on the way to get her kids some food at McDonald's.

The brief exchange of words between them lasted only a few seconds before Ann pulled out again to leave.

Up the street, Pedersen still watched. Something else immediately caught his eye. "I seen John coming out of the garage seemingly in a hurry. Got in his car, backed out rapidly, and exited, started down the street. And . . . I looked down there and seen Ann's van. It was just rounding the curve and John was right behind her. He seemed to be in a big hurry."

CHAPTER 6

MISSING

After both parents left, Joann and Glenn busied themselves while waiting for something to eat. Glenn played Nintendo games. Joann telephoned one of her close friends, Kristin Best, a classmate who had often spent the night with her in the Racz home. After they chatted for a while, and then hung up, Joann felt time seemed to drag. They spoke again, twice, by phone. Joann expressed her concern about why it was taking so long for either of her parents to bring back something to eat.

Ann and John had been gone approximately an hour when Carol Kuwata, driving four of the Brownies home from the bowling event, delivered Katelin to the Fortuna house. As they pulled to the curb, Joann heard Katelin's soft, high voice say, "I don't live here anymore. I live in a condo now." Unaware of Ann's move, and familiar with childish imagination, Kuwata said, "Oh, come on, Katelin." The driver watched as Katelin climbed out, walked to her front door, opened it, and waved to signify the presence of a family member inside.

Katelin would later vaguely recall being distressed

about her parents' absence, and standing outside near the air conditioner, crying.

The exact time John returned to the Fortuna house would turn out to be the subject of confusion and controversy. When asked later, Joann Racz at first guessed he had been gone only a few minutes. Other sources suggested that it might have been anywhere from two to four hours.

When the door finally opened, John walked into the house alone. Watching Glenn play his Nintendo games in the family room, Joann looked up, fully expecting to see her mother come in, carrying bags of hot food. Instead, John offered them a meager bag from McDonald's. The whole thing seemed peculiar to both kids. They also didn't understand why the french fries were ice-cold. But it disturbed them even more when John said, "Your mother said she was going away for a while to think things over." He didn't respond when they asked when she would return.

Joann called her friend Kristin again to report that her father had finally returned, and to complain about the cold food.

In Kristin's home, her mother detected brewing trouble by her daughter's chagrined expression. She asked Kristin about it, and the teenager replied "Something's weird! Joann's mom and dad were gone a long time and he came back with ice-cold french fries." The words struck the mother as nothing more than typical adolescent drama. It would be a long time before the full implication became apparent.

The soggy, limp fries failed miserably to satisfy the Racz children. They had expected to eat pizza for dinner, so John told them he would treat them at a nearby restaurant.

They piled into his Honda at about seven o'clock and drove about a mile before turning into a strip mall, where John led his trio into a pizza parlor. With their stomachs full, they returned to the Fortuna house. All three children wondered where their mother had gone, and why she would mysteriously decide to take a trip or "go away to think." A terrible sense of confusion and fear gripped them. This wasn't like her at all.

The hours passed and Ann still didn't return. John told them they would sleep in the house, but this only added to their anxiety. They would need a change of clothing to attend school on Tuesday, and everything they owned was over at the condo. Plus, their schoolbooks, along with personal possessions, were stuffed inside backpacks lying in the back of Ann's minivan. John assured them that everything would be taken care of.

Later that night, over at the Peachland condo, managers William and Cheryl Freet grew concerned about Ann and her kids. They had agreed to make some necessary repairs in the condo, and had tried all afternoon to gain access. Checking again, long after dark, they could raise no one and observed no lights showing through any of the windows. They believed that the new tenant would have mentioned any plans to be away overnight, and wondered if something had gone wrong.

Getting ready for school on Tuesday morning, Joann and Glenn dressed in the same clothing they had worn the previous day. John called neighbor Brenda George, explained that Katelin had only her Brownie uniform, and asked if he could borrow an outfit belonging to Brenda's daughter for Kate to wear to school that day. When Brenda walked over to deliver it, John asked if she would pick Katelin up from school that afternoon and for the rest of the week. The puzzled woman said she would be glad to help.

Joann struggled with emotional stress the entire day. She fretted all evening, and decided to call Pastor Glenn Thorp from a bedroom upstairs, where her father couldn't hear. When Thorp answered, Joann explained her anxiety. She couldn't believe that her mother hadn't returned to the Fortuna house to pick all three of them up and take them back to the condo.

Thorp tried to reassure Joann, pointing out that he expected to see Ann on Thursday evening at a counseling session appointment with both parents. But he said he would check to see if she might have returned to the condo that night. Thorp drove to Peachland and knocked on the door of Ann's unit a little after nine o' clock. No lights were on and no one answered. He scribbled on the back of his business card: *Ann, Please give me a call when you return. Joann was concerned about you—I will not reveal this address. Love, Glen.* Thorp stuck it in the sliding glass door and left.

Glenn Racz needed a change of clothing by Wednesday morning, so John turned to Brenda George again and borrowed some of her son's clothing. A short time before she planned to pick up Katelin from school, Brenda received another mystifying call from John. He said that he was at a bank in Los Angeles and would be delayed. Would she watch Katelin until he arrived home? Brenda knew that John had taken time off from work that week, and couldn't understand why he needed to go all the way to Los Angeles to do any banking. He didn't arrive home until seven-thirty that night, and offered no explanation for being so late.

Earlier that afternoon, Joann had grown tired of wearing the same skirt and blouse, and walked over to the condominium after school. Maybe she could find some clue about her mother. Joann discovered that she could gain access through the sliding glass door by pushing hard near the malfunctioning latch and opening it. Seeing nothing to help allay her fears about Ann, Joann gathered some clothing for herself and her siblings to take with her. As soon as she arrived back at the Fortuna house, she saw something that made her heart race with a flicker of hope. On the kitchen table lay the schoolbooks, pens, and pencils. Over to one side of the room, she spotted her backpack and Glenn's, along with her cosmetic kit, all of which had been left in the back of Ann's car. Did this mean her mother had returned?

She raced into the living room to find her father and asked, "Dad, where did all of this stuff come from?"

"Your mother dropped them off," he replied in a flat, emotionless voice. He added a brief comment that Ann had said the kids preferred to stay with their dad. Joann wanted to know just what that meant, but he offered no elaboration.

At the most recent counseling session with Pastor Glen Thorp, Ann and John had scheduled the next meeting for Thursday, April 25, at four o' clock. A few hours before the appointed hour, John called Thorp and said that Ann would not be able to come that night. It struck Thorp as peculiar because Ann had never been absent nor even tardy for any of their church meetings. In the past, if she had needed to change the schedule, she called well in advance. In view of Joann's request, and the fact that he hadn't heard anything from Ann, he felt the hair on the back of his neck bristle. It surprised Thorp even more when John agreed to come alone.

Racz arrived at the church office close to seven-thirty, and their conversation generally speculated about why Ann hadn't shown up. Thorp noticed perspiration on Racz's forehead, as if he'd been involved in some physical exertion, and a couple of scratches on his face, perhaps made by a fingernail.

By Friday morning, several other people grew worried about Ann. Emi Ryan called Brenda George to ask if she had heard from Ann. Both women felt creeping intuition of something really being wrong. Separately they talked to a few other mutual friends. None had heard anything from the missing woman. In consensus they asked Brenda to speak with John and try to get more information.

Brenda chose to do it by telephone and called John that night at ten o'clock. Recalling it later, Brenda said, "I told him that I had spoken to Ann's friends from her church group and also to Emi, and we were all very concerned because we realized that none of us had seen Ann and none of her relatives had seen her."

Racz's answer did nothing to ease Brenda's worry. He said simply she's all right, safe, and not to worry. Then he added, "When I think she may not come back, it makes me want to cry."

The whole conversation left Brenda even more uneasy.

Growing tension among Ann's friends paled next to the whirlpool of conflict and confusion in Joann Racz's mind. Trying to maintain hope, yet fearing the worst, she didn't know which way to turn. Why wouldn't her father say where her mother went and when she would come home? Why wasn't there a note or a phone call from her mom? None of this made any sense, and Joann fought against the dark suspicions eating away at her. She decided to call her cousin Kathy, Emi's daughter.

As soon as Kathy answered the phone, Joann asked, "Have you seen my mom?"

Puzzled, since she hadn't yet heard of Ann's disappearance, Kathy asked, "Well, what do you mean? That you haven't seen her?" She listened while Joann explained what had happened and expressed her foreboding. After trying to reassure the teenager, Kathy said she would go to the condo to see if she could find anything out. She drove to Peachland that evening and looked unsuccessfully around the carports for Ann's minivan. At the condo, she saw no lights on and found the doors locked. Deeply troubled, she left.

Joann called Kathy again on Saturday, from a girlfriend's home where she stayed all night, and once more on Sunday while her father visited with Pastor Thorp. The telephone conversations consisted mostly of attempts to console one another. Kathy agreed to go over to the condo again on Monday.

Through that weekend, Brenda George continued to fret about her neighbor's unexplained absence. Ann had gone on trips before, and she had always discussed it with Brenda well in advance. Later musing about it, Brenda said, "Ann would leave an extremely detailed itinerary, exactly where she was going and who with and where they would be staying, all the details exactly." Brenda had even taken care of Katelin during one of these journeys, and Ann had provided specific instructions of child care. "I think that was how I got to know our mutual friend, Dee Ann, because she and I shared the baby-sitting on at least one of the trips."

Dee Ann Wood had spoken briefly with Brenda on Thursday about Ann's absence, but didn't put much importance on it at first because she realized that the separation had been in effect only a few days. Perhaps Ann had decided to get away, alone, for a short while.

Reviewing it later, Dee Ann said, "It was the following Sunday, April twenty-eighth, that Kathy called me, about ten o'clock at night, and asked if I had seen Ann. I told her yes, that I had been with her a week ago Friday. Kathy said no one had seen her since Monday, including her kids. I thought, 'Oh, my God!'" A remark that Ann had once made leaped forward in Dee Ann's mind. Ann had said that if she really did leave John, he might kill her. At the time, it had seemed like just an offhand rhetorical comment. Now it assumed horrific proportions. Was it just a throwaway statement made for shock value, or did she really harbor that fear? "I thought, 'Oh, my God, he did kill her then.' But it was so stunning to me because I had pooh-poohed her when she said she was afraid. I had warned her to be careful and not underestimate John—the fact that she didn't think he was picking up on the clues when she did things. I thought that was kind of naïve. And it seemed to me that she was kind of overreacting the night she wanted to hide her car. I thought she could just avoid trouble by not answering the door, and I didn't think he would break it down. But I didn't see the danger that he might actually take her life. I was alarmed. If she hadn't been seen from Monday until Sunday, there was no other explanation. She wouldn't have just walked away, for many reasons.

"I asked Kathy, 'What do we do now? Where are the kids?' She said they are at John's. Then she mentioned something about herself and her mother planning on talking to Glen Thorp that night or on Monday. I said I thought it was a good idea to speak to the pastor."

Pastor Thorp held services that Sunday, with John Racz in attendance. He announced to his congregation that their friend, Ann Racz , had separated from her husband and was away. Thorp asked for their prayers. Among those in attendance, Roma Prior and her husband, both in their late sixties, decided to do more than pray. Having known Ann and John for ten years, they invited John and the kids to join them for dinner on Monday night. Roma also spoke to other church members, who agreed to deliver home-cooked meals to the Fortuna house the remainder of that week.

John Racz returned to his teaching job in Compton on Monday morning. His principal, Peter Danna, welcomed him back and expressed hope for everything being under control at home. With his infallible knack for remembering time frames, he recalled meeting Ann only one time, the previous Christmas at a party in John's classroom. While Danna spoke, he noticed a scratch mark on the side of John's face, extending down below the jawbone onto the neck, nearly two inches long. It brought to Danna's mind the image of what a raking fingernail might do, but he gave it no serious thought.

Racz said nothing to Danna about his wife being missing, but later that day at his appointment with Pastor Thorp, he mentioned a new development. He said that Ann had called and informed him that she had left her car at a lot called Flyaway in Van Nuys, about fifteen miles south of Valencia. Flyaway provides travelers with parking, airline counter services, and bus transportation to Los Angeles International Airport. To Thorp, John seemed to be implying, without specifically saying it, that Ann was on a long trip. Neither his voice nor expression reflected any emotion. Thorp asked Racz if he knew Ann's destination. No, John said. This exchange, combined with what he already knew, troubled Thorp and elevated his growing suspicion. He later said, "Ann would always call me when she was going on any trip to any place, and would always keep me informed."

That evening John took the kids over to the Prior home, where they ate dinner with Roma and her husband. Of course, Roma asked about Ann. John said that he hadn't seen her since April 22, and didn't know where she was. But, he added, Ann had called him yesterday afternoon. He claimed that he had asked her to come home, but she wouldn't even tell him where she was calling from.

Kathy Ryan had promised Joann she would check the condo again on Monday. She arrived late that day and used information Joann had give her about how to enter through the sliding glass door. Inside, she walked through the silent rooms. In the kitchen, the tiny refrigerator Kathy had given to Ann sat on the floor, with a half-filled paper bag of groceries resting on top of it. Across the patterned linoleum floor, on a light wood-grained counter, Kathy saw a package of Boboli pizza crust next to a jar of Ragú pizza sauce. The entire kitchen looked as if Ann had walked out in the middle of cleaning chores, planning to return within a few minutes and put things away. It certainly did not resemble the usual compulsive tidiness of Ann Racz.

In the other rooms, Kathy searched for any evidence indicating that Ann might have actually taken a trip. In one bathroom, Kathy noticed something that suggested exactly the contrary. Ann's curling iron lay next to the washbasin, and her cosmetics stood neatly in the medicine cabinet. Very few women go away—even overnight—without these personal items.

Glancing elsewhere in the condo, Kathy looked for anything with Ann's neat, calligraphic writing style. She knew that her aunt always made meticulous, detailed notes and entries on planning calendars. Nothing turned up to even hint at a trip.

Kathy did find a written note from Glenn. He had apparently walked over from school, just as Joann had, to retrieve something he needed:

> *Mom,*
> *I just came to take my Legos for a project. Joann got really mad but I sort of feel that was the right thing to do. I guess Dad sort of was the one who started it so it's not all your fault or all Dad's fault. I love you.*
>
> *Glenn*

Frustrated and sick with worry, Kathy left empty-handed, unable to offer anything that might help dispel Joann's fears.

Ann Racz had been a regular volunteer worker on Tuesdays at Hart High School, where Joann attended. Her absence on the last day of April magnified the pain for Joann, her friends, and regular staff members, who had known and admired Ann.

The level of anxiety among Ann's relatives and friends darkened their existence with dread, like overhead smoke from an approaching brush fire that sometimes devastated the hillside country where they lived. Images of Ann suffering a terrible fate ravaged Dee Ann Wood's thoughts. She had to do something—she at last picked up her phone and called Pastor Glen Thorp. In their conversation, she asked Thorp to call Ann's sister, Emi, at her home in Mesa, Arizona, near Phoenix.

Emi Ryan had suffered an internal storm of ragged emotions during the past few days, struggling to keep her heart in one piece. Pastor Thorp's call allowed her to express her worries. They exchanged information each of them had about Ann's actions before she vanished, including her affection for Bob Russell.

As soon as Thorp ended his discussion with Emi, he decided he had to make one more telephone contact in an attempt to locate Ann. If she had really gone away, it might be to join someone she apparently loved. When Bob Russell answered Thorp's call, though, his words made the pastor even more convinced that something terrible had happened. Russell had no idea where Ann might be and said he hadn't heard from her.

Thorp called Emi back with the bad news. Only one reasonable course of action remained to be taken now, and Emi authorized Thorp to act on her behalf.

CHAPTER 7

FLYAWAY MYSTERY

On Wednesday morning, May 1, 1991, Glen Thorp drove to the Santa Clarita Valley Sheriff's station and filed a missing person report.

A deputy sheriff, dispatched to the Peachland condominium, found the sliding glass door unlocked and conducted a brief search inside for any clues that might lead to finding Ann Racz. Observing that the resident had apparently still been in the process of moving in, with many possessions still in packing boxes, the deputy glanced into the bathroom, where he spotted cosmetics and a curling iron near the washbasin. This didn't look good. He reported his observations to a lieutenant, who forwarded the information to a specialized force.

Sergeant John View, supervisor of two detectives and a secretary making up the Missing Persons Unit (MPU), took on the Racz case. The absent woman's name rang a bell in View's memory, and the image crystallized when he saw her husband's name. He and John Racz had worked together early in their careers at the Firestone substation in South Central Los Angeles.

A muscular man, with dark, wavy hair, friendly eyes, and a broad grin topped by a brushy mustache, View and his small missing persons force handled over 1,200 reports annually. More than 95 percent of the missing people turned up alive and well within a few days. A few of the remainder were never re- solved, or ended in tragic results with the discovery of a dead body, some due to accidents and others victimized by killers.

Describing his unit's procedures, View said, "Any case that was reported as a missing person to one of the sheriff's stations was sent to sheriff's homicide. Missing adults, that is. And as a sergeant, I would review them and pass them out to the two detectives so we'd have an equal caseload." Detective Sally Fynan inherited this one. Her short reddish hair and twinkling eyes brought to mind the sparkle of actress Maureen O'Hara.

Fynan interviewed Joann Racz on Monday, May 6. The wor- ried teenager told of being picked up from school by her mother on that fateful Monday, two weeks earlier, and being taken to the Fortuna house. At about four o'clock, her mom, and then her dad, went to McDonald's to get some food for the kids. Sometime later, only her father returned, bringing cold french fries. This shocked Joann because she was certain her mom would come back, especially since Joann needed her schoolbooks. A couple of days later, she said, her books, along with notepapers, folders, a pencil bag, and her makeup kit, turned up in the house. Joann's father, she said, explained that her mother had dropped them off.

Fynan took notes of her interview with Joann, including a comment from her dad that had confused the girl. Mr. Racz, she said, claimed that her mom informed him that all of the kids had expressed a preference to stay with their father. Her brown eyes brimming with tears, Joann told Fynan that it wasn't true. Actually, when her mother had talked about a di- vorce, Joann had asked her if the children could alternately stay with each parent for perhaps a week at a time.

Inquiring what else her father had said, Fynan learned that

he spoke of giving his wife $8,000 on the Monday that she had left, and that he had talked to her by telephone when she called him a few days later. Joann indicated to Fynan that her mother had never gone away like this before. Also, her mom had left things in the condominium that she would definitely need on a trip, including her curling iron and clothing.

Emi Ryan had traveled from her home in Arizona and met with Detective Fynan after Joann's interview. To Emi, the whole set of circumstances reeked with suspicion, and she emphasized to the investigator that Ann "is a very stable person." This type of behavior, or sudden unexplained departure, didn't fit at all with her normal conduct.

For a third interview on that same Monday, Fynan contacted Pastor Glen Thorp. He could offer nothing new. He said that he had met with John Racz for a further counseling session two days earlier, on Saturday, but nothing helpful to solving the mystery had emerged.

Making a last stop that afternoon, Fynan faced John Racz. He openly admitted to the detective that he and his wife had marital problems. Yet, it still had astonished him to find, on Thursday, April 18, when he returned home from work, that she had moved out. A note Ann left informed Racz that she was leaving him.

Racz told Fynan that Ann had called late that evening, but she refused to say where she and the children were staying. After another phone call on Friday, they had agreed to seek counseling with Pastor Glen Thorp, which took place on Saturday. In that meeting, said Racz, Ann had confirmed her intentions to end the marriage. She did, however, agree to bring the children for a visit on Sunday, April 21. She kept her commitment, and they again visited Thorp.

The detective listened as Racz told of taking his children out for Chinese food, and his wife picking them up at the restaurant

afterward. The next day, he said, Ann took care of some banking business regarding a certificate of deposit that had matured,
came to the family residence, and gave him his share of it.

Fynan's detailed notes reflected Racz's narrative of subsequent events that day in which Ann had picked up the children
and brought them over to his home, but did not contain any reference to Katelin being dropped off later by the Brownie driver.

According to the detective's written record, Racz stated that
the kids came into the house, then joined Ann in the backyard,
where they talked together. Ann, he said, enjoyed traveling, so
he decided to provide her with the opportunity to go on a vacation and think things over. Not only that, but he would give
her all the money she needed so she would no longer think of
him as a tightwad. After the backyard conversation, Racz
claimed, he assured her that he would take good care of the
children during her absence. At that point, Ann said good-
bye to the kids and left.

As Racz continued his account, Fynan made more entries
in her notebook. He told her that he met Ann on April 23 at a
nearby Carl's Jr., where he gave her $8,000 in cash. The next
afternoon, he said, they met again, at four-thirty, inside
a nearby Tips restaurant and he handed over even more
money—$17,000 in cash. Racz volunteered that he had bor-
rowed it from his credit union in the form of two cashier's
checks. En route to his appointment with Ann, he had stopped
at two different banks and cashed them. According to Racz,
he hoped that these gifts would convince Ann not to end their
marriage. She had insisted, though, on going away to think
things over, and she refused to tell him her destination.

Once again, Racz insisted to Fynan that Ann had made a
collect call from LAX on the afternoon of Friday, April 26, to
state that she was going away to think about things. He also
said that her car was parked at Flyaway in the valley and that
he could either leave it or pick it up as she was taking a shuttle to the airport. He had chosen, he said, to go the Flyaway

parking area and move the car from the sun to a shady spot because there was a VCR inside it. This comment seemed strange. People familiar with the large parking area knew there were no trees or other ostensibly shady areas in it. And how would shade protect a video recording machine?

It is a routine function for investigators hunting missing people to check with the Los Angeles County Coroner's Office. Detective Fynan did this on Tuesday, and followed up by also contacting the county medical center, jail, and the Los Angeles Police Department (LAPD). She noted, "These checks met with negative results." She also probed the National Crime Information Center (NCIC), a database operated by a branch of the FBI to provide nationwide information flow for various law enforcement agencies. Nothing related to Ann Racz turned up.

Curious about John Racz's claim that he had moved Ann's car to a shady spot in the Flyaway lot to protect a VCR inside it, Detective Fynan, accompanied by Sergeant John View, drove to the facility in Van Nuys. They found her 1989 Plymouth Vista minivan parked in row D10, next to a large trailer house. During a short period of time each day, it would provide a modicum of shade. The Plymouth was locked, but the investigators peered through the windows, looking for any obvious signs of foul play. They saw nothing to indicate a struggle or any sign of bloodstains. Fynan noted the driver's seat was set in the far back position, obviously for a taller person than Ann to drive it. Someone had left the windows down just a crack. An "unknown object in the rear of the van" was covered with a blanket or a sunshade.

Because no evidence yet existed to suggest the commission of a crime, the officers saw no need to impound the vehicle. As far as they knew, Ann was on a vacation and could return at any time to retrieve her car. Before any additional measures could be taken, a lot of footwork remained to be done.

Fynan and View took the next step by visiting all six airline counters in the Flyaway building. They interviewed personnel at Continental, Delta, U.S. Air, United, Northwest, and American Airlines. At each stop, they showed the representatives a color photo of Ann Racz, stated her name, and asked if this person had purchased a ticket at any time since April 22. None of the airline people recognized the person in the photo, nor did they have any records of a ticket purchase by Ann Racz or Ann Yoshiyama.

A compelling sense of something amiss in this case kept View and Fynan digging, even beyond the typical missing person hunt. They decided to have another chat with Pastor Thorp at his home.

Sensitive about possibly saying something that could be considered privileged information, Thorp chose his words carefully. It wouldn't be correct to reveal anything that Ann or John had told him at their private marriage counseling meetings. He told the investigators that he had known the couple for approximately eighteen months, and that Ann had worked for the church on a part-time basis. She and her husband had been having marital problems, which was pretty well-known by most of their friends.

Asked what had precipitated his visit to the sheriff's office to report that Ann was missing, Thorp admitted that Emi Ryan, Ann's sister, had asked him to do it after conferring with Dee Ann Wood, Ann's best friend. They had both been deeply concerned due to not hearing from her for quite a while. Thorp said he had last seen Ann at about five-thirty in the afternoon of April 21, after a counseling session with John at the church office.

Still showing caution and reluctance, Thorp remarked, "I told both John and Ann that because of their strained marital relationship, I think it is best for you not to meet alone, but to have me or another party present." Another get-together had been scheduled for April 25, he said, and he planned to continue meeting with them until their scheduled divorce court hearing on May 14. "John did come to my office on April twenty-fifth, but Ann did not. He indicated to me that Ann had taken him up on his offer for her to go away and he stated that he had no idea where she went."

With hope that he might help the detectives track Ann down, Thorp decided to add a little bit more. He told them that Ann was afraid her husband would stop her from leaving him and that's why she was being so secretive about her plans. "In fact, she didn't even tell me until the day before she actually moved." At the last meeting Ann attended, he said, she had been very "pro-divorce" and appeared to have made up her mind. She felt that she should have custody of the children, since she wasn't working and could look after them full-time. John, Thorp added, had also expressed interest in having the children. "It really didn't seem to be a big problem."

"When did you first think something serious was wrong?"

"I first felt it on Tuesday, April twenty-third," Thorp said, "when their oldest daughter, Joann, called me and asked if I had heard from her mom. I felt then that Ann's disappearance was totally out of character."

During the sixteenth day of Ann's absence, a Wednesday, Detectives View and Fynan accompanied Joann to the condominium. They walked through the eerily quiet rooms, which had now gathered a light patina of dust, and collected several items, including a pair of letters addressed to Ann and the note on a business card left by Pastor Glen Thorp.

View listened as Joann spoke. He noted her recollection of hearing Ann say, several months ago, that she planned to divorce John and that she wanted to make it as easy as possible on the children to leave. Ann had also confided in Joann about fearing her husband because he had been a cop, but she didn't think he would hurt the kids. According to Joann, View wrote, her father had been both protective and possessive of her mother, and demanded to know at all times where she was.

* * *

The two investigators drove the short distance from Peachland to John Racz's house on Fortuna Drive. They had made an advance appointment with him, but upon arrival, they found no one home. The investigators chose to wait, and after more than half an hour, John Racz showed up. He invited them to sit in the living room, then instantly disappeared. Glancing at one another, the officers bristled at this behavior bordering on rudeness. After another interminable wait, Fynan rose, went through other rooms, found Racz, and suggested he join them. He complied, muttering something about attending to the kids. Immediately he asked, "Is this conversation on the record and should I tape-record it?"

Wrinkling his forehead and wondering if he had heard this guy correctly, View replied, "Yes, it is on the record, and you can certainly record it if you want to." Family members of a missing person usually show up punctually and have a little different reaction to the visit of officers who are trying to help find the loved one.

After a series of questions and answers, View jotted in his notebook that Racz hadn't heard from his wife since the collect phone call she made on Friday, April 26, and that he reiterated his previous account of events prior to her disappearance. Appearing uncomfortable, Racz addressed View directly and asked if he would come upstairs for a one-on-one chat. Sergeant View hesitated, then walked up a flight with him.

Now in private, Racz turned the conversation to their time as colleagues at the Firestone sheriff's station years ago. They hadn't been buddies, or even friends at the time, just two deputies assigned to the same location. Yet, John suddenly wanted to reminisce about the old days. It struck View as quite odd, and he reminded Racz that the purpose of today's meeting was to find information that might help locate Ann.

"Why would you two think I had anything to do with her disappearance?" Racz asked.

Taken aback, View replied, "I'm here to find out what happened to your wife. I'm not accusing you of anything."

In a demeanor that View would later describe as "starting to break down," Racz launched into a diatribe, admitting that he was having marital problems, like all people have. He remarked that he was a good father, and that Ann was on a trip.

"That's what we're here to find out," View said, thinking that perhaps the conversation might turn productive. Instead, Racz spoke in disjointed phrases about enjoying his time as a deputy, that he was a good father, and not knowing why people would think he had anything to do with Ann's absence, or harming her. View asked what the marital problems were about, but when Racz started to explain that it was of a sexual nature, View stopped him, not wanting to hear those kinds of details. He said, "John, we're here to find out what happened to Ann, and the best way to do that is go downstairs and talk to both of us and tell us where she is."

Back in the living room, the interaction didn't change. View would later say that in his opinion, John Racz was being evasive, and would say nothing more about where Ann might be—other than she's on a trip to an unknown location.

Trying to break the stalemate, View suggested that maybe he and Fynan should talk to the three kids. Perhaps they might have heard something that would provide a clue. However, Racz snapped, "I don't want the children upset and I don't think it would be a good idea for you to interview them." After some persuasion by Sally Fynan, Racz reluctantly allowed a brief conversation with Joann, but not with Glenn or Katelin.

Before View and Fynan left, Racz voluntarily handed them a key to Ann's minivan, still parked at the Flyaway lot.

* * *

The next interview took place on Friday when the team telephoned Emi Ryan at her home in Arizona. Emi admitted knowledge that Ann had planned for some time to leave her husband, and said they had last spoken, by phone, on April 21. Ann loved to travel but had always gone with someone, never by herself, Emi said. Regarding the chance that her sister would leave without any word to friends or family, and remain incommunicado for two weeks, Emi said it absolutely would not happen. In the most extreme of circumstances, Ann might go away for a day or two. And nothing would have caused her to leave without saying good-bye to her children.

A visit to Dee Ann Wood's home by View and Fynan followed. Yes, Wood said, most people regarded her as Ann's best friend, and as such, Ann often told her things she might not reveal to relatives or other pals. Ann had privately disclosed an abiding concern over possible violence from her husband if she tried to leave him. John had injured his hand twice in a fit of anger by slamming his fist into a door frame. Ann had also told her confidante that she worried about the guns he kept, and felt that he might use them if provoked.

Feeling that she shouldn't hold back any information— despite commitments of secrecy to Ann—Dee Ann spoke about her friend's relationship with Bob Russell. He lived near San Francisco, she said, but that is not where Ann had gone. Dee Ann knew this after her recent telephone conversation with Russell. The poor guy hadn't heard from her either, and worried like everyone else. The relationship between Ann and Bob, said Dee Ann, had been going on approximately one year, mostly through near-daily phone calls and letters, with only three or four actual meetings.

When Ann traveled, was it her custom to park at the Flyaway in Van Nuys and take the shuttle to LAX? To this question, Dee Ann said that her friend never used Flyaway. "I usually took her to the airport for her trips, and when I couldn't, someone else did."

Over the next few days, View and Fynan spoke with several people, including Emi's daughter, Kathy, Ann's divorce attorney, and briefly with Bob Russell. All three served primarily to confirm information already compiled. A survey of hospitals in the county proved only that Ann had not been admitted or treated by any of them. The investigators checked with her credit card provider, and arranged for notification in the case of any new activity on her account. They obtained her dental records and forwarded them to the Missing Unidentified Persons System (MUPS), a database operated by the U.S. Department of Justice (DOJ).

By the middle of May, John View and Sally Fynan conferred with their supervisor about the case of missing Ann Racz. The circumstances appeared suspicious. View summarized them: "She was a responsible individual, dedicated to her family. Based on our observations at the condo, it was very unlikely for her to do something like this." The detective itemized additional factors for consideration:

- She had been reported missing by her pastor and his input about marital strife.
- Her decision to separate shortly before vanishing.
- The fact that she had felt it necessary to keep her new address a secret from John Racz.
- Ann Racz had feared her husband, as mentioned by other individuals, family, and friends.
- The fact that we could not establish that she had got on any airline and went on a trip.

Bottom line, said View, "I believe the case needed further investigation beyond the resources of my unit. It needed to be investigated by the Homicide Division."

CHAPTER 8

LIVING LEGENDS

Most law enforcement detectives labor in relative obscurity. Sometimes a high-profile case may splash an investigator's name in the news media for a while before the fame turns threadbare and fades like an old pair of jeans. Now and then, though, a selected few become legendary.

Louis Danoff and Frank Salerno belong in a Hall of Fame for lawmen.

Known as Louie "the Hat," for his habit of covering advancing baldness with a variety of fedoras during most of his career, Danoff had been actively involved, along with Salerno, in a variety of headlined manhunts for notorious killers. These included the "Hillside Strangler" murders committed by Kenneth Bianchi and Angelo Buono, and the hideous slayings perpetrated by "Night Stalker" Richard Ramirez.

Louis Danoff joined the LASD in October 1966. After twelve years in patrol cars, he took a promotion to homicide detective in 1978. He would eventually investigate more than one thousand killings, including the mystery of Julie Church, who had vanished from Lancaster in 1981. In 1991, he still had trouble coming to grips with the not guilty verdict for Steven Jackson, who had been seen leaving a bar with Julie.

With the muscular body of a wrestler and rugged facial features above a strong chin, Danoff could turn bad guys into quaking jelly with one of his patented stares magnified by pilot-style eyeglasses. Few criminals knew that this lion had the gentle heart of a lamb when it came to compassion for victims. He would eventually become a de facto member of Ann Racz's family as "Uncle Louie."

Frank Salerno had served thirty-two years with the LASD, seventeen in the Homicide Division. Highly recognizable in countless newspaper photos by his trademark graying, close-cropped beard contrasting with a dark mustache and easy-going brown eyes, Salerno's features brought to mind Perry Como with whiskers. But it would be a serious mistake on the part of a killer to think that this soft-spoken homicide sergeant couldn't be rawhide-tough in his pursuit of justice. He had been the team leader in the Night Stalker investigation. Additionally, Salerno had looked into the bizarre drowning death of Natalie Wood near Santa Catalina Island.

To Salerno, high-profile slayings were no different than routine cases. They all required common sense, logic, and hard work. He had spelled out procedures in a program developed for training sheriff's homicide detectives.

Discussing basic investigation techniques, Salerno said, "Normally, with almost all homicides, you start with a crime scene, and you build your case from the victim out. When you have a body, obviously you're there to collect evidence." The objective, he explained, is to find links that will identify the perpetrator and connect that person to the victim's death. "When you don't have a crime scene to go to, per se, you still start with the victim. There is a saying in homicide we teach, and that is you learn as much as you can about your victim. The more you know about the victim—the closer you are to the victim—the better your chances for solving the crime. The victim becomes your best friend. You want to know that person in death as well as you would have in life. So that's where you start, especially when you don't have a body. You want to know the victim's life patterns. And as you learn more, you determine if something occurred that caused the victim to do something they normally wouldn't do, or break a life pattern."

The starting point, said Salerno, is close to home. "You begin with those people who surrounded and knew the victim." From there, you go where the leads take you.

In a missing person case that evolves into a suspected murder, the urgent focus turns to locating the body. Often that presents a huge challenge. One of the main obstacles in the case of Ann Racz, said Salerno, was the terrain of the Santa Clarita region. The geographic features around Valencia consisted of endless mountains, canyons, lakes, ravines, and a spiderweb of dirt roads crisscrossing the peaks and valleys. Her remains could have been easily hidden anywhere in underbrush extending hundreds of square miles.

It was quite unusual, Salerno acknowledged, for a missing person case to be turned over to the Homicide Bureau. Describing the factors that led to such a move in the Ann Racz search, he said that her life patterns, and the sudden breaking of them, pointed to foul play.

He and Danoff inherited the case on Monday, May 13, 1991. Sergeant John View and Detective Sally Fynan brought the facts to Salerno, laid out the suspicious factors, and requested that homicide take it over. Salerno agreed, and asked Louis Danoff to partner with him as they had on the Night Stalker task force.

After reviewing all of the written documentation prepared by View and Fynan, Salerno and Danoff followed the tried-and-true methodology. They started "with those people who surrounded and knew the victim." Using a teamwork approach,

Salerno requested Detective Sally Fynan to stay with them on the probe. "We asked her to continue helping, including notifications of the Department of Justice, checks with the coroner's office, surveying local hospitals, the jail system, and other routine things. I believe we also had her check some of the mental institutions and told her to keep those checks going on a regular basis until they were no longer needed. In addition, we arranged for her to flag all the checking accounts and credit cards to determine if there was any activity on them."

Explaining the term "flag," Salerno said, "The particular institution, for example, if it's Bank of America, or Nordstrom, or Macy's, was contacted and their security was asked to flag that account. So when there was any activity on it, they would notify us at the sheriff's department as to what had taken place with it." The officers would be especially interested to see who made the transaction, when, and what might have been purchased.

Investigations begin with tiny, routine steps. First on the checklist, Salerno sought out California Department of Motor Vehicles (DMV) data, including photos of Ann and John Racz, their descriptions, and information about her vehicle. He incorporated these facts in composing flyers to be posted on hamburger hill sites, and for distribution to various agencies. Over the next few months, new information and photos would be included on additional flyers.

Even though the missing persons duo had interviewed several people, Salerno and Danoff chose to duplicate these efforts with different slants.

Fynan and View had collected a few papers and possessions from the Peachland condominium, and turned them over to the homicide team. Salerno and Danoff examined them, including a receipt from the Hughes Market in Valencia dated April 22, 1991, at 1:51 P.M. It listed purchases of mushrooms, shredded cheese, sliced pepperoni, Boboli pizza crust, and Ragú sauce. Acquisition of these groceries by Ann Racz indicated a specific intent by Ann, and a pattern of her routine that had been suddenly broken, one of the tenets of investigating body-less cases.

Numerous other slips of paper, letters, business cards, and notes recovered from the condo gave the detectives insight into Ann's daily life, her methodical organization, and her meticulous preparations for tasks she routinely undertook. These materials served as building blocks in getting to know the missing person intimately. It became obvious to Salerno and Danoff that this woman had not simply stopped every-thing on a sudden whim and deserted her family and her life. The whole thing reeked of foul play.

In the late afternoon of Tuesday, May 14, Salerno and Danoff drove to Van Nuys to visit the Flyaway airport service firm. Based on View and Fynan's information, they had no trouble locating Ann's white minivan parked approximately in the giant lot's center, on the east side of a large camper-trailer and truck. They knew of John Racz's statement about moving the vehicle to a shady spot to protect a VCR on the backseat. His rationale seemed odd, to say the least. Salerno arranged for an aerial photographer to make a pictorial record of the scene.

That same day, at about 6:45 P.M., Salerno made his first contact with John Racz by telephone. Introducing himself, he said, "I'm Sergeant Frank Salerno from sheriff's homicide." Ordinarily, when the spouse of a missing person receives such a call, they react with various levels of emotion, fear, panic, or distress. None of this seemed evident in Racz's voice or be-havior. He didn't bother to ask why he was being contacted by people who investigate murders.

After noting this unusual reaction, Salerno asked permis-sion to tow the car to a police impound lot for examination. Racz's name on the registration slip made his concurrence a necessity. He granted it without question.

Salerno explained that Racz would be able to take possession of Ann's minivan the next day. Racz's next comment struck another odd note. He asked, "Do I have to pick it up?"

In reply, Salerno said, "Mr. Racz, the fees are going to build up on a daily basis. We, at the sheriff's department, will cover a couple of days. But you do need to pick it up. Is there a problem with that?" Racz uttered something to the effect that he didn't want the kids to see their mother's car.

At this point in Salerno's career, very little in the behavior of human beings surprised him. He asked, "Do you have a friend or a relative where you can store the car temporarily until the situation is straightened out?" Racz said he could probably find someone.

As he had in contacts with Sergeant View, Racz steered the conversation not in the direction of his missing wife, but instead to his previous tenure as a deputy.

John Racz asked, "Do I know you?"

"I don't know you," Salerno answered.

"When did you go to homicide?"

Keeping it on a courteous level, Salerno said, "In 1976."

"Well, I was at Firestone then. I may have seen you then."

It took Salerno a while to understand just what John Racz was talking about. The investigator hadn't yet learned of Racz's employment as a deputy sheriff years earlier. Ignoring the irrelevant comment, Salerno asked, "Have you heard from Ann?"

"No," said Racz. "As a matter of fact, she didn't show up for court today." A divorce hearing had been scheduled for that Tuesday, May 14. Racz's comment sounded as if he fully expected Ann to be there, despite his ongoing insistence that she had left town on a trip to think things over. His off-key comment sounded like a choir member singing the wrong tune.

After ending the conversation, Salerno ordered Ann's vehicle to be transported from the Flyaway lot to an impound yard. With Danoff, Salerno examined both the exterior and interior of the Plymouth. They noted that the driver's seat had been pushed back the maximum distance to accommodate a taller person than Ann. In the backseat, they saw a boxed VCR partially covered by a blanket, along with a Target store receipt. The transaction had been completed on April 22 at 12:45 P.M.

Wedged between the ceiling and the driver's-side sun visor, Salerno found a small slip of white paper and a ticket issued by a machine at the Flyaway entry gate. The yellow ticket bore the date April 25, ten o'clock in the morning, three days after Ann had last been seen by family and friends.

Salerno unfolded the white paper and read a brief penciled note, apparently intended for John Racz: *I'm glad you are becoming more reasonable about all this as time goes on— I think it helps to get along for the children's sake. Thank you.* In place of a signature, the writer had entered a large *A*. Salerno bagged it for fingerprinting.

In accordance with Salerno's standard procedure in which "you start with those people who surrounded and knew the victim," the two investigators began Wednesday, May 15, with a series of phone calls. They contacted Bob Russell, Emi Ryan, Dee Ann Wood, and Cheryl Freet, owner of the condominium Ann Racz had leased. With the first three, the conversations centered on establishing that none of them had seen Ann recently. They also discussed her lifestyle habits. Salerno asked Cheryl Freet for a key to the condo.

The sharp contrast between the demeanor of these four and John Racz impressed Salerno and Danoff. The relatives and friends all demonstrated deep anxiety about Ann's safety, while the husband appeared unmoved by her absence.

From Bob Russell, they learned of the post office box Ann used for her Monday Flowers business, and as a conduit for correspondence with him. Salerno arranged for a warrant to search the box. Among several envelopes inside, they found a letter addressed to Ann from Russell. It surprised them to learn that John Racz's name also appeared on the box rental agreement, but it remained unclear whether or not he actually had access to it. Salerno had a decision to make. After they examined the mail, what should they do with it? Give it to John Racz, because his name was associated with the box? Salerno decided to have each item returned to the senders, including the letter from Russell. Later explaining this, he said, "Not knowing exactly what we were dealing with, how the situation was going to turn out, we had a male individual who was corresponding with a married woman, and the husband had possible access to the box. Common sense told us we should do that."

Near sunset that Wednesday evening, Salerno and Danoff, accompanied by Sally Fynan, drove to the Racz home on Fortuna Drive. She had called John earlier and set up an interview appointment. This would be the first meeting between John Racz and the two homicide investigators.

Another aspect of Racz's puzzling behavior manifested itself when the trio arrived at the address and parked near the curbside mailbox. As they emerged from the vehicle, John Racz and his youngest daughter, Katelin, walked out the front door, turned toward the rounded cul-de-sac, stepped into the street, and began playing catch. They completely ignored Salerno, Danoff, and Fynan.

It couldn't have been accidental, considering the complete absence of other cars on the street, and no other pedestrians in sight. Racz and his daughter tossed the ball back and forth, no more than twenty-five feet in front of the police vehicle. Stunned by the rude act, the officers stood and watched, amazed at this man's peculiar attitude. Finally Salerno turned to Fynan and said, "Sally, get his attention. Tell him we're here." He reasoned that she was best suited to break the ice, since she had met with him a few days earlier.

Fynan called out to John Racz, who turned, appeared surprised, and said, "Oh, Sally." He walked toward them with

Katelin by his side. John directed the trio to the front door, opened it, and led them inside.

Expecting him to suggest places to sit, the officers faced yet another social faux pas. Recalling it, Salerno said, "We entered the house and really didn't get any direction from him as to where to go. Generally, we look to the individual who is the homeowner to direct us. 'I'd like you to go to the kitchen, dining room, living room.' He didn't do any of that. . . . We sort of wandered in like a herd." Somehow they ended up in the dining room and sat around the table.

The first words from John Racz also seemed strange: "Should I tape-record this?"

Salerno replied, "If you feel you have to, go ahead." Never before, in a search for a missing spouse, had he encountered such disconnected behavior. Racz promptly walked out of the dining area. After a short time, sounds came from another room, and Salerno assumed it meant Racz was searching for his recorder. When the noise ended, long minutes of silence set in. The detectives stared at one another in disbelief. Finally Salerno called upon Fynan again. "Sally, go find him."

She brought John Racz back and he sat down nonchalantly. Salerno then spoke. "Mr. Racz, we are here to assist Detective Fynan in locating your missing wife." Ann had been gone a little more than three weeks without contacting any of her relatives or friends.

"She is not missing. She is on vacation," Racz responded instantly.

"So you know where?"

"No," said Racz. He added that he had called Ann's aunt Kay, the woman with whom she had taken several trips, but the relative in Hawaii said she hadn't seen or heard from Ann.

With professional calm, Salerno continued by inquiring about Ann's background, how they met, when they were married, and Racz's job with the Compton School District. Racz answered the questions, told them about Ann's being born in Hawaii, the family's move to Los Angeles, her education, employment as a teacher, their meeting in 1969, marriage, and births of three children. He also spoke of being a deputy sheriff for twelve years and retiring due to a back injury.

Asked about Ann's flower business, Racz described her delivery each Monday of fresh flowers, in vases, to several doctors. The home-based business had been in operation about two years, he said, and he thought she did it primarily for fun.

Regarding Ann's church activities, Racz acknowledged her deep involvement, volunteer work a few days each week, and regular attendance at services while he just joined her on holidays. Recently, he said, she had been receiving a small amount of pay from the church for part-time work.

Salerno led into the marital problems, and later spoke of it: "He said approximately two years prior to our conversation that he noticed things starting to change . . . that she was letting the house go, although she was still taking care of herself. She was fastidious about that, as far as taking care of herself. He indicated that she told him of being tired of house routines, the kids, and that she wanted to get away."

For most of their marriage, said Racz, they had traveled together, but in recent years, Ann had taken trips to other countries with her aunt. One of those vacations, to Russia, had lasted a full month, said Racz, and he stayed home to take care of the kids.

Volunteering the next comment, Racz said that when Ann returned after the long absence, their relationship "sexwise" was better for several weeks; then "it went back to the way it was before the trip."

Ann had been unhappy recently, Racz commented, then added that she had been corresponding with someone named Bob in the San Francisco Bay Area for quite a while. He said, however, he had never seen or read any of the letters.

Racz appeared tense when he described her most recent trip. About a year ago, he said, she had traveled again with her aunt, this time to Hawaii and Japan. Salerno later recalled the part that seemed to bother John. "While she was in Honolulu, she had purchased a wedding band for herself. It upset him that she had not purchased one for him. And when we asked about that, he told us that she had said, 'The next time we go to Hawaii, we will buy you one.' It would be to replace their original matching wedding bands."

Back to the subject of Bob Russell, Racz told of Ann traveling twice up north. Salerno recalled, "Ann had asked him about taking a trip to visit with Bob, who had a daughter about the same age as Katelin. And she wanted to take Katelin and go up to the Bay Area and visit with Bob. She asked if it was all right if she stayed at Bob's house. He said no, he didn't think it was right to do that." During the three days of her trip, said Racz, he believed she stayed at a Motel 6.

The second journey north wasn't quite as clear to John Racz. Salerno said, "There was a time when Ann was picked as a representative from the local PTA in the Santa Clarita Valley and she took a trip up there. I believe she asked about spending an extra day to visit Bob, and Racz said he didn't know if she did, because she was only gone the specific time she originally said she was going to be gone."

Her contacts with Russell, John Racz told the investigators, caused friction. "They had talked and argued about it. But he didn't like doing it in front of the children, so he would take Ann upstairs to talk about it. And Ann—I don't remember if he used the word 'hated'—but she did not like that and it would give her knots in her stomach. She would really become upset about going upstairs to the bedroom to discuss this with him," Salerno stated.

Years later a misconception circulated about Ann attending a high-school reunion a couple of weeks before she vanished, reconnecting there with Bob Russell. The reunion came up for discussion in the interview with John Racz and he asserted that he had not gone with her. Racz had no idea whether or not

Bob Russell had attended. Russell himself, though, eventually cleared it up by stating that he had not been at the reunion.

Satisfied with the background information they had discussed, Salerno turned the conversation with John Racz to his activities between April 18, moving day for Ann, and April 22, when she vanished. "We asked him specifically to take it day by day and tell us what he did on each of those days."

According to what John Racz told Salerno, he got up at five o'clock on Thursday morning, April 18, readied himself for the long drive to Compton, then woke Ann up. He hugged and kissed her, reminded her that they planned on eating dinner that night at a local Mexican food restaurant, and left for work at six. At about three or three-thirty, he called home to tell her that he had a meeting, but no one answered. Not long after that, he left the school and stopped at Carl's Jr. on hamburger hill, had coffee and read the paper, then drove home, arriving close to six o'clock. Inside the house, it startled him to see some of the furniture missing and that his wife wasn't home. The thought ran through his mind that she had left him. A note he found in the kitchen confirmed it and said that she would call later that night.

Continuing his version of the events, Racz said that he went across the street to neighbor Don Pedersen's home, who told him that he had seen the moving van and Ann loading things into her car.

Sometime between nine and ten that night, Ann did call. She told him that she had, indeed, moved out, but she didn't want to talk long on the phone. The kids were okay, she said, and she would be back in contact on Friday. According to John, he begged her to meet him somewhere that night, but Ann turned him down. She also refused to reveal her new address. To John, the call sounded as if it were made from a pay phone.

The following night, he said, Ann kept her promise to call again. She repeated that the kids were okay. He asked if she would agree to join him in a meeting with Pastor Glen Thorp for counseling, and Ann said she would. Once more, she rejected his plea to meet in person right away. Even though Racz wanted to continue talking with her, Ann cut the conversation short with an excuse about being tired and wanting to get the children to bed. Again, the call seemed to be from a public telephone.

On Saturday morning, Racz told Salerno, he contacted Pastor Thorp to arrange for a meeting. When Ann called, he gave her the early-evening appointment time at Thorp's office. She showed up punctually at seven-thirty. In the discussion with Thorp, Ann could not articulate exactly what her concerns were as to the marriage, but she did make her unhappiness clear. According to John, he gave her a letter, the first of two he wrote, telling Ann that he wanted her back and that he would do anything to keep the marriage together. This would even include sleeping in separate bedrooms until they could resolve some sexual issues. Ann indicated she might be willing to give it a try, John Racz asserted.

Salerno knew that John Racz's claims about the letters were true. Sally Fynan had found them in the condominium and turned them over to the homicide investigators. He wondered about the claim that Ann had considered patching it up.

A subsequent discussion between Salerno and Pastor Thorp revealed that Ann had been unequivocal in rejecting reconciliation. She had, though, agreed to bring the children over to the Fortuna house on Sunday to visit John. In John Racz's statements to Salerno, he said that he attended church that Sunday morning, and arranged with Pastor Thorp to set up another counseling session. She brought the children over, as promised, that afternoon. At about 4:30 P.M., he and Ann kept the appointment. Racz said that he gave her his second letter, a plea for her to return on the condition that he would try to be a better husband, but she remained adamant in her decision to end the marriage.

On a more practical level, he reminded Ann of some tile work set to begin at the house on Monday, and she needed to cough up her share of the cost. They agreed that she could cash a maturing joint CD in the amount of $13,242, keep $2,000 for expenses, and give him the remaining check for $3,000 on Monday. Before leaving the counseling session, said John Racz, they made another appointment for the evening of Thursday, April 25. He told Salerno that he still held out hope for salvaging the marriage and for Ann's return. "I'm determined to get her back," he declared.

Moving on to the final day of Ann's known existence, Salerno asked Racz about the events of Monday, April 22. Racz said he called in to the school principal that morning to report that he would be absent. He waited for the tile workers to arrive, but they didn't show up. Ann came over by herself in the early afternoon, said Racz, and without exiting her car, she gave him the money according to their agreement. He told her he wanted to see the kids, so she left, picked them up from school, brought all three of them to the house a half hour later, and parked inside the garage.

This claim would subsequently raise questions when Salerno learned that Katelin had not arrived with Ann, but had been delivered later by the Brownie driver, Carol Kuwata.

After the kids went into the house, said John Racz, he asked Ann to go to the backyard patio with him, where they had a discussion.

Racz made no mention of the children sitting in the car for nearly a half hour before getting out, and that Ann never left the car, as neighbor Don Pedersen would report. Both Glenn and Joann would also tell the detectives that their mother stayed in her car. The detectives noted the discrepancy.

In recalling John Racz's account of events that day, Salerno said that in the backyard conversation John told Ann that he wanted the marriage to remain intact, and if it didn't, he might commit suicide. John also claimed that he offered to cash the check Ann had just delivered and give it to her on Tuesday. In addition, he would borrow $17,000 from another joint CD, this one in his credit union, and hand it to her on Wednesday. If she wanted to travel, she could go away and think about the marriage situation. She could take as much time as she needed, on the condition that she would come back.

When John Racz acknowledged to Salerno that all of their bank accounts, including CDs, were jointly owned by Ann, it seemed strange that John would be offering to get the money for her. She could easily withdraw it herself. He asked if Ann had accepted his offer. Racz said she indicated "she would try it."

At the end of their discussion in the backyard, said John, they walked back into the garage. He called the children and told them to say good-bye to their mother. Without giving them any hugs or kisses, he said, Ann left.

A short time later, according to John, one of the kids said something about being hungry, so he went to McDonald's to buy some fast food for them.

Racz's tale about Ann's sudden departure for an extended trip raised more questions in Salerno's mind. He asked, "Did you discuss with her anything about arrangements for the children's clothing, books, homework, medications, or their daily needs?" John said there had been no such discussion. Nor had the children brought up any of these needs when saying good-bye to their mother. Racz mentioned that he told the kids, "If your mother doesn't come back, I will go to Target and buy you some clothes."

"Did you go get the food for them?" Salerno inquired. Yes, said Racz. He drove the short distance to McDonald's, near Lyons Avenue on hamburger hill. That evening, Racz said, he took the kids to a pizza restaurant for dinner.

Needing some details about the missing woman—"for obvious reasons, clothing, jewelry, handbag, whatever, to assist us if an individual was found alive, dead, or partial remains"—

Salerno asked how Ann was dressed at the time she left. Racz said that she wore pink pants and maybe pink-and-white shoes, but he couldn't remember anything more.

"Can you describe any jewelry she had on?"

Later discussing John Racz's answer, Salerno stated, "He said she was wearing a diamond ring on her right hand. She had won it on a television program. I asked him how much it was worth. He estimated about a thousand dollars. And he also said she was wearing on her left hand that wedding band she had purchased on her trip to Hawaii."

Asked to describe the Hawaiian ring, Racz said it was black and gold. "Was that the same wedding band you told me about a little while ago, the one that made you angry?"

Racz acknowledged that it was, indeed, the same ring.

In response to a query about any tattoos, scars, or other physical characteristics of Ann, John described a scar "that ran from her navel to an area of her groin, which was the result of a tubal ligation she received when Katelin was born." He also noted that Ann didn't smoke, didn't drink, didn't use drugs, and that she was "a very sound person."

Regarding John Racz's allegation that he offered to give his wife money the next day, Salerno asked him for details of events on Tuesday, April 23. Racz said that his children went to school, wearing the same clothing they had worn on Monday. He drove to a bank and cashed the roughly $8,900 check Ann had given him. She arrived at the house between one-thirty and two o'clock in the afternoon, pulled into the driveway, and asked him if they could go somewhere to talk. They went in separate cars to Carl's Jr. on hamburger hill.

"What did you talk about?" Salerno asked.

John couldn't seem to recall, only that Ann wanted to know how the children were. He claimed he handed her $8,900 in bills from the check he had cashed. And they made arrangements to meet at Tips restaurant, just one block away, on Wednesday, so he could give her additional money.

"What was she wearing when you met at Carl's Jr.?"

"I'm not sure. I think it was the same outfit she wore on Monday."

To Salerno, the whole picture seemed cockeyed. Racz wanted him to believe that this meticulously neat, organized woman drove away on Monday with plans to go on a trip, yet showed up the next day wearing the same clothing. She certainly had access to the condominium. Why would she not change clothes, as any woman would?

"Wasn't that kind of unusual for her?" Salerno asked.

"Yes," Racz answered. "She normally changed clothes every day." He added that her routine included getting her hair done every couple of months. She was "immaculately groomed, and would not go out of the house without her hair being perfect and her makeup in place. She never left without looking good." Even though Ann showed up at the restaurant wearing clothing from the previous day, said Racz, "she still looked good to me."

With that, John suddenly remembered something else from their meeting at Carl's Jr. He had asked her for the kids' backpacks and Glenn's flute, all lying in the backseat of her car, and she gave them to him. Instead of placing them in his vehicle, he said, he walked home, carrying the packs and flute.

The story grew more bizarre to Salerno with every new utterance from John Racz's mouth. "Why did you do that?"

"I wanted to make Ann feel bad. I wanted her to feel sorry for me . . . I guess."

To the detectives, that rationale sounded as valid as the Night Stalker's claims of innocence. Curious about the distance from Carl's Jr. to the Fortuna house, Salerno and Danoff later measured it and found it to be exactly nine-tenths of a mile, much of it uphill. Racz chose to walk it, carrying heavy books and backpacks, rather than put the stuff in his car and drive home. Then, later, he walked back to get his vehicle. Yeah, that made sense!

Racz next answered the detectives' questions about Wednesday, April 24. He said that he went to a bank in Los Angeles and borrowed $17,000 against a $100,000 CD, taking it in two checks. Back in Valencia, he cashed both checks at a Security Pacific Bank, planning to give the money to Ann.

"Why didn't you just endorse the checks and give them to her?"

"Because I didn't want her to think of me as a cheapskate."

Salerno and Danoff, both of whom had seen every type of scam possible, wondered if the story of giving cash to Ann might just be to avoid a specific problem. If he had given her checks, it wouldn't be difficult to find out whether they had ever been cashed, and if so, where.

After leaving the bank, said John, he drove around to kill some time, and then went to Tips restaurant, near the Carl's Jr., where he had met Ann on Tuesday. He had a cup of coffee, waited, and she showed up at about four o'clock.

"Was she still wearing jewelry?"

"Yes, she still had on the diamond ring and the black-and-gold wedding band from Hawaii." Asked if he was certain, Racz replied in the affirmative. And he recalled that "she really looked good."

"And did you give her the seventeen thousand dollars?"

"Yes, I did."

"Was it just a bundle of cash, or packaged, or what?"

"It was in a Security Pacific Bank envelope."

According to John Racz, Ann repeated her intention to go on a trip, but she wouldn't say where or how long she planned to stay. He didn't pressure her to tell him. They walked out of the restaurant that afternoon at about four-thirty, and he drove home alone, John said.

On Thursday, said Racz, he didn't hear from Ann at all. He kept the appointment by himself with Pastor Thorp that evening.

The next day was the last time he heard from Ann, Racz told the detectives. She called him collect and said that she was going away. She had parked her car at the Flyaway in Van Nuys and said he could leave it there or pick it up, whatever he felt like doing. During this call, Racz added, he could hear cars in the background. She asked him to take good care of the children and said she would contact him again soon.

"Did you ask her how long she would be gone, to give you some estimate as to how long you would be taking care of the children?"

"No."

About an hour after the call, said Racz, he drove to the Flyaway lot, found her car, and moved it to a shady spot.

"John, why did you move the car?"

Racz said that she had left a new VCR in the backseat, and he wanted to protect it.

"Why didn't you just take it with you?" He had no answer. "Did you notice anything else in the car?" Salerno wondered if Racz would mention the handwritten note, signed only with a capital *A,* that they had found tucked under the sun visor. Racz acknowledged seeing it, and said it was in Ann's handwriting.

"Did she usually sign her name with only the first letter of her name?"

Racz said that she didn't, and he appeared upset that Ann hadn't even taken the time to write her name.

"Why didn't you take it with you?"

"I didn't know what to do with it." It seemed improbable to the investigators that he had even found the note. It hadn't been visible until they searched the car. His comment just added one more oddity in this whole story that had more potholes than the mountainous dirt roads above Valencia.

"Is that the last time you saw her vehicle?" No, said Racz. He had driven over there again about a week later, with Katelin along for the ride. But he didn't want the little girl to see her mother's car, so he parked some distance away and walked over to it.

Salerno wanted to know if Racz thought Ann no longer loved

him. Appearing to give it some thought for a few seconds, he said that he believed she had "fallen out of love with" him. She was no longer "demonstrative" toward him, and didn't feel for him "like [he] felt for her." But he didn't think she had left him for another man.

Once again, Salerno asked Racz if he had any idea where his wife had gone. Despite his earlier denial of having any idea, he now said he thought she might be in Hawaii. Salerno noted that Racz had previously spoken of talking to Ann's aunt Kay in Hilo, who said she hadn't seen Ann or heard from her. So there seemed to be no logic at all in the supposition that Ann had gone to the islands, and not contacted her aunt.

Nearly finished, Salerno mentioned that they would like to interview the two younger children, and for the first time, Racz showed signs of stress and turned defensive. "Why do you want to do that? Why do you need to talk to my kids?"

"John, it's just a part of the investigation. It's something we have to do. They are two of the last people who saw your wife." Racz uttered something about the officers wishing to poison their minds. Salerno shot back, "Why would we do that? All we want to know is what they remember."

Still resistant, Racz said he wanted to see a list of the questions to be asked before he would grant permission. And he insisted on being present during any interrogation. Salerno explained, "John, that's not going to be possible, because there may have been something that Ann shared with them in confidence. Something they would not tell us if you were there. For example, she might have told them she was leaving you and to keep it a secret."

By way of additional explanation, Danoff commented, "They should have been talked to earlier, but they weren't, and now we need to talk to them." Of course, both men knew that Detective Sally Fynan had already interviewed Joann, but no one had yet spoken to Glenn or Katelin.

Still wearing a stern expression, John Racz said he would

think about it and let the officers know. Then, as if they were all good friends in a social atmosphere, he began talking about the old days when he served as a deputy. He rushed upstairs and brought down a roster of Firestone station personnel, and asked if the trio knew any of them. His whole demeanor changed from solemn reluctance to animated interest. The three investigators recognized a few names and chatted briefly about them, mostly to be polite.

Before leaving, Danoff said he would like to take a few documents with him to be copied. He said, "I would like to see your personal phone book so we can make contact with those people listed, to see if we can get a lead as to somebody who may have seen or heard from Ann. Also, I'd like to make copies of your phone bills for the first four months of this year." Racz surprised them with his ready compliance. He produced the personal phone listings, and telephone bills for January, February, and March. But, he said, he couldn't find the one for April, and may have thrown it away.

To the detectives, it sounded suspicious. The April bill would be the most crucial one.

The strange behavior of John Racz intrigued Louis Danoff and Frank Salerno. In all their years of experience, they had never met anyone quite like him. And no potential homicide case had ever presented so many challenges.

CHAPTER 9

STRANGE EVASION

Santa Clarita and the area around hamburger hill, off Lyons Avenue, appeared to most travelers in 1991 to be an ordinary, perhaps dull, place to stop for some fast food before undertaking the long, mountainous drive north.

It is anything but dull. The region is rich with history. Long before establishment of the Interstate Highway System in the 1950s, the tortuous "Ridge Route," between Santa Clarita and Wheeler Ridge, about sixty miles, served as the only link between Northern and Southern California. Two narrow lanes snaked along mountaintops in endless hairpin curves and life-threatening precipices. Solid-tire trucks and Model T Fords crept along for nearly a full day to cover the undulant, serpentine stretch. Decades of improvements dropped the highway into lower valleys and widened it several times. I-5, now eight lanes wide in some segments, peaks at over four thousand feet before descending down a stretch called the "grapevine" into the flatlands of San Joaquin Valley. At today's breathtaking speeds, it takes less than an hour to breeze through.

Lyons Avenue leading to hamburger hill is named after Cyrus and Sanford Lyon, twin brothers who foreshadowed the fast-food center in 1855 by purchasing a stagecoach stop to serve passengers. It stood only about four miles from the present-day glut of eateries. Sanford Lyon, with two other men in 1869, poked around in Pico Canyon a short distance from hamburger hill and established the first successful oil well west of Pennsylvania. Purchased eight years later by petroleum entrepreneur Alex Mentry, it was the center of a community built around his thirteen-room mansion and called, of course, Mentryville, which still remains.

A stunning disaster struck the region just before midnight, March 12, 1928. The St. Francis Dam, located in San Francisquito Canyon about twelve miles north of Valencia, collapsed and released the entire lake. A monstrous wall of water, more than 12 billion gallons, thundered down the canyon, taking houses, vehicles, and human beings with it. As many as 450 people died. The torrent surged past Santa Clarita and the present site of Magic Mountain, all the way to the coast fifty miles away.

Gunfights were common in those days, and notorious bandit Tiburcio Vasquez roamed the hills where an outcropping of colorful, jagged rocks—the Vasquez Rocks—are named after him. Silver-screen cowboys proliferated when motion picture companies discovered the picturesque region even before talkies came into fashion. John Wayne, Hopalong Cassidy, Gene Autry, and scores of stars rode the trails, shooting up everything in sight and chasing villains, especially on the set of a Western movie town built in Placerita Canyon.

Real-life criminals soon found the rugged terrain, carved with dozens of twisting canyons, a handy place to dump murder victims.

The search for Ann Racz necessarily centered on a possibility that her life had ended in violence, and that her body might be hidden somewhere in the region. On May 17, Frank Salerno asked the sheriff's office for special help. "We requested that one of the Homicide Bureau's helicopters, with an observer and heat-seeking technology, fly that area at a low altitude to see if they could locate anything of interest that could direct us to a site we could search for a body."

Explaining the need for heat-seeking equipment, Salerno said, "It gives you the possibility of finding a body that has been placed in a location such as this, heavily covered with shrubs, undergrowth, and trees. It picks up, in layman's terms, heat left in the body and pinpoints a spot to look at, even when the body is decomposing within a short period of time after death." But the system is not infallible, and in such a broad area, a corpse can easily be overlooked.

Much of hamburger hill's terrain, west of the fast-food restaurants, had been excavated for construction of new commercial and industrial buildings. Perhaps close examination would reveal a disturbance in the smooth surfaces being readied for layers of concrete to be poured. Or, in undeveloped hills and ravines, something might be spotted that could lead to discarded or buried human remains.

Administrators granted the request and scheduled the helicopter hunt for the next day, Saturday, May 18.

Salerno and Danoff used the remainder of Friday to visit Ann's Peachland condominium, joined by a fingerprint technician and a criminalist. As they walked through the living room, two bedrooms, kitchen, and bathrooms, it became obvious that Ann had not completed unpacking the things she brought from the Fortuna house. Nor had she repacked anything for a trip. Boxes still contained clothing and personal belongings. Her cosmetics stood upright in the medicine cabinet. Hair spray, deodorant, and other personal hygiene materials had been placed below the washbasin. On the counter, near a hand mirror and a mug containing toothbrushes and toothpaste, lay her curling iron, the cord dangling to the floor.

In one of the bedrooms, a convertible sofa, pulled out into

bed form, held a pair of afghan blankets. Joann would later identify one of them as her favorite possession, made for her by Ann.

Four matching brown vinyl suitcases and a red cosmetic case, still unpacked, stood on the master bedroom's floor. Examination of their contents convinced the investigators that none of the cases appeared to have been packed for an extended trip. And obviously Ann had not taken them with her when she vanished. Salerno noted that the appearance suggested someone moving in, not moving out or arranging for a vacation journey.

Atop a desk in the master bedroom, they found a book-type calendar, opened to a page for April 22. Salerno flipped through it and found carefully entered notations for birthdays and other reminders. On the July page, the fourteenth, he saw notations that Joann would turn fifteen on the same day that Emi and Jerry celebrated their wedding anniversary. Looking closely at all of the pages for April and May, the detective found nothing about a planned trip. No entries for daily activities could be seen after April 22.

That bedroom's closet contained Ann's clothing, carefully arranged on hangers, with no gaps between them that would suggest things had been removed for a trip.

Under the desk, they discovered a red nylon bag stuffed with various documents, some pertaining to the pending divorce. Another item caught the detectives' interest: Ann's passport. She certainly would not have gone anywhere outside the country without it.

Ann had evidently been to a local bookstore in recent weeks, as shown by a plastic bag marked with the store's logo. It contained a pair of books about coping with divorce. Other indications of her interest showed up on notepaper found in the trash basket, torn to pieces. When the criminalist taped it together, they found penciled research entries on the topic of do-it-yourself divorce, plus authors' names with book titles about the same subject. If any doubt existed about Ann's serious intention to end the marriage, these discoveries washed it away.

Foodstuff in the kitchen made it clear that Ann had planned to make pizza for dinner on her last day in the condominium. Salerno later spoke of it: "Prior to our going to the Peachland condo, we had learned from briefing by Detectives Fynan and View, from their interview with Joann Racz, that Ann had told Joann of her intentions on Monday, April twenty-second, that their dinner was going to be homemade pizza. We also took note of the fact that we were being told by John Racz that he had seen Ann on a number of occasions following that afternoon of April twenty-second, and it appeared to me that the pizza was still out to be made from that Monday afternoon. It also appeared from the condition of the condominium that Ann had never returned, which led me to wonder where she had been living, staying, or sleeping in that week that Mr. Racz is telling us that he is seeing her and giving her money."

Another discovery elevated suspicions even higher about Ann's alleged trip. The search produced her personal phonebook, something Ann certainly would have taken with her. Salerno arranged for copies to be made of the pages, and for most of the numbers to be called to question each individual about seeing or hearing from Ann since the day she vanished.

It touched the investigators' hearts to read three notes Joann had left in case her mother came home.

After nearly three hours and thirty minutes of searching the condominium, and processing what they found, Salerno, Danoff, and the two specialists left a little before midnight.

Voicing the reasonable assumptions reached by what he had seen, Salerno said, "It was becoming apparent, based on what we were finding and not finding, that Ann's life patterns had ceased. Other than John Racz's statements regarding the meetings after April twenty-second, there was no one else we came up with that had seen, heard from, talked to, or made any observations of Ann Racz. I mean that everything we learned about Ann, her organizational skills, the fact that she kept in contact with friends, that she had letters to be mailed on April twenty-fourth, twenty-fifth, and twenty-seventh, and those were not mailed. Her best friend had not heard from her. Her family had not heard from her. There was no indication of a trip anywhere that we found. She just seemed to disappear. According to what we were being told by everybody who knew her, this was not Ann's modus operandi, this was not her pattern. Her life patterns had just stopped. It was becoming, in my mind, fairly obvious that we were dealing with a situation where Ann had met with foul play."

While the helicopter flew overhead on Saturday morning, Salerno and Danoff drove the entire length of Pico Canyon Road, about three miles, until it transitioned into a dirt road. They scanned both shoulders, looking for any hint of a place where Ann's body might have been hidden. Finally, at a gate to the historic Mentryville community, they turned around. It disappointed Salerno to later learn that the aircraft had not used heat-seeking equipment. Neither the aerial nor the ground teams found anything useful to solve the mystery.

That afternoon the detectives canvassed the Fortuna Drive neighborhood, interviewing John Racz's neighbors. While visiting one of them, they spotted John returning home, and walked over to return his personal phone book and telephone bill records. Salerno took the opportunity to again raise the question of interviewing Glenn and Katelin. John hadn't changed his mind and expressed opposition to dragging his kids through any interrogation. After Salerno offered to let Sally Fynan do the questioning, on the basis that a woman might be more gentle in posing the questions, John Racz agreed to at least set a date for the interview. They penciled in Monday, May 20. He also said he would allow them to examine his vehicle on the same date.

During the conversation, John commented about Ann's luggage. He said she had won a nine-piece set of brown vinyl suitcases ten years ago, and five pieces of it were still in the Fortuna house. Salerno didn't know why John brought it up, but he mentally thanked him. The detectives had seen four of the suitcases in the condo. With all of her luggage accounted for, this news reinforced the probability that Ann had not taken an extended trip anywhere.

John Racz's objection to interviewing the children apparently covered only the younger two, Glenn and Katelin. That Saturday afternoon, Salerno and Danoff did speak with fourteen-year-old Joann Racz. She told them that last summer her mother had started talking about separating from John, and in March had confided that it would take place soon. Her mom had even bought a new television and VCR so the kids would have entertainment at their new residence, but the VCR didn't work right and had to be exchanged. Joann took the detectives through her recollections of April 18, moving day, and later on April 22, including the departure of both parents, separately, to go buy some fast food for the hungry kids.

A confusing point in Joann's narrative focused on the amount of time her father had been gone before returning with cold french fries. She couldn't recall whether it had been a few minutes or a couple of hours. Mostly, she felt hurt about her mother not saying good-bye, and then never returning. Ann had promised to cook pizza that night, so Joann fully expected her to be gone no more than a few minutes. The heartbroken teenager affirmed to the detectives that her mother had never said anything about going on a trip. The pain grew even worse soon afterward, Joann said, when she came home and found her backpack, books, and cosmetics in the house, all of which had been left in her mom's car. It shattered her when John said that Ann had dropped the things off, but she hadn't stayed to see her children.

In the weeks following Ann's disappearance, Joann said,

she had visited the condominium five times, gaining access via a faulty lock on the sliding glass door. Her hopes to find some sign of her mother's return slowly dimmed each time. She had written three notes and left them for her mother to find in case she came home.

After ending the session with Joann, Salerno spoke again with John Racz. He planned to move Ann's car from the impound yard back to the Flyaway lot.

"Why would you do that?" the detective asked.

"Just in case she comes home."

Salerno resisted the urge to shake his head. Racz had been insisting that Ann had left for a trip to think things over, which implied she would come back after making a decision. Now it changed to "just in case," which reeked with a whole new implication.

Continuing the process of getting to know Ann Racz, the detectives met on Monday, May 20, with Emi Ryan and Joji Yoshiyama, the missing woman's older sister and brother. They told of giving Ann a "family loan," to help her pay for a divorce, including attorney's fees. On the previous March 1, Ann had deposited it in her Monday Flowers bank account. Not one penny had ever been withdrawn.

After leaving the family members, Salerno and Danoff drove to Pastor Glen Thorp's office. He appeared reluctant to say much, still concerned about the delicate matter of confidentiality between a marriage counselor and his client. Picking his words carefully, Thorp spoke of Ann's apparent determination to seek divorce, and his efforts to change her mind. Thorp also revealed that he had visited John Racz at the Fortuna home on Thursday, May 2. Mr. Racz, he said, had told him that on his last meeting with Ann, they had argued.

Back in the Santa Clarita Valley station, the detectives prepared to keep their appointment with John Racz, set for seven-thirty that evening to examine his car. Close to six o'clock, a sergeant summoned Salerno to the phone. Sally Fynan's voice sounded troubled. She said that she had shown up at the Fortuna house to interview Glenn and Katelin, according to the agreement with John. But a problem had developed. "Mr. Racz has changed his mind about letting me talk to the kids. Will you speak to him?"

Salerno said he would. Later describing it, the detective recalled, "Racz expressed worry about us talking to the two youngest children. He made a comment that he was concerned about what questions Detective Fynan might ask the children. I believe at that point he said that some of her previous inquiries had put him in a bad light, that he wanted a list of the questions before we started. Also, he wanted to be present with his kids."

Controlling his voice to hide the growing impatience, Salerno asked specifically what Detective Fynan had asked that bothered Racz. "He couldn't articulate to me what those questions were. We discussed this some more but did not iron it out. And we didn't come to any type of agreement other than the fact that Detective Fynan was not going to talk to the two young children that evening."

Was John Racz simply being an overprotective father, or did he fear something coming from his kids' mouths that would create a serious problem for him? If Salerno suspected the latter, he put it aside for the moment. He asked Racz if he still planned to bring his car over to the station. Yes, said Racz, he would be there on time.

Racz kept his commitment and showed up at the front desk. Salerno met him and escorted him through a hallway toward an interview room, where Louis Danoff waited. At the door, Salerno said, "Please step in."

"I'd rather not," Racz replied. Instead, he walked over to a sergeant's desk and greeted the man whom he had known years earlier as deputies at the Wayside Honor Rancho. When the sergeant had left that post, he had written a short note to Racz. Now, in their conversation, Racz said he had kept the note all those years and still had it. He said something else to the sergeant that Salerno overheard: "Maybe you're in a position now to help me."

Salerno interrupted and again asked Racz to step into the interview room. They had no intention of interrogating him, Salerno explained, but simply needed him to sign a release form granting permission to process his vehicle. John Racz, though, still showed reluctance, asking, "What is it you're looking for?"

Danoff gave him a succinct one-word reply: "Blood."

Later recalling it, Salerno said, "We explained that if we did find blood, we would have to process it to determine if it was human, and it might take some time to determine if it had any importance in the case or even pertained to this particular disappearance. He questioned me, saying he thought we had said we were just maybe looking for prints. We explained that prints wouldn't have meant very much, since both he and his wife had access to the vehicle. The more we talked, it was starting to appear that we were not going to get his permission or signature on the consent form."

During this exchange, Danoff entered some observations in his notebook, which seemed to disturb Racz. He said, "Louie, you're always taking notes," then reached over and grabbed the pencil from Danoff's hand. He turned to Salerno and asked, "What if I don't sign that consent form?"

"John, we haven't forced you to do anything yet."

"What do you mean, 'yet'?"

Completely calm, Salerno said, "Look, John, we're not going to force you to do anything. It's your decision. If you don't want us to process the car, tell us so. We're not going to force you to do it." The important thing, Salerno said, was to keep everything focused on one objective: to find Ann.

"Where do you think she is?" John asked.

"I don't know, John. Where do you think she is?"

"Hawaii," John snapped, without adding any specifics.

Looking directly into Racz's eyes, Salerno kept his voice low. "If she is in Hawaii, why hasn't anybody heard from her? Her family is there, you know. Nobody has heard from her."

John fell silent, then changed the subject. He wanted to know which detective was in charge of the investigation, Salerno or Danoff?

Salerno, recalling that day, described his answer. "I tried to explain to him that we worked as a team, as partners. I wasn't in charge of Louie, and Louie wasn't in charge of me. We worked this investigation together and that we were both responsible for it."

Racz, his face a shade darker, asked a stark question: "Frank, do you think I did it?"

"Did what, John?"

Racz fell silent again for several moments. At last he mumbled something mostly unintelligible about having done nothing wrong.

Salerno waited, giving him the chance to clarify, but it didn't come. The detective spoke. "John, we've got an obligation to find Ann. It's an obligation to her, to you, and to your children. Especially the children. We should all be allies in this. This should be a team effort. We should all be working together to find Ann."

Racz didn't react to Salerno's comments, but he finally agreed to sign the consent form, on the condition that he could be present while they processed the vehicle.

Needing another signed consent to examine Racz's bank statements, for the purpose of verifying his claims of obtaining cash and giving it to his wife, Salerno made the additional request. Racz gave him a long, silent stare, then said he would have to think about it.

Later discussing it, Salerno recalled, "I asked him if he had any particular reason to delay his decision, and he said we had hit him with a lot, he was tired, and we were asking to talk to two small children and he wanted some time to think about it. This would also allow him to talk it over with his kids first."

Before the investigators could begin processing Racz's car, he asked how long it would take. Told that it would be some time, Racz commented that he had left the kids earlier that evening at a pizza restaurant, a place that provided games for children, and it would be closing soon, at nine. He needed to go pick them up. Salerno offered to send Sally Fynan to bring them to the station, and Racz agreed.

While Racz observed, and moved from person to person making small talk, a criminalist used a chemical called luminol in the red 1983 Honda's interior. Even if blood has been carefully washed away, luminol will reveal the invisible stains.

In this case, no bloodstains could be found.

After Racz took possession of his car, and left with the three children, the detectives still had more work to do. They drove to Ann's Peachland condominium, with the criminalist, and used luminol to see if latent bloodstains might show up. Again it produced nothing.

Due to John Racz's insistence that he had met Ann in two restaurants to give her $25,000, Salerno and Danoff realized the utmost importance of either verifying his claim, or disproving it. Ann Racz had been missing almost one month by May 21. On that Tuesday, Detectives Salerno and Danoff visited the owner of Tips restaurant, on hamburger hill. The owner provided Salerno with a listing of all employees, along with contact information.

The sleuths also stopped at McDonald's and Carl's Jr. to obtain similar lists. It would require a lot of telephone calls, driving, and footwork, but they needed to find out if anyone had seen John and Ann together on April 22, or anytime after that. Their first target of interest, though, centered on the alleged meeting and handover of cash on April 24, between 4:00 and 4:30 P.M. at Tips.

Within the next few days, Salerno and Danoff managed to find all fourteen of the employees except one—a woman who had worked there briefly before returning to her home in Thailand.

In personal interviews with each of the workers, the detectives produced photos of both Ann and John, then asked if they had been in the restaurant on April 24. Recalling it, Salerno said, "One of them recognized Mr. Racz as having been in there [at some other time]. I don't recall if she said he was a regular customer. But nobody recognized them as having been in there together, specifically on that date we were focusing on. One of them made a comment . . . on the fact that they were— I can't remember the word she used—a striking couple or a good-looking couple that she would have remembered." None of them could say they had ever seen Ann Racz in person.

At Carl's Jr., fourteen employees examined photos of John and Ann Racz. None could recall seeing them during the week following April 22, specifically Tuesday, April 23, the date John claimed they went to the restaurant and he gave her $8,000 in cash.

At McDonald's, the same results came from multiple interviews. No one had seen Ann Racz on April 22 or any time afterward.

Yet another visit to the Flyaway airport service in Van Nuys produced similar results. Every employee at the airline service counters stated they had not seen Ann Racz, nor did her name show up on any business transactions. Interviews with drivers from the various taxi companies, bus lines, and shuttle services serving the facility indicated that she had not been a passenger in any of the commercial vehicles.

Emi Ryan, Ann's sister, agreed to meet the detectives for one more examination of the Peachland condo. She aided them in collecting accumulated mail from the box at that address. In the stack of envelopes, they found two letters from Bob Russell, dated April 27 and May 2. Both of them expressed deep concern for her safety and hope that she would be able to contact him soon.

In the quest to know everything possible about Ann Racz, the detectives flew to the Bay Area for a face-to-face interview with Russell. He cooperated completely, and gave them a stack of 109 letters she had written to him between March 11, 1990, and April 21, 1991.

A visit to John at his Fortuna Drive home on May 24 by Salerno and Danoff still didn't produce his permission to interview the two younger children. Racz claimed he hadn't had a chance yet to discuss it with them. He changed the subject by asking if they had talked to "the guy in San Francisco." Salerno understood that he meant Bob Russell, and he said they had spoken with him.

All of the flyers distributed by investigators contained a portrait of Ann, but Salerno wanted a photo of her from head to toe, not just her face. If someone had spotted a woman fitting the description, a full-length picture might help the witness decide if it was really Ann. Racz didn't like the idea and said he didn't have such a photo readily available. He would look for one.

In another sharp turn of topics, Racz asked about the probability of Ann being "in trouble, if and when she showed up." No, Salerno told him, she would not be in trouble. Steering the exchange back to a more logical level, Salerno asked if John still had the final note Ann had left for him on April 18. John said that he probably had it somewhere, since he was a "saver." But he didn't know exactly where he had put it.

The detectives said they would return in a couple of days, expressed hope of speaking to the children, and would like to pick up Ann's note and a full-length photo of her if John could locate them.

They kept their promise on Monday, May 27, knocking again at John Racz's front door. Inside, Racz stated that he still hadn't found the note left by Ann, nor the requested photo. His inability to locate these items did nothing to convince Salerno and Danoff of Racz's sincerity. While they were asking, they threw in another request for the missing April telephone bill he had recently been unable to find. Racz said it still hadn't turned up.

"Have you discussed with Glenn and Katelin our need to ask them a few questions?" Salerno inquired. Racz said he still hadn't had a chance to talk it over with them. His two weeks of stalling on the issue did not appear to conform with the behavior of a person hoping to reunite with a missing spouse. And his next question to the detectives struck them as even more peculiar.

Racz asked, "How long has she been gone?" A truly distraught husband would probably know the exact number of days, hours, and minutes his beloved wife had been absent.

Salerno answered, "A little more than one month," then added his own query. "Is this the longest she has ever been gone without you hearing from her?" Racz muttered something in the affirmative, and that she usually sent a postcard or letter, or sometimes called him while away on a trip. He acknowledged usually knowing where she was.

The detectives left Racz, even more unsettled about his reluctance to cooperate, but no less determined to do what they knew had to be done. Just before sunset on the last day of May, they dropped by the house again. No one answered the door, so Salerno left a business card, on which he wrote a note asking when they could speak to Glenn and Katelin.

Two days passed with no contact from Racz, so the detectives made the trip again to Fortuna Drive. This time Racz opened the door. "Hello, John," Salerno greeted. "We were wondering if you have found the note Ann left on April eighteenth."

Inviting them in, John waited until they stood in the entry before answering with a curt "No."

"What about that missing phone bill?"

"I don't have it."

"When are you going to allow us to talk to the two kids? It's important to this investigation. Quite a bit of time has gone by. Have you had a chance to talk to them yet?"

Racz said he had spoken about it to Glenn, but not to Katelin.

Years of hard experience had taught Salerno the value of persistence. "John, it's important that we talk to them and we'd like to set up an interview appointment so that we can get it done." At last it seemed to work. Racz said that only Katelin happened to be home right then, and if Salerno wanted to, he could speak to her.

Surprised, Salerno said, "Well, if you remember, we had a discussion about Sally talking to the two younger children. We need to arrange a meeting to fit her schedule."

Racz, changing directions with the frequency of a hooked marlin, asked, "What if I refuse?" But apparently realizing the negative image it created, he followed up instantly: "Well, I guess that wouldn't look too good." Salerno mentally agreed, but repeated his previous assertion that they didn't plan to force him to do anything. The prospects for success, he said, depended on teamwork by everyone involved.

Asking both men to step outside, Racz steered them to the front patio. Speaking low, he explained that he didn't want Katelin to hear them talking and get the impression that he wasn't cooperating. After a few more minutes of conversation, Racz said he would call soon to set up a date for Katelin's interview with Detective Fynan.

Slightly buoyed, but still skeptical, Salerno and Danoff left and spent the rest of the day looking into Ann Racz's visits to banks on her last known day, April 22, and verifying that no transactions had taken place since then.

The skepticism proved valid when Racz failed to call. Salerno made the contact instead, and convinced Racz to schedule an appointment for Sally Fynan to talk to Katelin on June 4.

When she showed up, Racz told her he had changed his mind because he still hadn't had a chance to speak to his child.

It is not professional or productive for police officers to show anger. Even if they feel outrage and fury, it is best to never let it show. So when Danoff and Salerno showed up at Racz's home the next day, their faces reflected nothing but calm dignity. And even when the conversation circled again in repetition of everything that had been said before, both veterans masked any distress. Racz apparently felt so comfortable with them, he actually asked if he could ride along with them on the investigation.

"No," said Salerno, "that just isn't possible. In order to maintain the integrity of our findings, it must be between me and my partner and the sheriff's department, and not you as a citizen."

Perhaps because of their dignity and professionalism, John Racz at last agreed to an interview date of Monday, June 10, for Sally Fynan to question Glenn and Katelin. Still, he wanted Sergeant View, whom he had known at the Firestone station, to be present.

Fully expecting yet another cancellation when they arrived at the Fortuna house, Detective Fynan and Sergeant View couldn't believe it when Racz actually allowed the interview. Both Glenn and Katelin sat with them at the dining-room table and answered questions while Racz busied himself elsewhere. For the most part, it didn't produce any breakthrough in the investigation. Katelin remembered being brought home, wearing her Brownie uniform, by Mrs. Kuwata on the day Ann vanished. Glenn said he had been absorbed in his video games on that day and hadn't paid much attention to what else took place. Neither of them had known in advance that their parents would separate. The officers asked a few more questions, took notes, and thanked the children for their help.

Five days later, on Saturday, Pastor Glen Thorp called Salerno. He said something had been wearing on his mind and he thought he should report it. This information hadn't seemed important at the time, but now that Ann had been missing for nearly two months, it might be significant. Thorp reminded Salerno that a counseling appointment had been scheduled for Ann and John on April 25, and that John had called to cancel it, but at Thorp's urging, he had shown up alone. When Racz arrived, Thorp noticed scratches on John's right hand and on his face. The injury on the back of his hand looked fresh and had not yet scabbed over. A similar wound on his cheek ran all the way down to the chin.

Grateful for this new twist, Salerno thanked the pastor and noted the information in his growing portfolio.

More entries came on Monday, June 17, as the result of a conversation with Emi Ryan. The subject of Ann's ring, the black-and-gold one she bought in Hawaii, came up. When asked if she knew about the ring, Emi instantly said she did. As a matter of fact, she had it in her possession.

This news energized Salerno. Racz had twice claimed that Ann wore it when he had given her the money in meetings at Carl's Jr. and at Tips.

Emi also commented that she planned to attend Glenn's ceremony on Thursday, June 20, when he would graduate from the sixth grade. Salerno noted it in his calendar.

That afternoon both he and Danoff joined the family at Wiley Canyon Elementary School to watch Glenn march with classmates and accept his diploma. No one expected Ann to magically show up, but it disappointed relatives and friends when John also failed to be there for his son.

Most homicide investigations involve tips from the public, especially when news coverage is extensive and flyers are posted. Salerno and Danoff responded to countless calls from well-meaning tipsters. On June 25, they drove to a ten-acre plot of land on the north side of Lyons Avenue to explore what appeared to be fresh digging. That same evening, they hurried to Rockwell Canyon Road about two miles north of the McDonald's restaurant to examine another site of freshly turned earth and to peer into drainage pipes easily large enough for hiding a body.

Failure to find any trace of Ann carried both disappointment and relief. At least a glimmer of hope remained that she would miraculously return, alive and well.

From Ann's notes found in the condominium, Salerno had spotted the name Theresa Minch, a member of Pastor Thorp's Presbyterian Church. The handwritten records indicated that Ann knew Minch was going through a divorce, and had consulted her about the process. The detectives hoped that she might be able to recall if Ann had revealed specific reasons for wanting to end the marriage. After leaving John Racz on Monday, the investigators telephoned Ms. Minch, then drove to her home.

Minch welcomed the officers and spoke openly. She described her acquaintance with Ann Racz as a fellow church member, and the friendship they had developed. Ann, she said, had approached her with questions about the separation and divorce process. Both of their husbands had been in law enforcement and "had the mentality that goes with it." Salerno and Danoff suppressed the urge to smile, because they understood exactly what she meant.

Responding to their questions, Minch said that Ann had unequivocally planned to separate from John Racz and to divorce him. She undertook the project with her usual meticulous research and implementation, step by step, exercising extreme caution all the time to prevent John from knowing about it. John had been "verbally abusive" and Ann worried about her safety. At one point, Minch said, Ann divulged that she had been threatened by John. He had said, "If you ever leave, I will kill you."

CHAPTER 10

"NOBODY SAW HER ANYWHERE."

Considering a whirlpool of odd reactions by John Racz, inconsistent statements, and dubious scenarios in his stories, Sergeant Salerno and Detective Danoff needed to ask more questions of him. But the interview would have to be informal, since nothing in the investigation so far had turned up evidence to arrest him.

Salerno weighed just how to ask Racz to come into the Santa Clarita sheriff's substation for a meeting, but the onus bounced from his shoulders via a telephone call from Racz on June 28. John had a few complaints he wanted to discuss.

First, said John, he didn't know why his photo needed to be on the flyers being distributed, especially at local restaurants and businesses. Friends of his children would see them and ask embarrassing questions. And a few other things bothered him as well.

Voicing sympathy and understanding, Salerno invited Racz

to come in, sit down, and have a chat about his grievances. Racz agreed and arrived that same evening before seven o'clock. His younger daughter came with him, carrying her pet cat. En route, Racz said, Katelin had asked, "What if Mommy doesn't come back?" He didn't bother to tell anyone how he had responded.

While another officer attended to Katelin and the cat, Salerno led John Racz to a tiny conference room. Unknown to him, a video camera captured the entire session.

Louie Danoff invited Racz to take a seat on one side of the table, while he and Frank Salerno sat in folding chairs directly across from the interviewee.

Without a word or question about the investigation's progress, inquiry of any news about his wife, or a show of interest in the possibility of locating her, Racz voiced his complaints. His main concern related to his picture on the flyers. Salerno explained that they needed to find any person who might be able to shed light on Ann's absence, and the flyers could help accomplish this. A potential witness might remember seeing him in one of the restaurants with an Asian woman, even if they didn't recognize her photo. It would help corroborate his statements about meeting her at Carl's Jr. and at Tips.

Apparently unsatisfied with that rationale, John Racz shifted to complaining about black fingerprint powder left on his car after officers had examined it. Perhaps realizing the trivial nature of this lament, he trailed off into a low grumble, telling them to just forget it.

Grabbing the opportunity for a transition into the search for Ann, Salerno asked, "John, what do you want us to do? What do you suggest?" Racz had nothing to offer. Salerno cranked it up. "How do you think we can get beyond you as a possible suspect?" Still nothing came from Racz. Finally he rested his elbows on the table, held his hands together as if praying, and replied, "I don't know. I don't know. I—I'm worried about Ann."

Glaring, Danoff inquired, "Well, when did you start to worry about Ann?"

"I worried about—I started worrying about Ann, uh, when I started thinking that, you know, maybe she didn't take a vacation. Maybe she didn't go away to think about things. I don't know."

"When did you think that?"

Repeating "I don't know" several more times, Racz said, "A few weeks ago, maybe. But, uh, I'm at a point where I don't know if I should be worrying about her. . . . I've been worried about her for a while. But at the same time, when she comes back—if she comes back—people are gonna be angry at her too. It's a combination, you know, she goes away and doesn't tell anyone."

Without acknowledging the ambiguous ramble, Salerno produced a pair of photographs. In reference to John's statement about meeting Ann at Tips restaurant, Salerno asked, "Do you place either of these women at Tips?"

"Mmm, I think the lady on the bottom is the hostess at Tips. Or she does something there," Racz said.

Directing attention to the second photo, Salerno inquired, "You ever seen this one before?"

"I don't know, I'm not sure about her. I think the one on the bottom is the hostess. I remember she was a Japanese lady."

"Well, is this the one you said was there the day you and Ann went in there?"

"I think she was in there. Yeah."

"Are you sure?"

"You know, every time I go in there, I see her."

Still grimacing, Danoff let his expression become even more stern. "Let's don't play word games. . . . You told us that when you went in, that gal was the cashier."

Nodding, Racz mumbled, "Unh-hunh," but he wouldn't confirm the woman's presence on that day. "Every time I go in there, I usually see her. And I guess if she was there, then I saw her."

"John, we're not playing games here. We're talking about Wednesday, right, the twenty-fourth of April, when you gave Ann seventeen thousand dollars in cash at Tips. Was this woman there?"

Probably recognizing that Danoff and Salerno may have already interviewed the hostess-cashier and asked her if she had seen John and Ann in the restaurant on that day, Racz remained ambiguous. "I'm not positive. I think she was."

Moving on, Frank Salerno asked a few questions, trying for more specific responses. Racz seemed more interested in asserting his inculpability. "I know in my mind that I didn't do anything improper."

The word "improper" grated on Danoff. He snapped back, "Okay, if you know in your mind that you didn't do anything, John—see, if I'm sitting over there, you know what I'd do? I'd say, 'Goddamn it, I didn't kill my wife. I didn't do anything. Would you guys get off my goddamn ass, so I can move on.'" The detective let that sink in, and added, "Do you see? That's different from 'I know in my mind that I didn't do anything.'"

Racz didn't blink. "There are different personalities," he muttered.

Pressing a little harder, Danoff finally got an affirmative nod from Racz that both women in the photos were present in the restaurant that afternoon. To that, Salerno said, "All right. Now, John, they, along with every other employee working, *every other employee,* John, did *not* see John Racz or Ann Racz come in there."

"Well, I was in there," Racz insisted.

Danoff shook his head. "These are the kind of stumbling blocks we're getting. We're conducting an investigation, and we've got these barriers. We're trying to get over them. You say you want to help us get over them, John. But what I'm hearing is just verbiage. I don't think you really want to help us."

Staring at the tabletop, John replied, "Well, I'll go over there and talk to those ladies if you want me to—"

Frank Salerno interrupted. "No, you don't need to bother them. Please don't."

"But I was there. I was there and I got a cup of coffee."

Danoff didn't try to hide his disbelief.

Suddenly rising to his feet, Racz said, "I've got to go. My little girl is outside."

Danoff snapped, "Sit down." Even though nothing prevented him from leaving, Racz sank back into his chair.

Turning to a different subject, Salerno asked Racz to verify that he had learned on Friday, April 26, about Ann's car being at the Flyaway facility. Again the questions were met with vague, ambiguous replies. The detective asked if John had ever slammed his fist into a wall during an argument with Ann. This, at least, elicited a strong denial. When Salerno repeated the question, Racz leaped to his feet again, saying, "Okay, I'm gonna stop here."

Accused of not wanting to cooperate, Racz reminded the detectives, "Look, I came over here on my own, and I'm answering your questions—some of them."

Danoff's mouth formed a little smirk as he said, "Some of them. You got that right. There, you are being honest. For some reason, you don't want to answer all of them, John."

The accusation appeared to rattle Racz. His lips moved, but they spilled no meaningful sounds. "Okay. Because—okay. When, uh—"

"When what?" Danoff growled.

Instead of answering, John asked a question. "As—as far as you're concerned, there is no new information?"

In response Salerno said, "I didn't tell you that." His gambit appealing to the children's need to know what happened to their mother made no headway, so Salerno said, "Look, John, your wife is not out there running around spending twenty-five thousand dollars. Nobody in the world has heard from your wife. And nobody has seen her."

With a little more emotion, Racz answered, "Ann's going to show up. And you guys are gonna come to my door. And you're gonna say, 'John, we're sorry.'"

Danoff instantly asserted, "If she does, we'll be the first ones there, John. I guarantee you. We'll also be the very first ones there when we find her body. Okay, either way, I promise you that."

Undeterred, Racz kept on track. "Because—I can't deal with it. I can't deal with it if something—"

Danoff continued, "You're going to have to deal with it, John. You have to for your children. . . . You've gotta face it, John. You've gotta stand up and face them."

Lapsing into repetition again, John repeated, "I don't know" several times.

"Yes, you do know, John. You do know," Salerno said.

A slight quaver appeared in Racz's voice. "I have to—I have to go under the assumption that nothing's happened to her."

"You can't say that. Her life has ceased. Everything she's ever done is—"

Now louder, Racz croaked, "Oh, come on. Don't say that. Goddamn it, her life has not ceased yet. You don't know that for sure, yet. You're just—you're just saying that. And you don't know it for sure." A few more muffled grunts came from Racz's throat, but no distinguishable words.

"Your wife wanted to know if the move would affect the children's behavior. This is not your ordinary woman, John. She never went back to that condo. Do you know that?" Salerno questioned.

After a long silence, Racz replied, "I refuse to accept that."

"That's the problem, John. The problem is you are not accepting it."

If a crack had opened in Racz's bulwarks, he sealed it up

instantly. "I want Ann back. I don't need you saying this. You're just saying it."

"Only you can bring her back, John. . . . You're the key." Salerno paused, but Racz met it with a mute stare. "It isn't the end of the world, John. It's just being a man and owning up to something. But you're the key—this is not a lady that's going to leave her kids and just run away."

"Okay," Racz replied. "I—I don't know what to say. But I want Ann back."

"Well, help us then. Help us, John, help your kids."

Danoff grabbed the cue regarding the children and escalated it. "The hell with us. Help your kids. We got nothing to gain on this."

Hoping they had found a vulnerable spot, Salerno continued the refrain. "Listen, you know, win or lose, it doesn't matter to us. We're talking straight up here. The issue is not us, the issue is your kids. That's the real issue."

"Mmnh—mmnh," Racz groaned through closed lips. "And that's—that's what I want to concentrate on."

Salerno kept it going. "John, you're the key here. And you can say all you want, all this verbiage, and we can play all these verbal . . . but I'll say it again. You're a smart person and you know that it's not like anything else. It's not just going to go away."

If Racz had taken one step in the desired direction, he instantly retreated two steps. "But, uh, you know, I have to go. I didn't plan on being here this long. But I told you. You came that night and I talked for two hours. I mean, we went over everything."

"John," Salerno hammered, "we're not talking about a burglary here. We're not talking about grand theft. We're talking about your wife, okay? What if we talked for six hours? What if we talked a day? It's your wife. It's your family. It's not a stolen bicycle, John."

This produced only another muffled grunt.

"And that's the attitude you're coming across with. Yeah, we've talked for a few hours. Is that really enough? We're picking up stories from what other people are saying. But, basically, after the twenty-second, it's all your story. We're trying to confirm your activities, but you want us off it. Give us something to help us put it to an end."

Another unintelligible rumble came from Racz's grimacing mouth before he uttered, "Well, I don't know what to tell you."

Salerno recapped it: "Your daughter walks from the garage into the house. And she is the last person, other than you, to see her." He omitted the brief conversation Ann had held with a neighbor about Joann babysitting, and the sighting by another neighbor, Don Pedersen. "Nobody has seen Ann since then. Joann is the last person, other than you. It's as simple as that. So what do you want us to do? Nobody saw her at Tips. She never went back to the condo. Nobody saw her at Carl's. Nobody saw her at McDonald's. Nobody saw her anywhere."

"Yeah, okay, I—"

Interrupting, Salerno asked, "So what do you want us to do? Give us some suggestions, John. Your other two children didn't go out and say good-bye to her. . . . John, your other two children did not go outside and say good-bye to their mother. Joann and the kids were expecting her to come back that night, take them home, feed them pizza. They expected to go to school the next day, continue on with their life at Peachland—"

Now Racz interrupted him. "Well, all the children said good-bye to her. They were standing by the door and they said good-bye to her. I don't know."

Shaking his head in the negative, Salerno disputed him. "That isn't what they told us. That is *not* what they told us."

Racz repeated the assertion. "Well, they said good-bye to her."

Playing a new trump card, Danoff said, "Katelin, man, wasn't even home yet. She got dropped off after Ann left!"

Apparently unshaken, John replied, "Well, I don't know

what they told you, but I think all the kids were home. They—they were all home and they all said good-bye."

"Well, why would they say good-bye to her when she was just going to get some hamburgers for them? Why would there be any need to say good-bye?"

Another grunt came from Racz.

Salerno asked, "Did you go to McDonald's?"

Stammering a bit, Racz repeated the question. "Did I go to McDonald's? Yeah, I—I told you that before."

"What did you buy?"

"I bought some food for the kids. I bought them thick shakes and some hamburgers."

"Hamburgers? And a thick shake? For all of them?"

Dancing away again, Racz said, "Okay. Now, this—you know, in that article, and the flyer that you have up, you know, there's some discrepancies in that. And I don't want to, you know—I don't know if you want to—if that's the way you finally put it in there. I don't know if that was the . . . food I ordered. What did *you* order two months ago when you went to McDonald's?"

Chafing at the bit, Danoff snapped, "It wasn't two months ago when we asked you that."

Racz continued his argument. "You didn't ask me what I ordered when you . . . talked to me." In yet another mercurial switch, he announced, "I have to go. At what point can those flyers be taken down?"

Salerno's tolerance for evasion was exhausted. He reminded Racz that a great deal of time and effort had been spent trying to discover what happened to Ann. "You look closest to home first, John. That's the primary thing we teach every new homicide investigator. All right?" The answer came in the form of another grunt. "You know what that means, don't you, John? You look closest to home first?" A nearly imperceptible nod by Racz suggested an affirmative answer. "You look at those people directly around the victim . . . all right. Now, we're attacking this in a twofold manner. One, as a missing person. Right?"

Yet another mumbling nod.

"We can't get past home. And home doesn't want to help. All right? Every time we start going back over something, it's a hassle. You know, just like now when we asked if you remember what you ordered two months ago from McDonald's . . . you are bothered by everything we are doing, which would lead a normal, intelligent individual to believe there's a reason for that."

Danoff tossed a question like an unpinned hand grenade. "How long were you gone?"

"I was gone, uh—"

"How long were you gone?" No answer came. "Now, tell me you don't remember how long you were gone."

"I don't remember exactly. I went to McDonald's and I came back."

"Were you gone longer than thirty minutes?"

"No. McDonald's is only a little ways away."

"We know where McDonald's is. We spent a lot of time on hamburger hill. It's nine-tenths of a mile."

Racz stammered, "Okay, Frank and Louie, uh, okay Frank and Louie—"

"Were you gone thirty minutes?"

"Okay."

"See, John," Salerno reiterated, "we can't get by this 'closest to home' thing. This is the way it is. And we should be operating together, all three of us as a team. . . . John, you know what this has come down to? It has to do with life's experience. . . . It has to do with reading people, reading an intelligent person and not getting the right answers. We're not getting the right answers, John. You can't tell me how long you were gone. I might expect to hear, 'Goddamn it, Frank, I was only gone a few minutes. I can't tell you if it was seven-and-a-half minutes, Frank, but I know it was less than ten.' And you can't even tell me that."

"Okay."

Danoff stepped in again. "This is your story. There's nobody else feeding us any other story. Everybody else's story stops on April twenty-first. Joann's and the kids' story stops at about four o'clock, maybe a little after, on April twenty-second. Your story continues, but we can't confirm it. Is that when she went missing?"

Snapping back, Racz said, "That's when she left."

Salerno voiced his next words in razor-sharp tones. "It's like what I'm getting here is that you have something to hide. I mean, assuming your wife went missing, you would like to resolve that she's either alive somewhere, or she's not."

"I think my wife is still alive," Racz said.

"Why do you think she's still alive?"

"Why? See, that's what I mean. You're asking me questions—"

"Well, you just made that statement again."

"I didn't—I didn't do anything to hurt her. I don't think . . . I think she left on her own and I think she's still alive. I think she is. I don't—"

"Well, I hope you're right," Salerno said in a manner that made it clear that he no longer wanted to talk to John Racz on this day.

The sparring match had lasted nearly a half hour. Finally Danoff and Salerno ended the session. They watched John Racz walk away to take his daughter and the cat home.

Both detectives vowed to continue their pursuit until the mystery of Ann Racz could be solved and to one day sit in a courtroom while a jury weighed the guilt or innocence of the person charged with her murder.

CHAPTER 11

CANYONS, CAVES, AND BOOTLEGGERS

It is not commonly known that one of the most productive gold mines in California's history is twenty-five miles east of Valencia, near the high desert community of Acton. The discovery of precious minerals in the region shortly after the Civil War brought prospectors, who burrowed into the hills and gullies like giant gophers. Some of the tunnels, with colorful names such as Red Rover, Puritan, and New York, descended hundreds of feet. Henry T. Gage, who became California's twentieth governor, from 1899 to 1903, owned several of the mines. Years later, when his relatives reopened the New York pit, hoping to find a new vein of gold, they renamed it the Governor.

These caves and tunnels may have enriched a few in earlier eras, but they turned into daunting problems for homicide detectives in recent times. The odds of finding a murder victim tossed into one of the caverns bordered on zero. Yet, dedicated officers, like Frank Salerno and Louis Danoff, kept trying. With a team of helpers, they searched the Governor and Red Rover mine areas to follow up on tips and clues. "That area is known for a long time to be a site where bodies have been dumped. Around Santa Clarita, all the way up to Palmdale, Lancaster, and the Antelope Valley, it has been a dumping ground where bodies have been, you know, murdered and hidden for decades," stated Danoff.

Giving an example, Danoff explained, "Prior to this Ann Racz investigation, there was an LAPD murder in which the victims were missing and never found. A few clues turned up and we joined LAPD investigators. We set up a search in which we went back to the Acton area. We lowered video cameras into the mines. So we went up there in the search for Ann Racz and used the video camera technique again, but found nothing."

Spring weather in the Santa Clarita Valley turned into broiling summer heat. On July 17, Danoff met with Emi Ryan and her daughter Kathy inside the well-cooled ambience of Tips restaurant on hamburger hill. They reviewed the investigation's progress, discussed John Racz's behavior, and recapitulated facts about Ann's routines. Kathy brought a Thomas Guide mapbook of L.A. County, with certain pages marked, and gave it to the detective.

Back in his office, Danoff created a document containing Ann's dental chart, thumbprint, and a physical description of her to be circulated to every sheriff's department and coroner's office in California. He obtained her prints from records of her application to teach in Los Angeles County. The detective also asked that the information be distributed to all fifty Departments of Justice throughout the United States. This provided an opportunity for data to be matched in both civil and criminal case searches. On the slim chance that Ann had voluntarily left and might apply for a job somewhere, Danoff explained, she would probably be required to submit to fingerprinting. Occupations requiring fingerprints include teachers. The description included her height, weight, hair color, scars, and other information.

Because John Racz insisted that Ann had gone on a trip, Danoff arranged for Interpol to receive copies of the flyers. He wanted to be certain that if she entered any one of the 186 countries served by the international police agency, there would be a chance of her being seen.

Over the next couple of years, Danoff would renew the profiles, and arrange for redistribution of them.

Frank Salerno oversaw distribution of flyers to bus stations, LAX, Flyaway, other shuttle services. He made certain they were posted at all restaurants and businesses on hamburger hill near Lyons Avenue, and sent a few to the Firestone sheriff's station, where John Racz had once worked.

Homicide detectives do not have the luxury of limiting their investigation to a single case. Salerno and Danoff worked a thick stack of other murders simultaneously. While their dedication to solving the mystery of Ann Racz never flagged, they couldn't give it all of their time.

Summer and fall raced by with no encouraging developments. Christmas and New Year's Eve left only frustration for the investigators, as well as for Ann's family.

On January 13, 1992, four days before Ann would have turned forty-three, news of human remains discovered in the Antelope Valley struck Danoff with the force of a .45-caliber slug to the chest. He hadn't forgotten the frustration he felt seven years earlier when a jury had freed Steven Jackson from charges of murdering Julie Church. Now, construction workers excavating a site no more than 150 paces from Jackson's residence unearthed a skeleton. Dental records left no doubt about the identity of Julie, who had vanished in 1981. She had resigned from her job and stopped at a Lancaster tavern to celebrate. A witness reported seeing her walk out of the bar with

Jackson, the manager of a local board-and-care home. No one ever saw her again.

As part of the investigation team, Danoff had helped convince the district attorney to file charges against Jackson, even without finding the victim's body. A prolonged trial, lasting twenty-two months, had resulted in a not guilty verdict. The *Los Angeles Times* had carried the story of his exoneration on January 17, 1985, Ann's thirty-sixth birthday.

Never having doubted Jackson's guilt, Danoff still believed that Steve Jackson killed Julie. Now the detective felt grinding pain, knowing that this man could never be brought to justice. The Constitution's clause of double jeopardy gave him a free pass forever.

The lesson couldn't have been spelled out more clearly: don't rush to judgment! Danoff would continue digging into the case of Ann Racz until enough evidence could be found to avoid another courtroom failure.

To keep the investigation fresh, Danoff arranged for the story to be covered by a television show called *Murder One,* on February 22, 1992. He explained, "The purpose is to get information out to a vast number of people in far-off areas, and to keep public interest at a high level."

On the first anniversary of Ann's disappearance, Danoff paid a visit to John Racz. He brought with him the last letter Ann had written to Bob Russell, just to see how Racz would react. But it elicited no emotional breakdown, not even a wrinkled brow. It would later be implied that Danoff showed the letter to Joann during the visit, but he adamantly denied it. Instead, Danoff stated, Racz handed it to his daughter and allowed her to read it.

More tips came in the middle of May, leading Danoff to head up a search of the Santa Clarita Valley industrial center and the Magic Mountain Parkway, not far from the amusement park's array of thrill rides. Officers also spread out through the hills of Sand Canyon, Brandywine Canyon,

Placerita Canyon Road, and Meadstone Road. A few of the searchers trudged the dirt roads branching off these main thoroughfares. They found nothing useful.

In June, Danoff's search teams hunted the length of Los Pinetos Road, adjacent to State Highway 14, five miles from hamburger hill. This stretch, known as the Antelope Valley Freeway, branches east of I-5, just below Santa Clarita, passes through the old gold mine community of Acton, and takes travelers to the vast Mojave Desert. When NASA's space shuttles return from outer space, the route is filled with sightseers headed toward Edwards Air Force Base to watch the majestic aircraft land. Danoff had another type of viewing in mind on his drive to the desert. Hikers had reported seeing possible human remains, but their sighting turned out to be another false alarm.

A few of the tips Danoff received actually did result in locating bodies, or body parts. He explained what happens when these grisly discoveries are made. "Initially you go out there to examine exactly what has been found. Sometimes it requires an excavation. You bring in a team from the L.A. County Coroner's Office and they will do an archeological dig."

Another sweltering summer sent heat waves rising from the hills and canyons. On July 28, Danoff led another search in proximity to the Antelope Valley Freeway, along Spring Canyon, parallel to the road for several miles, then unpaved Heffner Road, ten more miles farther to the east, and finally Indian Creek Road, close to the old Governor gold mine in Acton. They returned to the same area two weeks later, this time with a horse-mounted posse. The rugged countryside and mounted lawmen could well have been right out of the Wild West days. After digging around a dozen possible burial sites, perspiring, and taking salt tablets to ward off heat prostration, they drove back toward Los Angeles, pulling horse trailers, empty-handed.

More mounted posse hunts took place that summer along dirt

trails crisscrossing the Santa Clarita Valley and the Antelope Valley. Riders from other Sheriff's Stations helped Danoff scour even more remote sites in the Santa Clarita Valley, Antelope Valley, Spring Canyon again, and Tick Canyon. "I went back many, many times over those areas. We'd had several telephone tips. The second reason is the Thomas Guide map book, the one Kathy gave us," Danoff said. One of those pages showed the back roads, including Davenport Road, of Aqua Dulce. It appeared that John Racz had marked these obscure routes.

Some of the search-and-rescue teams drove four-wheel vehicles along twisting trails and dirt roads. "We didn't know if she was disposed of, what kind of vehicle was available to take her to certain areas. And some of the areas you wouldn't want to go into without a four-wheeler. The areas I personally searched in this region, you could get into with a conventional car. It might be a little crazy, but you could do it and you could get out okay."

Time after time, the searchers came back with nothing. Maybe a lawman with less grit might have allowed repeated failures to dim enthusiasm, but Danoff had the hide of a rhinoceros. Before August ended, he led probes and excavation crews in digging up twenty-six possible burial sites they had identified. In the miserable heat, during which fires often ravaged rural L.A. County, Danoff took the precaution of having fire-suppressing teams accompany his gang into dry forests and brushland.

Before August came to a close, Danoff received a phone call from a woman who belonged to Ann's Elizabeth circle group at the Newhall Presbyterian Church, along with Dee Ann Wood and several others. Pamela Cottrel had first contacted Dee Ann Wood to ask her advice about contacting the detective, and Wood had encouraged it. Cottrel informed Danoff that she had observed something the detectives should know about, and wanted to tell him before she moved out of state. Her husband, a military pilot, had been transferred to

Wright-Patterson Air Force Base in Ohio, and the family would soon be moving there.

Both Salerno and Danoff listened as Cottrel said, "I have noticed a lot of construction in an area not far from Ann's home, a lot of earthmoving. I have a daughter who wants to be an engineer and build things. She asked me if we could go watch the bulldozers. So we sat by the side of Lyons Avenue and observed the heavy machinery covering and reconstructing hillsides." Much of it took place within a half mile of the McDonald's on hamburger hill, but, Cottrel said, she and her child also visited several other sites. "They were getting ready to pour concrete and I made a note of that. I used to help my dad pour concrete on the farm, so I was familiar with the procedure."

The investigators had also seen construction work in those areas, but noted a few specific sites Cottrel mentioned for follow-up examination.

Worry plagued Danoff and Salerno that Ann's body might have been buried on a site excavated for a new building, where she could lie underneath a thick layer of concrete for decades. On September 10, 1992, based on Pamela Cottrel's observations, they searched an area being readied for future buildings at Newhall Ranch Road, about four miles north of hamburger hill and east of Magic Mountain. It would have been an ideal place to dump a murder victim before the bulldozers moved in. But it proved to be futile, as similar efforts had in the past.

Danoff contacted the popular television tabloid *Hard Copy* in October and arranged for the airing of a segment on the missing woman, hoping that someone with viable information might see it. The nationwide, and even international, coverage might eventually turn up something.

More expeditions took place when fall weather turned Santa Clarita's trees into bursts of golden colors in November. Danoff led groups of searchers through a half-dozen sites that month. On November 28, several people met the sheriff's team at an assembly point and led them to a man-made cave. Danoff crawled into the hidden, dark cavern. Aptly named "Bootlegger Cave," it had been the hiding place for illicit booze during Prohibition in the late 1920s. Among the detritus accumulated for most of a century, the detective found an area inside paved with cement. He could picture crates stacked there containing bottles of bathtub gin, and men, clad in pin-striped suits, black shirts, and white ties, carrying tommy guns and hauling the liquor away in Model A Fords.

A couple of weeks before Christmas, Danoff and Salerno revisited the Bouquet Canyon area and a dirt road extension of Newhall Canyon Road. The final search of 1992 also marked another ending.

It turned out to be Frank Salerno's last effort on the case. In January 1993, he took a medical leave of absence from his job, and remained away until he retired the following August. Nevertheless, Salerno kept in contact with his partner's persistent efforts to untie the Gordian knot of Ann Racz.

CHAPTER 12

"She's Out There Gallivanting."

After Sergeant Frank Salerno left the case, Detective Louis Danoff refused to let go. He kept in contact with principals in the case, led hunts into the local wilderness, and handled the distribution of flyers and bulletins involving rewards being offered for information leading to Ann's whereabouts. Funding for the rewards came not only from Ann's family, but from several sources collectively called "The Friends of Ann."

Another television news-documentary show, *Prime Suspect,* aired in January 1993, featuring Danoff describing the hunt for Ann Racz.

Under his direction, searchers fanned out to numerous places within Southern California, including the Santa Clarita and Antelope Valleys, as well as other areas of rural L.A. County. Deputies and volunteers saturated hamburger hill restaurants and businesses with the posters.

In the same manner that Inspector Javert pursued Jean

Valjean in Victor Hugo's classic *Les Misèrables,* Louis
Danoff stayed on John Racz's trail. He suspected that his
quarry, though, had done more than steal a loaf of bread. On
February 1, 1993, Danoff drove to Marian Anderson Elementary School in Compton and waited outside in the parking lot
until John Racz came out to his vehicle. He asked the surprised teacher if he had heard from Ann. Racz said he hadn't.

"Not even on her birthday a couple of weeks ago?"

"No, I didn't," John barked. "I have to go."

Danoff refused to be shunted away and kept Racz talking,
but John diverted the conversation to his own experience as a
deputy years earlier. "I was a sergeant, you know." It struck
Danoff as incredulous that this man wanted to talk about himself
rather than ask if any progress had been made in finding Ann.
Not a single question about the investigation. Finally John did
say, "If you get any new information, will you let me know?"

"Yeah," Danoff snapped. "I will definitely tell you."

Ann Racz's family appreciated Danoff's continued pursuit
of answers, but they decided to seek some of their own. On
the second anniversary of Ann's disappearance, Takeo, Joji,
and Emi drove to the Fortuna house for a meeting with John
Racz, in hopes that he could shed some light on what happened to their beloved sister. Afterward, each of them documented the event for possible future use.

Joji Yoshiyama wrote:

> *At approximately 5:15 p.m., on April 22, 1993, Emi,*
> *Takeo and I went to John's house to visit the children and*
> *have a talk with John. . . . After a few minutes of polite*
> *conversation with John and the children, we asked John*
> *if we may talk to him alone, so he sent Katelin and Glenn*
> *outside while Joann did something in the kitchen and*
> *later went upstairs.*
>
> *Takeo, Emi, John, and I talked in the living room.*
> *I told John that I wanted to hear his story about Ann's*

*disappearance; that maybe if we talk things out we might
be able to figure out what might have happened to Ann.*

*He started his story on the Thursday (April 18) that
Ann left the house. Things were normal in the morning
when he left for work, so he was surprised when he got
home later that day to find out that Ann had left. John
said that Ann wrote him a note saying that she will call
him later to explain about her leaving.*

*John then said that he and Ann had met with the Pastor
for counseling, either on Saturday or Sunday, he doesn't
remember the exact date. He said that on Sunday evening
Ann met the children and him at a restaurant for dinner.*

*I asked him about Monday, the last day the children
had seen their mother. John said that when he got home
from work on that Monday, the children were at the
house waiting for Ann to pick them up. Emi had to
remind John that Katelin was not at home at that time,
and John's response was, "I don't remember."*

*John then said that Ann left to get the children some-
thing to eat. I asked him if that was the last time he had
seen or talked to Ann, and he said, "Yes."*

*He went looking for Ann when she did not return,
could not find her, so got some food for the children,
can't remember what he got them. Takeo then asked him
about meeting with Ann to give her some money. Then
[John] suddenly remembered that Monday was not the
last time he had seen or talked with Ann. He couldn't remember if it was Tuesday or Wednesday night that he
had met Ann at a restaurant to give her some money.*

*So again, I asked him if that was the last time he had
seen or talked with Ann, and he said "Yes."*

*I asked him if he had told the children about meeting
with their mother that evening and he couldn't remember. I reminded him that the children had not seen or*

heard from their mother since Monday, so his meeting with Ann should have been told to the children.

He still claimed he does not remember whether he told the children about meeting Ann. We had to remind John that the meeting with Ann to give her the money was not the last time he had talked to Ann because he claimed that he had a call from her on Friday, from the airport.

So again I asked him if he had told the children about the phone call since they had not heard from her for almost a week now. And again, he said he does not remember whether he told the children about the call from Ann.

I asked John if he really believed that Ann would leave the children without a word of her whereabouts or not contacting any of us. His answer was, "I don't know."

So I told him that he does not know Ann as he claims, because Ann would never leave without letting her children or her family know [what] her plans might be.

I was very surprised when John said that he had no idea that Ann wanted to leave him. He said he thought that everything was fine, but then I told him that I know for a fact that Ann had told me she had asked John for a divorce and he refused. So how can he say that everything is okay?

I told John that we appreciate having the children for family gatherings once in a while, and we would like our relationship with the children to continue. John agreed to this, but asked why he couldn't be included in our family gatherings. He was reminded by Emi that if Ann were here they would be separated or divorced by now, and so his presence would make everyone very uncomfortable, especially our mother.

John said that he was very upset about people pointing their fingers at him, neighbor children asking if he had done something to his [wife]. So we told John that we cannot control what other people think and say to him.

Two things I noticed about John during our conversa-

tion with him. First, his responses were very deliberate. One can see that he was really thinking before answering. He would speak very slowly, and yet many of his answers were, "I don't remember."

The second thing I noticed was that John would not look at me when answering the questions. I cannot speak for Emi or Takeo, but I felt frustrated and yet relieved after talking to John. Frustrated because we did not learn anything about Ann's disappearance. And yet relieved because we got to tell John our family situation in regards to this matter.

Louis Danoff's workload of other homicide investigations busied him, but he kept Ann's case a top priority in both his mind and his heart. On May 4, 1993, he led another hunt in the hills north and west of Magic Mountain. Soon after that, searchers trudged along dirt roads in undeveloped sectors northwest of a Valencia industrial center and the Santa Clarita riverbed. "These were close to the area where Ann Racz lived," Danoff explained. "Because they are isolated and rural, there is a good possibility that if you want to secrete somebody there, it would be a good hiding place."

In several expeditions, K-9 teams joined Danoff's reserve law enforcement officers, as they did on May 15, 1993. Acting on a clue, they trudged over the Santa Monica Mountains near Malibu. It wasn't far from John Racz's final duty station during his tenure with the LASD. More probes of canyons and caves rounded out the year and continued through 1994.

Ann's status remained a mystery, but certainly not from lack of effort by Detective Louis Danoff.

Ann Racz would have celebrated her forty-sixth birthday on Tuesday, January 17, 1995. Instead of anticipating a party, her family dreaded the upcoming fourth anniversary of her disappearance into an unknown universe—without a single clue indicating that she might still be alive. Ann's three children suffered immeasurable pain, and her siblings endured a grinding, hollow helplessness.

Emi traveled from Arizona after Christmas and New Year holidays to spend some time with her daughter Kathy. Married the previous May, Kathy had become Kathy Gettman.

Over the meal, Emi made a decision. She needed to talk to John about some things, and she couldn't postpone it any longer.

Back in the Fortuna house, Emi told Katelin how much she had enjoyed her visit during Christmas. John sat watching television. Speaking to both John and his daughter, Emi revealed that Grandma Matsue had taken sick in late December forcing her into bed for three weeks. John remained glued to the TV screen, apparently disinterested.

Raising her voice, and speaking directly to John, Emi said, "Before she dies, Grandma wants to know what happened to Ann." John refused to divert his eyes from the screen or to answer.

Determined, Emi said, "John, can you tell me something?"

Still no response.

Louder, Emi insisted, "John, can you answer me?"

Finally he grunted, "I don't know where she is." Frowning, he added, "She's out there gallivanting somewhere."

Her stomach churning with frustration, Emi asked, "How can you say she's out there, and she's not contacting her kids or her mother? If she could, she would have called her kids, or her mom, or me, a long time ago."

Without turning toward her, John muttered, "She can call us anytime."

Adding a little fuel to the tension, Kathy jumped in. "How can she do that, or reach you, since you changed your phone number?"

John tore his eyes away from the television, glared at

Kathy, and snapped, "You keep quiet. You have nothing to say about this."

Protective of her daughter, and angry, Emi said, "She can say what she feels. She's an adult and knows what she's saying."

John growled, sotto voce, "I don't want to talk about Ann in front of the kids."

"Okay," said Emi, "let's go outside and talk."

John rocketed from his chair and headed toward a door to the garage, with Emi one pace behind him.

As soon as they entered the garage, John whirled, leaned down, almost nose to nose with Emi, and yelled, "She's out there fucking!"

The "F" word may not hold the vulgar voltage it once did, but to a lady approaching her fifty-eighth birthday, its blatant usage resonated with obvious insult. She later recalled her reaction. "I slapped him across the face. He yelled it again. I slapped him again. He said it again and again, right in my face, and every time he said it, I slapped him. It happened four or five times."

Still within inches of John's face, Emi shrieked, "How can you say that? Ann is missing and she's not alive anywhere. If so, she would have contacted us."

John's eyes flashed sparks as he repeated the accusation. "She's out there fucking." Emi slapped him again. They repeated the furious exchange at least three more times.

At last, Kathy dashed out the door, pried them apart, and placed her own body between the combatants. Pounding her fists against John's chest, she screamed, "Get away from my mother!" John shouted, "Keep away from me, you—you—fat bitch." Emi pulled Kathy away and told her to go back into the house. The daughter reluctantly complied.

Now appearing frazzled, John demanded of Emi, "Why are you doing this?"

After reining in her fury, Emi said, "I just want you to tell me where Ann is and what you did to her."

"I did nothing to her," John asserted. "You're talking crazy. Why are you accusing me of doing something to her?"

"Because she disappeared without a trace. Because since that Monday, April the twenty-second, there have been no notes, no letters, and no phone calls from her or from anyone who could have seen her."

Later speaking of it, Emi explained, "When the sheriffs checked his story, they couldn't verify anything John had said. And his story changed from what he told me that first week, and later when Joji, Takeo, and I talked to him in April 1993. But all he did is say again that I am crazy."

With vitriol boiling again, Emi continued her barrage against John Racz. She pointed out that the children don't even talk about their mother. "Why? People ask me how come. Neighbors ask me why they don't talk about their mom at all. And even when the kids are with me, they never bring up Ann until I say something. Then they talk about her very reluctantly."

"They talk about their mother. And I tell them nice things about her," John answered.

Emi shook her head. "Okay, then why don't you tell me what happened that day she left?"

"I don't know."

"You're the last person to see her. And I know you did something to her."

"You talk crazy. I love Ann."

"How can you say you love her, and then accuse her of those awful things you just said?"

"Well," John snorted, "you can love a person and still say the truth about them."

"You're sick," Emi hissed.

"When Ann comes back—"

Emi interrupted with an incredulous laugh. "You know that Ann can't come back. You killed her!"

Ignoring the dramatic indictment, John continued. "When Ann comes back, will you back me up?"

Emi almost choked. "What are you talking about?"

"When Ann comes back, and wants the kids, will you help me out?"

This sudden swerve from all logic or reality struck Emi like a scene from *Jerry Springer*. "You're crazy and you're sick. How can you sleep at night, knowing what you did?"

His face blank again, John replied, "I sleep good at night because I did nothing to Ann."

"Well, I have a terrible time sleeping," said Emi, "because worrying and thinking about Ann keeps me awake. How can you be so apathetic with your wife missing? Aren't you worried that something might have happened to her?"

"No. She's the one who left and she can come back at any time. It's up to her. She's the one who left."

"I think you are the one who got rid of her."

Raising his eyebrows as if perplexed, John asked, "How can you talk so crazy, Emi?"

Regulating her voice to sound calm and collected, Emi replied, "There are a lot of things that make me say this."

Later recalling the confrontation, Emi enumerated the reasons. "For one thing, he never, never called the sheriffs and asked if they had heard or learned anything new. And the things he said the first week and what he said two years later were different. Even the things he said at first didn't make sense. Then the money—which we didn't know they had—made me think he did it for greed. He was not going to split it with Ann. And pride. He could not stand it that Ann wanted to leave him. He told me that I was talking crazy. He said again that Ann was out there fucking somewhere. So I slapped him again."

At that point, John barked, "If you hit me again, I'm going to call the sheriff's office."

Bristling with defiance, Emi said, "Good! Call them. I would like them to come here."

"They'll arrest you."

"Good! I have lots to say to them. In fact, I'll call the sheriff's office for you, right now."

The door through which they had exited the house opened again and Kathy came out once more. She had apparently been listening and said, "Mom, we should leave. John is just repeating things and not saying anything worthwhile." Kathy turned toward the family room and called out for Glenn and Katelin to come say good-bye.

Emi said to John, "All right, we're going to go now." She started toward her car.

His voice now dripping with saccharin, John addressed his daughter. "Katelin, Aunty Emi is leaving now. Go give her a hug."

Amazed at the chameleon change, Emi embraced her young niece and her nephew, then took a few steps toward the car. But she wheeled around, approached John again, and said, "If there's anything you want to tell me, anytime, or if there's anything I can do, let me know. I may be the only person who can, or will, help you."

At her car, Emi remembered a bag of cookies she had brought for Glenn, and she called him over. As she opened the trunk, John came to her. "Wait, Emi, there's something I want you to hear." Turning to his son, he said, "Glenn, don't we talk about Mom? Don't I say nice things about her?"

The boy, now fifteen, stared at his father a few seconds, then gazed at his own feet and said, "No, not really."

Emi tried to see John's face, but he had turned away. He spoke to the boy. "Glenn, I love your mom. You know I love your mom—"

Unable to stand it, Emi interrupted. "Stop it, John. Don't do this for me or in front of your kids. I just wanted to know if you normally or naturally talk to them about Ann. I didn't want you to do it for my benefit." She said good-bye to Glenn and Katelin, immediately climbed into her car with Kathy, and sped away.

During the drive, Emi commented that throughout the entire altercation, John had never lifted his hands to defend himself or fend off the series of slaps to his face. Kathy replied, "Mom, he had both hands in his pants pockets the whole time."

The next morning, Emi drove over to the Fortuna house again, to see Joann. She told her niece a little bit about the previous day's confrontation. According to Emi's later recollection, Joann said, "He's so stupid, and I hate him so much."

Surprised, Emi advised, "But you live here, so you must do the best you can and don't get him mad. Just take care of yourself and the kids."

Emi and her eighteen-year-old niece comforted each other, and Emi left, still besieged with doubt, questions, and suspicions.

Later speaking of the distressing event, Emi said, "For Jerry and me, religion and church played a very big part of our lives during our search for the truth and missing Ann. She was always in our prayers. For many years after she disappeared, I attended daily Mass in the morning, praying for answers about Ann. I did this until the time when I had that bad argument with John in the garage and then I felt that God wasn't listening to me anymore. I did not attend church for a whole year after that, not even Easter Mass or Christmas Mass. Then I decided that I needed to have faith for myself, my family, and especially to find out what happened to Ann. I talked to my priest. I wanted to come back to church. Jerry helped me through it. He is my strength, as always. And, as always, church and religion play a very big part in our lives. Belief in God and prayers helped us through those very difficult years."

CHAPTER 13

A FIRE
IN THE BELLY

The fires of determination still burned inside Louis Danoff, and he led new probes in February 1995 that extended the search to neighboring Kern and Ventura Counties.

The daily business of homicide investigators sometimes took them to the local L.A. County District Attorney's Office. Danoff and his colleagues became familiar with the one-story Newhall building on West Valencia Boulevard, about five miles north of the Racz home. In room number 1, conferring with attorneys about ongoing cases, they probably passed a rookie prosecutor named Beth Silverman. Any testosterone-laced man couldn't help but do a double take at the vivacious brunette with an effervescent smile, wavy dark hair tumbling past her shoulders, and mirthful brown eyes unable to conceal a glint of mischief. Silverman had recently completed training as a new DDA, and joined the small Newhall office in 1996 to handle misdemeanors.

Whether or not they took notice of her at that time, Danoff and other officers would eventually become well aware of Silverman.

Over the full five years since Ann Racz had vanished, Danoff never rejected a reasonable clue, nor did he ever hesitate to launch another search. "One of the reasons why I was doing all this stuff is that people would see us out there and would want to help. They would approach us, or later make contact, and tell us new information that might be useful. They see you, and they know why you are there. I know that I was approached many times. When they realize that we are still active on the case, still searching, they want to help us out. I always believe that something is going to come out of it. At least you are out there trying."

During the entire investigation, month after month, year after year, Danoff received not a single telephone call or letter from John Racz to inquire about their progress, to ask if any news had surfaced about his missing wife, or to offer his help in searching for her. The only contact he initiated came shortly after the videotaped interview, to complain about his photograph being included on the posters and flyers. Racz wanted to know when they would be taken down. It seemed to the detectives that a truly innocent person would be doing everything he could to aid the search. And even though John Racz had a reputation for frugality, wouldn't it have been a prudent move to offer a reward?

Unfazed, Danoff continued to enlist the help of news media to keep the case alive. TV and radio stations sent reporters to cover the searches, sometimes leading to more tips from the public.

Danoff's perseverance, combined with his strong personal interest in the case, created a powerful bond with Ann's family. Several of her relatives began calling him "Uncle Louie." He repeatedly attended the annual April 22 memorials they held for Ann. Except for the first one, the detective never saw John Racz at any of them.

In the final month of 1996, a fire ravaged the hills along the old Ridge Route from Templin Highway to Highway 138, burning away decades of brush and undergrowth. With hope of greater visibility, Danoff headed up another team of searchers, which walked miles along the twisting old road.

As spring greened up the blackened area, and early wildflowers bloomed, new bands of volunteers and reserve officers made themselves available. They gathered on March 17, 1997, to search an area in Valencia at the rear of a real estate office. Someone had called in to report the discovery of unearthed human bones. The investigators did find a few shreds of old clothing, but the bones turned out to be refuse from a restaurant serving barbecued ribs.

Not every detective could keep the belly fire burning in the manner of Louis Danoff—he needed no extra fuel—but Emi and Jerry Ryan stood ready to provide it if they thought investigator interest seemed to be dwindling. Through frequent phone calls and occasional letters, they kept in frequent touch with Danoff. "They asked me questions as to what I was doing. They sometimes came up with things that they wanted to pursue," Danoff recalled. Emi kept him supplied with photos, information about the family, and whatever support the detective requested.

Looking back over the frustrating years, Danoff said, "On old and unsolved cases, you work them a little bit different than you do your fresh ones. One of the things you do with cold cases is try to encourage family involvement, get them working with you. It's old information and sometimes they can get something the detectives can't get. Sometimes they can find people you need to interview. You want to be working with the family. The other thing with old cases is that you want to keep them alive. And the way you do that is go to the media, as opposed to new cases where you tend to stay away from the media because you don't want to compromise information. It's kind of odd. There's an old saying that if you don't solve your case in eight days, you know you're in trouble. That's not true. Actually, the older the case, the better some aspects of it are. People talk to you, when they wouldn't if the case was recent. Even in gang cases, what they wouldn't talk about today, five years down the road they will tell you everything. The information is better. Another thing is, as the investigator, you're asking more inclusive questions. At first, you are trying to get more background information, in a more narrowly constricted scope. You go back later and you're basically dealing with a wider scope of information about your victim, more information about their past."

On April 22, 1997, Danoff, as usual, attended the memorial for Ann. Ten days later, he received information about skeletal remains found alongside Tujunga Canyon Road. The homicide team found them and arranged for examination by the coroner, who concluded that they were probably remains of an Asian female. Danoff leaped into action and retrieved the dental chart for Ann Racz obtained by Sally Fynan from Ann's dentist six years earlier. He delivered the chart to the coroner for comparison by a forensic odontologist. It concluded, as all the other hope-filled efforts had, in a dead end.

Nearly every deputy working the Santa Clarita or Antelope Valley areas knew of Danoff's quest, and kept him posted on breaking cases that might be remotely connected. "They saw me out there enough . . . and if they got anything or they knew that somebody had found something of interest, I was getting a call from them. Also, I was in and out of the coroner's office enough on this particular case, I knew the personnel . . . ," he added. "I was in touch with these people enough that they knew what I was looking for, and if there was something I had missed, they would let me know."

After the memorial of April 22, 1998, Danoff contacted another television show, *Eye on America,* and arranged for coverage of the case. It seemed to produce results one month later when a caller said that a human jawbone had been found next to the Angeles Crest Highway. Danoff made his usual visit to the coroner's office and talked to the investigator who rolled on it. Teeth clinging to the bone did not match Ann Racz's dental charts.

To save time and travel, the coroner's office, in November 1998, finally bent their policy and allowed Danoff to leave a copy of the dental charts with them for future use.

The endless routine of skeletal remains being discovered, and Danoff responding, continued through 1999. On July 4, Danoff arranged for the Los Angeles *Daily News* to include an article about Ann Racz in their ongoing series covering unsolved crimes. It kept his string intact of convincing various newspapers to publish at least one article on the case every year. He explained, "It's easy for people to go on with their daily lives and forget. As I said, with an old case, you try to keep it alive." He even contacted the *Rafu Shimpto,* a Japanese-English newspaper, and convinced them to run a story.

Two weeks after attending the ninth memorial for her, "Uncle Louie" grieved with Ann's family when they lost their beloved matriarch. Grandma Matsue Yoshiyama passed away, never knowing what had happened to her youngest daughter. Danoff stood silently with the family at the funeral on May 5, 2000.

Nearly two more years of searching and coping with frustration occupied Danoff's every spare minute. Finally he reached the end of his official career, as had his partner and friend, Frank Salerno. Louis Danoff retired on March 30, 2001.

If anyone thought his departure meant the end of his quest, they couldn't have been more mistaken. Danoff signed up as a volunteer reserve officer, at a salary of a dollar per year, with the objective of contributing to the volumes of documentation and assisting with future searches.

He also continued to hound television producers, and convinced them to cover the case on a series called *Vanished.*

At the eleventh memorial for Ann, on April 22, 2002, Danoff once again joined her family at the Newhall Presbyterian Church. The assembly gathered near a rosebush planted in her name, and a small bronze plaque posted in the garden with white raised words *In Remembrance of ANN, April 22, 1991.*

Perhaps nudged along by Danoff, and probably because of a nationwide surge in solving cold cases, the sheriff's department changed the status of the Ann Racz files from cold case to an active investigation once more. They handed it to Sergeant Delores "Dee" Scott on May 10, 2005. For Scott, it would be the second time she faced the challenge of working an investigation in which the victim's body hadn't been found. The Homicide Bureau's work had helped convict a Long Beach man named Bruce Koklich of murdering his wife in 2001.

Danoff immediately volunteered to aid her in any way he could, and worked the case until September 10, 2005. He acted as liaison to several key people, including Bob Russell. In those months of duty, Danoff looked into at least thirty possible grave sites based on tips he received.

CHAPTER 14

GROWING UP
IN PAIN

Ann's three children endured a barrage of conflicting emotions during the seemingly endless years investigators searched for their mother. It is not difficult to understand how profoundly the circumstances impacted Joann, Glenn, and Katelin. Their mother had ostensibly deserted them. Their father reportedly refused to discuss it or explain precisely what had happened. Instead, he reinforced the tale of her departure to take a trip and think things over, adding that she didn't care enough about her kids to keep in touch with them. To adolescents, the confusion and hurt is immeasurable.

Emotional pain in children can be manifested in multiple ways. In some cases, a child suffering internal conflicts might react with antisocial behavior, aggressiveness toward peers, bed-wetting, and poor performance at school. Others might internalize the stress and withdraw from all social interaction.

Criminal behavior in adults is often rationalized by pointing out unendurable childhood experiences.

The Racz children apparently coped with the problem as well as anyone could.

Joann's metamorphosis from a fourteen-year-old child into young adulthood included periods of sentimental reminiscing about her mother. Each time she heard the song "Unchained Melody," the 1950s version by Al Hibbler, or the 1965 Righteous Brothers rendition, it would take Joann back to the times her mother would cry at hearing the tune on radio oldies stations. Vocals by the Beatles and the Bee Gees brought on the same nostalgic recollections.

A powerful respect for Ann remained with Joann. "Mom was very outgoing, but not loud. She attracted people, wanted to be involved in the community, friends, church, neighbors, school. She took these things very seriously. Especially education. I remember her telling me how important school was. That was number one. Friends and fun were important, but school came first. She loved her arts and crafts, which was fun for her. She was fond of holiday family gatherings for Thanksgiving and Christmas."

Asked if her mother had been strict, Joann smiled and said, "Oh, yeah. I wouldn't say she was above and beyond in being strict, but she wanted to make sure we knew the rules were important. She wanted structure, but was very fair about it. And reasonable."

A certain amount of regret also permeated Joann's recollections. "I feel that I was really close to my mom, but not as close as I wanted to be in that last year. I was fourteen, and when you are twelve to fourteen, you try and kinda step away from all that and ignore your parents and get into fashion, friends, music. You want to steer away from hanging out with your mom a lot. While I wanted to be close to her, it's a time when you are being steered in other directions. I was definitely inclined to pay more attention to my friends, being cool. I wish I had been closer, but when I think back on it, I feel we had a good enough relationship where she could tell me certain things, but, of course, not the adult situations that were happening. I could tell she cared a lot about me and that made us close."

Punishment for misdeeds, said Joann, came from both of her parents. "The worst punishment I had was from my dad. On a few occasions, he got his belt out to spank us—a couple of times. But Mom never spanked us. Dad was pretty strict, but Mom did all the work with the kids. I was eight when I got my last spanking."

Pointing to a piano in her living room, Joann explained that it had belonged to her mother and it reminded her of a moment from the past when she had taken lessons. "I was refusing to play the piano, and Mom said how terrible that was. She didn't play it, though, but she was very musical, and would often sing in the car. She knew all the words."

Looking backward in time, Joann considered the painful months and years following Ann's disappearance. She spoke of it haltingly, with moisture glistening in her eyes. "I was really in shock. All three of us were. We were kinda stumped, and didn't know what to think. I know sometimes maybe, when my sister and I would cry, that was probably the stem reason of what we were trying to get out. Other things might have triggered it.

"After Mom was gone, our relationship with Dad changed. Everything was kind of hush-hush, like we're not supposed to be talking about all that kind of stuff. So I feel like for me, that made things kind of change. When I'd be talking to Glenn and Katelin and he came in, we'd have to stop. Things changed, where I had to be careful of what I said in front of him. We kids talked a little bit about it, but it was too much of a mystery to even come close to getting any answers. We speculated among ourselves a little bit, but didn't get too deep into it. We didn't analyze it, because it was just too hard. I did in my own mind, tried to analyze every little thing. All three of us probably did, but somehow we couldn't share it. We didn't want Dad to know, because he discouraged us from dwelling on it. For the first couple of years, especially the first year, I was kind of in denial. I brought it up to Dad but didn't make a big deal over it. And I'm sure Glenn and Kate had their own little things too. I had some blowouts with Dad because I was the oldest. I stuck up for my mom. In denial, though, I would wonder, 'Did Mom really just leave us?' She could be alive, but I was back and forth. After about two years, I told myself that my dad had something major to do with it and he's hiding it. I had nothing but intuition to go on, but it seemed like the handwriting was right in front of my face. I just had a feeling, and let myself go with my intuition. You get the right answers sometimes when you go with intuition. I didn't want to keep thinking, for five more years, that my mom was just out there somewhere. I had friends tell me she could be alive. But while I hoped she might be—really, after a year or two—I was pretty much thinking that my dad was hiding something."

It became apparent to Joann not long after her mother vanished that sheriff's detectives seemed to be focusing their investigation on John Racz. She wondered if he had killed her. Joann recalled her suspicions. "I think I began to believe in that first year that he might have done something to her. It was in the back of my head that I knew something was up. At first, I thought okay, maybe she had to escape. She was hurting so bad she needed to escape and create a new life. But that was so small in my mind, and the odds of her doing that were so slim, I couldn't really accept it. It took me about a year to see that she wasn't going to come back. It was way too weird, his story about going out and knocking on doors to find her. I didn't go for that. My mom had told me a couple of things beforehand that made me feel like she was scared."

Speaking of the prolonged investigation into her mother's absence, Joann recalled, "I talked to Louis Danoff a lot, from the time I was sixteen years old. He's the one I would always have lunch with. Gosh, I feel like he's done all he can to help. He had passion for my mom and the case. With the other detectives, like View and Salerno, I have a place for them in my heart for all their hard work. I know the passion they put into it, and it made me realize how seriously they took it. And I really appreciated every ounce of work they did. I talked to Louis on many occasions and he took notes. He was always there to find out from me what was happening with us. They were really good. The whole team, including Sally Fynan. They really helped me out."

Joann's brother and little sister also struggled with conflicting emotions. Speaking of Katelin's reactions, Joann said, "She seems more withdrawn. I totally understand what she's gone through, because I went through the exact same thing. I have been her before, I have been that person. Like when people call, I don't call back—'Just leave me alone.' I've been immature, like that whole growing up through high school, so I understand. She is very intelligent and street-smart too. She's still trying to get used to the facts about what happened to our mom and everything that followed. I think she knows in the back of her head what really happened."

About five years after Ann disappeared, a peculiar thing happened involving Katelin and their father, said Joann. It still bothered her.

John had taken Glenn and Katelin to play in the snow at Mt. Pinos, near the community of Frazier Park, about forty-five miles northwest of their home. Joann had to work, so she couldn't go with them.

Glenn wanted to use the sled they brought. After agreeing on a time to meet his son back at the car, John took Katelin for a walk toward another area of the mountain resort. Glenn found a perfect slope and occupied himself with their sled for hours. He kept his part of the bargain and went back to the parked car precisely on time. His father and sister failed to show up, however. The boy, now sixteen, waited for nearly two hours, until panic drove him to the local police station.

At one o'clock the next morning, Joann's ringing phone woke her up. A police officer informed her that her brother had reported his father and sister as missing. The youth was at the station and needed a ride home.

"I immediately dropped everything and my heart was broken," she later recalled. Frightened, confused, and furious, Joann imagined nightmarish possibilities. "I thought I had lost my sister." How could this happen? Something so easy as a day trip to the snow, and suddenly her father and sister have vanished? Shouldn't a former cop know how to avoid this? Wouldn't a schoolteacher understand how to keep kids safe? "My brother is alone at the police station at one o'clock in the morning, I have to work the next day, and I'm freaked out that Dad and Kate are gone. I'm so scared and angry."

Joann made the long drive to pick up her worried brother and brought him home. "I remember feeling so empty, unsure— another one of those mysteries. Who knows what's happening? And, of course, the next morning they were found."

Racz and his twelve-year-old daughter had been located by a search-and-rescue team. "They were brought in. Freezing cold. My dad and my sister explained to me how cold it was. Kate said they really were missing." Relieved, but still troubled by the incident, Joann couldn't shed nagging suspicions about the entire incident. She never found satisfactory answers.

As the years crept by with no resolution about her mother, Joann experienced endless gut-wrenching feelings. "Yeah, I felt helpless. It was so depressing and sad that it could have happened. And there was no proof. I felt there was nothing I could do to move forward or to do something about it. Yet, I wanted to. I have a voice. I can do something. But, honestly, I wondered if I would end up dead myself if I let this thing take my life over. By the time I had my own daughter, and things got very hectic for me because I have this major responsibility. I can't let myself be depressed and unstable, especially around my child. So I tried to move on. I knew something was going to happen. I knew it wasn't going to be like having grandkids and stuff and still not knowing what happened. I just knew something was going to happen. I knew that my dad was going to be questioned. When he and I used to have these crazy brawls, fights, usually during high school and after that, they'd be very bad. They were about a lot of things, but the underlying thing was always about my mom. I don't hate my dad. It's just when you are young, you go through all of these confusing feelings. I knew when we were fighting that something was going to pop up in his face and I would have nothing to do with it. I mean, I couldn't control it, but I didn't want to be the catalyst. I could have, but I didn't want to create the circumstances that would prevent me from ever talking to my dad again. Things would be just way too deep and drastic for me to ever start anything. I had to move on, but I felt like we were going to see something happen. I didn't know when, and it seems like it popped up and began to unfold a lot quicker than I thought it would. But anytime would have been the right time."

CHAPTER 15

A NEW LOOK

Sergeant Delores Scott, the new lead investigator on the Ann Racz case, had already served twenty-three years with the LASD. When she started, in 1981, Scott followed the pattern experienced by nearly all rookie deputies, being assigned to a custodial facility, the L.A. women's jail. Patrolling in a black-and-white vehicle came next on the streets and highways of northeast Los Angeles. Promotion to detective landed her in the Sex Crimes Unit, where she coped with the full spectrum of deviant behavior. Next came five years in the Narcotics Unit, a tour that included undercover work.

While Scott could be as tough as needed in her law enforcement work, she still maintained a soft-spoken elegance. This quality often gave her a strong advantage in dealing not only with criminals, but also in gaining the confidence and cooperation of witnesses.

Top performers among sheriff's detectives usually land in homicide, and Scott made that move in 1992. Seven years later, the brass recognized Scott's outstanding work by promoting her to sergeant in the upscale Marina del Rey station, handling missing persons cases. She stayed there a year, both supervising and investigating more than two thousand incidents.

Recalling it, she said, "The cases are typically very routine. You receive the report, and, typically, once you make a couple of phone calls to the person who made the report, it's not unusual that the missing individual has already returned home." Others require investigation, though. As Frank Salerno taught, "You basically get a sense of the missing person's life patterns, their daily routines, and then you follow those leads."

Of the unresolved segment, Scott observed, "We investigate even more thoroughly. You start at the person's home and if suspicious circumstances are involved, some of these cases, maybe two or three a year, are handed over to homicide because we believe that foul play is involved." Scott added that during all of her time in that assignment, only two cases in that small category remained unsolved. The others were all found dead. The Ann Racz mystery was one of those two.

After her year in Marina del Rey, Scott moved again to homicide, working the Missing Persons Unit, including the highly publicized Bruce Koklich case. In 2005, she began looking into unsolved cold cases, with the Ann Racz mystery at the top of the stack. Asked about the backlog, she said, "Believe it or not, we had about five thousand cold cases in our library."

Scott's philosophy of investigation combined two levels of "smart." She believed that you can be "book smart" or "commonsense smart," or both. She also understood the importance of establishing warm relations with the missing victim's family. In addition, Scott would have an investigative advantage over her predecessors with the use of three data banks: fingerprints, dental records, and DNA.

Responding to a question about where an investigator begins on a long-standing cold case, Scott smiled and said, "All right. You get a large cup of coffee and then you open the case file and you start reviewing whatever is in there. Because, you know, in this particular case, it was fourteen years old." She explained that fourteen years is certainly no record. "There have been some cases forty or fifty years old. You try to familiarize yourself with everything that was done in the initial stages, with the victim, the witnesses, and any possible suspect. . . . It's like reading a book." Of course, she acknowledged, you make contact with the original investigating officers if they are still available. "You can get a sense from them as to the personalities of the people involved."

A daunting task faced Dee Scott as she waded into the Racz mystery: "Most cold cases, all the information is contained within one folder. Unfortunately, with this case, it's a four-drawer cabinet, stuffed with reports, documentation, and other data. And I'm a slow reader."

In line with the protocol of learning everything possible about the missing person, Scott and Detective Robert Taylor flew to the San Francisco Bay Area in May to question Bob Russell. Back in Santa Clarita, they spoke to Dee Ann Wood and Pastor Glen Thorp for more orientation.

Just as Frank Salerno and Louis Danoff had partnered on the Racz investigation, Dee Scott took on Deputy Cheryl Comstock as her teammate in late spring 2006. Comstock had been chasing crooks for almost thirty years, half of them in homicide. Slim and light-complected, with short blond hair, contrasting with Scott's dark brown tresses, Comstock could fit into any social environment with her dignity and graceful bearing.

After digesting the thick volumes of records, Scott and Comstock talked to the initial investigators, and "roundtabled it" with other people in the Cold Case Unit. Familiarized with the bulk of what had transpired since April 1991, they initiated their new probe, beginning with more interviews of key people.

Diving headfirst into the fieldwork on June 9, 2006, the two women drove to the Fortuna house for a face-to-face meeting with John Racz. Before arriving, they wondered if he would ask about any progress in finding his wife. He didn't. Nor did he invite them into the house. They stood on the front patio to talk. In the conversation, Scott explained about the DNA data bank, and told him they were in the process of taking biological samples from Ann's family members for potential future comparison to unidentified bodies or body parts. It would be on an entirely voluntary basis. Before Scott could ask Racz if he would consent to giving a fluid sample, he interrupted.

Evidently, John Racz thought it more important to chat about other things. He told them of his tenure as a deputy, mentioned his various assignments, asked both women if he had ever met them during that time, and what class in the Sheriff's Academy they were from. Politely redirecting him to the point of this visit, Scott tried again to ask if he would help. Instead, Racz raised another question. Could he tape the conversation? "It's up to you," Scott replied. "We don't have an issue with it."

Motioning for the detectives to follow, Racz led them into his garage, opened the trunk of his car, and lifted out a large vintage video camera. They trooped into the living room, where Scott again started to further explain the DNA process. She told him that it would not be invasive at all, that it's nothing more than a cotton swab, like a Q-Tip, used to take a small amount of saliva from inside the cheek. But Racz paid more attention to setting up his camera and getting it to work. "He kept wanting to change the subject and didn't know whether he wanted to give us a sample. He said, 'Why don't you leave the forms here. I will read them over. You know, I want to cooperate, but I don't know if I can.' He kept going back and forth pointing that big camera at our faces. If Cheryl was talking, he would go to her and ask for her name, rank, and file number. Then he'd pull the camera over to me and ask me the same thing. If he asked a question, and Cheryl started to answer, he would say, 'No, I want the sergeant to answer it.' He was trying to take control of the conversation," Scott recalled.

Veering away from the DNA request for a moment, Comstock asked if Ann had disappeared in 1991. Racz replied, "That's when she left." He added, "I didn't do anything to hurt her, I don't think. I think she left on her own. I think she is still alive."

An hour of futile attempts to obtain the DNA sample passed, and the two detectives finally left empty-handed.

Calling on Katelin, now age twenty-two, Scott asked her consent to give a DNA sample by swabbing a small amount of saliva from her mouth. She explained that in the case of a missing female, it would be best, ideally, to obtain DNA samples from both of her parents. But since Ann Racz's parents were deceased, the next best option is to obtain samples from the missing woman's children. These would be analyzed and entered into databases for future comparison with any biological remains found. Katelin readily allowed it and agreed to an appointment for an interview within a few days.

Next they visited Glenn Racz. "When we first met Glenn, he was very forthcoming, friendly, very likeable, and gave us his true account as he recalled," Comstock said. He had no objections to swabbing the inside of his check for a saliva sample.

Joann's turn came the next day, June 10, and she, likewise, cooperated in a friendly manner.

At the second meeting with Katelin, a few days later, with a tape recorder running, the young woman seemed receptive, friendly, and responsive to their questions. Asked if she thought that Ann had abandoned her children, Katelin unequivocally expressed belief that her mother would never have voluntarily chosen not to see her kids again. On the contrary, she said, she remembered her mother to be devoted to all three of them. Comstock recalled that Katelin spoke openly of her father too, saying he had told her long ago about giving Ann "$10,000" before she went away and left her car at the Flyaway lot.

A few months later, it stunned the investigators when Katelin dramatically reversed her opinions and her demeanor toward the detectives.

And it mystified both women when Glenn, like his sister, later turned reticent and uncooperative. They realized that each of the siblings had probably been negatively influenced by someone, or some event.

Exactly as Louis Danoff had done, Scott kept close contact with the coroner's office to see if any "Jane Does" might possibly be Ann Racz. And she faithfully followed up on discoveries of partial human remains. Scott's new slant on the investigation included the use of recently developed database search engines for comparisons of any fingerprints, credit history, Social Security records, property acquisition, and other similar tracking data, both in California and in Hawaii. Information about Ann was entered into MUPS for ongoing comparisons. Contacts with hospitals, mental institutions, and other similar organizations took place under Scott's direction. She even utilized e-mail to disseminate bulletins across the country.

New flyers and information sheets developed by Scott included "age progression" images of Ann Racz, developed by computerized graphics to reflect how she would probably look after the passage of fifteen years. The current bulletin, distributed throughout the United States, to Interpol, and to news media on June 16, 2006, offered the only reward still outstanding for information about Ann. It came from Emi and Jerry Ryan. John Racz still made no contribution.

On that same date, Dee Scott held a news conference, hoping to generate new interest and leads. Explaining it, she said, "We wanted to bring the case to the forefront again, and we believe the media is obviously a great tool to get the attention of a vast population of people. . . . Putting the information out there could bring forth new witnesses."

Coverage of the conference by news media resulted in one telephone call. It came from Kristin Best, Joann's close friend at the time Ann vanished. Scott and Comstock arranged to interview her in two weeks, on June 30.

More travel followed. Before June ended, Scott and Comstock flew to Florida to meet with John Racz's widowed mother and his sister. Looking for anything in John's background that might explain his unusual behavior after his wife had vanished, they took extensive notes. In August, they crossed the Pacific to Hawaii for an interview with Ann's relatives who still lived in Honolulu and in Hilo. None of them had heard from or seen Ann at any time since she vanished.

Forging ahead with the new investigation, Sergeant Scott and Detective Comstock found that John Racz now had a girlfriend, an Asian-American woman. In interviews conducted on June 21, they spoke to her and to Larry Baker, Ann's divorce attorney. The girlfriend had little to say about John. The attorney stated that his contacts with Ann had left him believing that she was afraid of her husband.

John Racz had long refused to landscape his backyard, despite Ann's pleading. Not long after her disappearance, he evidently had a change of heart and covered the bare dirt with green lawn surrounded by sections of concrete slab.

On the chance that Racz might have used the plot as a burial ground, Dee Scott obtained a search warrant and led a team of officers to the Fortuna home on June 24. The group included an "electromagnetic company." Scott explained that "it's kind of high-tech for me, but I understand it's a company that operated with a GPS (Global Positioning System) in order to detect anomalies under the ground."

Geophysical methods of searching for a buried body

are controversial and subject to variables in operator skills, interpretation of data, and reliability of equipment. These techniques include ground-penetrating radar (GPR), electrical resistivity, and electromagnetic surveying. All of them are relatively new as forensic technology. They do not actually locate bodies, but can detect anomalies in the ground at suspected burial sites, such as disturbed soil, air pockets, and chemical alterations caused by decomposing flesh.

The use of modern technology had no better results than the old-fashioned method of using long metal rods to probe the ground. According to Scott's subsequent comments about the search of Racz's backyard, equipment malfunctions caused the disappointing failure.

Scott and Comstock kept the appointment with Kristin Best on June 30. The woman who, as a teenager, had been Joann's best friend during their high-school days recalled something about April 22, 1991. She said that Joann had telephoned her several times that afternoon and evening. In the first conversation, Joann told of being dropped off at the Fortuna house by her mother, who had left to buy some food for the kids at McDonald's. In follow-up calls, Joann said her father had also left, and expressed worry because her mother had not returned. Joann finally called to complain that her father had come back with french fries, and they were ice-cold.

To the detectives, Kristin's statements carried substantial weight. Her words provided corroboration that the fries Racz bought were cold. In addition, Kristin's estimation that Joann's calls came over a period of about two hours stamped an estimated time frame on the length of Racz's absence that afternoon.

* * *

Because malfunctioning equipment had led to failure in the June 24 search of Racz's backyard, the detectives returned on Friday, July 7, with a new warrant and a different company specializing in buried body searches using radar technology. This time they discovered four "areas of interest." After stringing crime scene tape and securing the yard with a deputy, the officers arranged for a contractor to show up the next day and remove sections of concrete paving.

On Saturday morning, Scott arrived bright and early, followed by the contractor, an excavation crew from the coroner's office, and a cadaver dog with handler. Hours of work, scanning, digging, and probing produced nothing helpful. As the law enforcement team disbanded and left, the contractor prepared to replace broken concrete sections.

Over the next few weeks, Scott and Comstock met with Kimiko "Auntie Kay" Jewett, Pastor Glen Thorp, Compton school principal Peter Danna, and the managers of Peachland Condominiums. They also arranged for new technology fingerprinting examination of the Flyaway parking lot entry ticket.

Now it came time for a decision by the Los Angeles District Attorney's (LADA) Office. Did they have enough evidence to move forward with the case?

In a 1965 comedy-drama film titled *How to Murder Your Wife,* Jack Lemmon plays the role of Stanley Ford, a man who makes the mistake of marrying while drunk, then fantasizes about murdering the woman. When she vanishes, Ford is arrested. He tells his lawyer, "There's no body. You can't try a person for murder without a body."

That statement parroted what most people believed for many decades.

CHAPTER 16

TOUGH DECISIONS

<u>Ronald Bowers:</u>

When sheriff's detectives first brought the case of John Racz to us in the DAs office, I knew they faced nearly insurmountable obstacles. Even though it had been more than twenty years since a jury found Steven Jackson not guilty in the murder of Julie Church, the defeat still resonated at all levels of law enforcement. If the great J. Miller Leavy couldn't convince twelve people, good and true, that a murder could have been committed even though the victim's body had never turned up, then who could? The raw, festering wound of the Church case bled freely again when workers found Church's body a short distance from Jackson's residence, after the defendant had walked away a free man, never to face another trial related to her death.

My office routine, on the seventeenth floor of the Criminal Courts Building in downtown Los Angeles, included meetings with deputy district attorneys to assist in their preparation for trials. Even before they filed a case, I would be brought in to create a visual presentation for the top brass to aid them in the decision-making process.

On a smoggy Wednesday, in the late summer of 2006, I looked up from my work on a couple of PowerPoint presentations and saw DDA Shellie Samuels coming through the door. A sheriff's homicide detective accompanied her. Shellie stands a slim five-six, wears her dark hair in pageboy style, which frames horn-rimmed glasses, and uses a no-nonsense approach to problem solving. She immediately began speaking in her matter-of-fact voice, telling me that she needed some help in developing an important presentation. To me, her demeanor conveyed unhappiness that it must include slides to explain the details. In my infinite wisdom, I recognized this wasn't the time to tell Shellie that I was too busy to help with her project.

Nevertheless, I invited her and the detective to come in and sit down. Shellie's frown deepened when she saw that I had only one guest chair. She grabbed another one from an office across the hall, returned, and introduced me to Sergeant Delores "Dee" Scott. I thought I recognized her as one of the investigators of a murder several years earlier, in which Bruce Koklich had been convicted of killing his wife—even though searchers had never located the body.

Shellie started explaining to me that the sheriff's Homicide Bureau wanted the DAs office to consider filing charges in a cold case from the eighties. I think my shoulders slumped a little at the prospect of hearing about long-faded evidence and unavailable witnesses. Even though I didn't have the time, I asked her to give me a short version of the facts. I knew that Shellie was a fast talker, so I figured it couldn't take that long.

She said it involved a wife who had been missing for sixteen years, and her body had never been found. I sat up straight again. "No body" cases have always intrigued me. Very few of them ever wound up in front of a jury. My experience told me that if law enforcement worked more closely with seasoned and creative prosecutors, more of these cases could be filed and won. Now eager, I wanted to hear what Dee Scott and her investigation had turned up in the way of evidence.

Scott said the victim's husband had been a schoolteacher, then a sergeant with the sheriff's department, and returned to teaching. Wow! This remarkable combination piqued my interest even more. She told me that the female victim had moved to a condominium with her three kids and hired a divorce lawyer. Rattling off names and ages of the children, Scott added that this woman had resumed contact with an old boyfriend resulting in a romantic relationship. A pastor/counselor had tried unsuccessfully to patch up the marriage and he turned out to be the person who made the missing person report. It all sounded liked the plot of a mystery novel.

Asking Scott to slow down, I grabbed a pencil, drew a set of squares, and asked the suspect's name. She said it was John Racz. I entered the name in the first box, and Dee immediately corrected my misspelling of it. In other boxes, I printed names and ages of the three children, and identities of other key people.

Next we tackled the events, with Scott and Shellie both describing what they had learned. One minute they told me about Mrs. Racz moving into the condo, and the next minute about the pastor reporting her missing, and the divorce papers being served, and then jumped back in time to a wedding in San Diego.

I struggled with the overwhelming onslaught of baffling details, and wondered if they hoped to convince me by the sheer volume of information that murder charges must be filed. But I knew that our administrators would ask the tough questions and look for the meat in all of these bones. As tactfully as I could, I suggested we slow down so I could develop a timeline to help sort out this jumble of facts.

Shellie mentioned that she had other pressing business, asked Sergeant Scott to work with me on the dates involved, then left.

I looked at Scott and saw an understanding smile playing on her lips. She opened a folder and pulled out a lengthy, detailed timeline already prepared. It listed all of the facts arranged in chronological order, and it gave me a great deal of what I needed to develop a presentation for Samuels. Actually, the layout contained too much. I realized that I would have to reduce it to essential facts required by administrators, who always appeared to be in a hurry to find the bottom line.

With Scott's help, I roughed out a calendar depicting events between Sunday, April 14, 1991, when Ann Racz leased the condo, and Tuesday, May 14, 1991, when she didn't show up for the divorce hearing. By filling the in-between calendar days with important facts, I soon had a sequential summary. But, because April 22, when Ann disappeared, overflowed with events, I needed to build a separate timeline sheet for that day alone. Trying to be as graphic as possible, I decided to make it in the form of a clock. The first entry at 12:45 P.M. showed Ann's VCR transaction at a Target store. Moving on, it listed her bank transactions, grocery shopping, delivering checks to her husband at the Fortuna house, picking up Glenn and Joann at school, returning to the home, and leaving to buy fast food at McDonald's.

As I scrutinized this clock chart, the key problem became apparent to me. It involved a major question: did John Racz have sufficient time to kill his wife? Sergeant Scott admitted that with the passage of so many years, some of the witnesses had trouble recalling precise events and exact time frames. She had worked long and hard on the in-vestigation, and I understood the importance of carefully wording my questions to her. Yet, I needed to know if the window of opportunity reasonably existed for Racz to commit the crime and possibly dispose of his wife's body. This could very well be the Achilles' heel of this case.

Backing away from that crucial point temporarily, I listened as Scott filled in the blanks about other facts. Together we weighed various possibilities and scenarios. Using a computer map program, we looked at distances both Ann and John would have driven. The DA's decision makers, and eventually jurors, would want to know the routes traveled and where the couple may have crossed paths, but we could only make educated guesses.

I studied the map and realized that it tended to spotlight the big problem. How could John have enough time to drive to McDonald's, purchase fast food, meet with Ann at the restaurant, or some other secluded place, kill her, somehow cover up or dispose of her body, and drive back to the house? Sergeant Scott mentioned that the oldest daughter, Joann, thought that her father had been gone only five or ten minutes. If her time estimate proved correct, we faced a serious quandary. Trying to figure out possibilities for expanding the narrow window of opportunity, I concentrated on the Brownie leader who brought Katelin home. If she could pinpoint the exact timing, it might help. We also knew that John had taken his kids to a pizza restaurant at about 7:00 P.M. But we still needed more.

The doubts I expressed didn't ingratiate me with Sergeant Scott. She firmly believed that John Racz had killed his wife, and she didn't enjoy hearing me punch holes in that theory. Over my long career, I've had to make thousands of tough decisions about filing criminal charges. Prosecutors learn that we are not the most popular acquaintances of detectives, especially when we tell them that the evidence they have gathered is insufficient.

Reminding myself that the decision of filing or rejecting the Racz case lay in other hands, not mine, I proceeded with my visual aid preparation. And I changed my role of pinpointing problems to identifying for Scott certain things I would need for a presentation, such as photos and documents.

At that point, Shellie Samuels popped her head back in and asked how it was going; I think she could tell by the expression on Sergeant Scott's face. Shellie announced that she had to run. Before she could leave, I asked when the big meeting would take place. In two weeks, she said, then asked, "What do you think of the case?"

I had to be truthful, and answered, "This case has reasonable doubt written all over it." Not waiting for the predictable reaction, I added, "The motive evidence appears strong, but the opportunity evidence needs to be worked on."

As Shellie turned to make her exit, she said, "Dee, see what you can do on the critical times. Get the stuff to Ron that he needs." She turned the corner and disappeared in a flash.

I understood the consternation Dee Scott felt, and soft-pedaled my next words. I told her that if she could get me the needed information, I would prepare a strong PowerPoint presentation. I had no qualms about her sincerity and desire to see this thing through to completion, and I wrote out a list of information I needed.

My confidence in Dee Scott proved accurate by her return only one week later with a stack of things I had requested. While I drafted more elements for Shellie Samuels to use in her pitch, Scott answered questions for me. We inserted better information about Racz's window of opportunity, discussed his motivation, and examined inconsistencies in his statements, along with his odd behavior. Only one point came up for dispute. Regarding Racz's apathy, Dee wanted to enter the words "Had little interest in finding her." This lack of interest, Dee said, indicated a consciousness of guilt. I contended it might weaken the prosecution, since Racz had repeatedly claimed that Ann had left on a spontaneous vacation and chose to make it permanent. That would give him rationale for not filing a missing person report or spend resources searching for her.

Sergeant Scott had a different interpretation. She insisted that Ann's leaving for a temporary vacation might be plausible, but no one could possibly presume—after sixteen years—that John Racz still believed in the extended vacation, and thus had no interest in knowing what happened to Ann.

I had to concur with Dee's reasoning and I used her wording.

Two weeks later, Shellie presented the PowerPoint show to top administrators. Everyone listened and seemed to understand the facts. Vigorous debate followed, with the pros and cons bouncing back and forth like a volleyball game. Finally the senior member, after asking a few questions, announced, "Go for it."

The committee made two other decisions. First, the question came up as to whether the case should be taken to a preliminary hearing or to a grand jury. They chose the grand jury route.

Second, in view of Shellie Samuel's heavy workload, they decided to hand over the prosecution duties to a bright, aggressive deputy district attorney named Beth Silverman.

With her usual dynamo energy, people skills, and ability to hone in on the essential elements of a case, Silverman contacted every witness. She worked with them to review documentation and their personal memories as to what happened and when it happened.

Her preparation greased the skids, and the grand jury proceedings, in early October 2006, moved forward with relative ease. Grand juries don't issue verdicts of guilt or innocence. Consisting of ordinary citizens who serve a set term, they listen to a prosecutor and a few witnesses, then decide if there is sufficient evidence for criminal charges to be filed. Despite the absence of a smoking gun—or even a body—Silverman convinced the jurists that circumstances pointed to John Racz's possible involvement in his wife's death. They issued an indictment for him to be tried for that crime, along with a warrant for his arrest.

Accompanied by three deputies, Sergeant Delores Scott drove to Los Angeles International Airport on the morning of October 21. They waited in the customs section for arriving international flights and watched for passengers from a Korean Airlines jet originating in Indonesia. John Racz came into view at about 9:15 A.M., with his Asian girlfriend. Scott stopped him, advised him that he was under arrest on charges of murder, and snapped handcuffs on his wrists.

* * *

Joann Racz later recalled her reaction to the news. "I got a call from my sister. She asked, 'Did you hear what happened?' I said no, and instantly got freaked out and scared, thinking maybe she got in a car accident, or maybe she had gotten robbed. I said, 'No, what is it?' She said, 'Dad got arrested at the airport.'

"I just, it was kinda like the most devastating thing for me to hear. I was totally shocked. I had it in the back of my head that it might take place someday, but when I really got the news, with no advance notice, it was just stunning. And it was sad because of the embarrassment for him at the airport, the embarrassment in jail. He was with his current girlfriend. They had been together a couple of years. And it was so unexpected. You're coming back from a vacation and a long international flight, which is freaky enough, with delays and all. But to have people take you right there. I could not imagine. I just felt so bad that it was the type of situation my dad got himself into. I had nothing to do with it, though. He put himself in that situation. When my sister told me, it was pretty devastating."

Within a few days, Racz posted a million-dollar bail and went home. Looking back in time, Joann said, "I took my daughter to the Valencia house to be there. Glenn met us at the house. Katelin went to pick him up from jail and brought him back. About an hour later, my dad and Kate arrived. I just recall seeing him step out of the car, with his clothes wrinkled and his hair a little bit messed up. He actually looked pretty clean for being in jail for five days. And he had a big smile on his face, he was happy to be home. If that was me, I'd be screaming and ripping apart the door. Get in quick and take a shower. He didn't even unload his suitcase from the trip. Oh, he had gifts, he had clothes, you know. Actually, it was probably extremely overwhelming for him to have to come home to us kids like that. But he had a little chuckle about it, like 'God, I can't even believe I was there. What the heck is going on?'

"For me, I'd be crying, screaming, cursing. But he was like

'Thank God, I never want to go there again.' No crying or sadness. I didn't want him to feel humiliated, and I wanted to show him that we were there for him."

The bail enabled Racz to remain free pending the outcome of the trial, which would be held more than seven months later in the San Fernando Courthouse.

Known for her intelligence, meticulous organization, and dependability, Ann Racz retained her youthful vigor and beauty despite prematurely graying hair and a troubled marriage.
(Courtesy of Jerry Ryan)

LOCATIONS

Aerial view in 1991 of "Hamburger Hill," including McDonald's, the site of Ann Racz's final destination. The wide swath of excavated land between Old Road and Pico Canyon Road is covered today by commercial buildings. Does Ann's body lie somewhere beneath them?
(Courtesy of the L.A. District Attorney's Office)

A gathering of the Yoshiyama family near their home in Hilo, Hawaii, 1955. Back row, left to right: Takeo, Matsue, Jerry, Emi, and Joji. Ann, age six, stands next to her seated grandfather.
(Courtesy of Joji Yoshiyama)

Jerry Yoshiyama holds three-year-old Ann in Hilo. Before World War II, he worked there as fishing fleet manager and auctioneer of the daily catch. After release from the wartime internment camps, he sold life insurance.
(Courtesy of Joji Yoshiyama)

Ann Yoshiyama was a high school student when she formed a lifetime connection with classmate Bob Russell. *(Yearbook photo)*

After earning a teacher's credential, Ann married John Racz in Hollywood, July 1972. *(Courtesy of Jerry Ryan)*

John Racz and son Glenn in 1984, when John was a deputy sheriff. *(Courtesy of Jerry Ryan)*

Joann Racz straddles her father's lap while Ann holds their only son, Glenn. Ann's mother, Matsue, couldn't have guessed that she would outlive her youngest daughter. *(Courtesy of Jerry Ryan)*

Ann wears a star-shaped pendant emblematic of John's tenure as a Sheriff's Deputy. She replaced it with a sapphire pendant given to her by Bob Russell. *(Courtesy of Jerry Ryan)*

The Racz family owned and lived in this upscale home in Valencia, not far from Magic Mountain. John dreaded the idea of divorce and division of community property. *(Author photo)*

The Peachland condominium complex where Ann moved, no more than two miles from the Racz home. Friends thought it was risky for Ann to remain in such close proximity to her husband. *(Author photo)*

Carports for residents at Peachland. It would be easy for John to find Ann's white minivan parked here. *(Author photo)*

John Racz beaming with pride at his newest daughter, Katelin, 1984.
(Courtesy of Terry Wood)

Dee Ann Wood with her baby, Ian, and Ann with little Katelin at a double baptism ceremony.
(Courtesy of Terry Wood)

Attending a niece's marriage in San Diego, Glenn, John, Ann, and Joann appear happy, but she is masking her fear, having already decided to move out with the children and divorce John. *(Courtesy of Jerry Ryan)*

Detectives Louis "The Hat" Danoff and Frank Salerno, legends with the LA County Sheriff's Office, had worked on numerous high profile murders, including the Nightstalker and the Hillside Strangler cases. Both men labored to solve the mystery of Ann Racz. *(Courtesy of the L.A. District Attorney's Office)*

John Racz told detectives that Ann had parked her car in the Flyaway lot and taken a shuttle to Los Angeles International Airport. He claimed to have moved her vehicle to a shady spot. A parking receipt disputed the date he said it entered the facility. *(Courtesy of the L.A. District Attorney's Office)*

Danoff and Salerno interviewed John Racz about his wife's disappearance, but the former deputy sheriff gave only ambiguous answers to their questions. *(Courtesy of the L.A. District Attorney's Office)*

Pastor Glen Thorpe in 2008. He provided marriage counseling to Ann and John, and suffered internal conflict when asked to reveal what she told him about her fears. *(Photo by Ron Bowers)*

When Ann vanished on April 22, 1991, she had planned to cook pizza for her children's dinner that night in the condo, and she mysteriously left ingredients on the counter. *(Courtesy of the L.A. District Attorney's Office)*

Even though John Racz claimed that Ann went on a trip to think things over, investigators found her makeup and curling iron in the condo bathroom, items every woman takes when traveling. *(Courtesy of the L.A. District Attorney's Office)*

Louis Danoff and Frank Salerno in Judge Coen's courtroom during the trial. *(Photo by Ron Bowers)*

Ann bought a ring in Hawaii, inscribed with the word KUUIPO, meaning "sweetheart," and told her lover it symbolized him. John Racz said she wore it on the day she vanished. *(Author photo)*

Emi, Ann's sister, actually had the KUUIPO ring in her possession so she knew that John lied. She holds it on a paper roll and displays a newspaper dated after Ann's disappearance. *(Courtesy of Jerry Ryan)*

Emi Ryan with her two nieces, Katelin and Joann, who grew to adulthood under stress and conflicting emotions, wondering why their mother never came home and if their father had anything to do with her fate.
(Courtesy of Jerry Ryan)

Joann Racz holds the blanket Ann made for her. She once told her mother that it was the single possession she would take with her in case of emergency. *(Author photo)*

After the case had gone cold for more than a decade, Detectives Cheryl Comstock and Dee Scott of the L.A. Sheriff's Office renewed the investigation. *(Photo by Gregory Bojorquez)*

Ron Bowers and Dee Ann Wood at the McDonald's where John Racz was suspected of confronting his wife and killing her. But how did he dispose of her body? *(Author photo)*

The San Fernando courthouse where John Racz faced trial for murder.
(Author photo)

Barbara Kaplan hoped to be a juror in the Racz trial, and was the last one selected. She expressed disgust that the defense may have tried to turn Ann's children against their mother by revealing private love letters.
(Author photo)

EVIDENCE ANN IS DEAD
☐ NOT HEARD FROM OR SEEN FOR 16 YEARS
☐ No contact with children, family, Bob, Dee Ann, Pastor & Friends
☐ Did not remove money from any of her bank accounts
☐ Did not use credit cards or order new cards in her name
☐ Did not use her Name or Social Security number
☐ Did not finalize her much-wanted divorce

EVIDENCE DEFENDANT KILLED ANN
☐ MOTIVE TO KILL
☐ Defendant was frugal person, did not want to share comm. prop.
☐ Defendant was controlling person; angered by Ann disobeying
☐ MEANS TO KILL
☐ Defendant had weapons, trained to subdue people & render unconscious with stakehold
☐ Defendant was much larger & stronger than Ann
☐ Defendant had ability to instill fear in Ann
☐ OPPORTUNITY TO KILL
☐ Defendant followed her to McDonald's
☐ Defendant was gone for substantial amount of time
☐ DEFENDANT'S DEMEANOR
☐ Defendant was not concerned Ann was missing
☐ Defendant was uncooperative with detectives in locating Ann
☐ CONSCIOUSNESS OF GUILT
☐ Made up story re: meetings with wife to give money
☐ Made up story re: receiving phone call from LAX / Flyaway
☐ Planted victim's car at Flyaway in Van Nuys
☐ Tried to destroy, manipulate & suppress evidence
☐ LIED TO DETECTIVES & OTHERS
☐ Gave multiple inconsistent statements
☐ Where met with Ann to give her the money
☐ When last spoke to Ann
☐ Amount of money given to Ann

Deputy D.A. Beth Silverman supplemented the investigation, found crucial evidence, and despite huge obstacles, prosecuted John Racz. *(Author photo)*

John Racz, at the defense table in court, posted a million-dollar bail so he could remain free during the three-month trial. *(Photo by Gregory Bojorquez)*

Jerry Ryan and his nephew, Glenn Racz, after Glenn had earned a Master's Degree in engineering. *(Courtesy of Emi Ryan)*

Ann's best friend, Dee Ann Wood, kneels at a memorial rose bush and plaque for Ann at the Newhall Presbyterian Church yard. *(Author photo)*

The plaque's simple words pay homage to the woman who vanished in April 1991 and was never seen again. *(Author photo)*

Glenn Racz and his sister Joann attended the 2008 memorial for their mother and expressed their love for her. *(Courtesy of Jerry Ryan)*

The memorial gathering on April 22, 2008, the seventeenth anniversary of Ann's disappearance, included (left to right) Louis Danoff, Bob Russell, Beth Silverman, Don Lasseter, and Frank Salerno. *(Photo by Ron Bowers)*

is no need for her to check in with our office manager, Kiki Clemons. Everyone in the Major Crimes Division knows Beth is there. She makes no apology for being loud, and her acquaintances recognize it as part of her persona. I don't know of anyone who can spew out more words in one breath than Beth. Her rapid-fire delivery can completely disarm opposing counsel. She is neither shy nor reserved, doesn't hesitate to express her opinion, and is never accused of being indecisive.

Most of these characteristics originated in Beth's childhood. She grew up comfortably in Westlake Village, an affluent community surrounding a man-made lake in the western extremes of San Fernando Valley. Her father, a physician specializing in obstetrics and gynecology, hoped Beth and her older sister would enter the same profession. The sister did, and practices with her dad. Their younger brother migrated to San Diego and prospered in financial investments. But Beth seldom follows others' footsteps.

Beth takes her job so seriously. She is one of the hardest-working litigators I've ever known, and argues her cases with the skill of Clarence Darrow. I once asked her if she had been a member of the debating team in high school. "Nah," she replied, with her trademark smile, "I was a cheerleader." She also confessed to being a counselor at summer camp, specializing in gymnastics. And like many sun-worshiping teenagers, she loved spending as much time as possible at the beach. Amazed, I asked if she later worked long hours in college on homework. Wrong again. "I was a sorority party girl," she laughingly admitted.

After graduating from Agoura High School in 1985, Beth wanted to escape the Southern California environment and expand her horizons. At the University of Wisconsin, she majored in journalism and considered writing as a profession but soon sought a new direction. One of her sorority sisters, the governor's daughter, interested Beth in the grand theater of politics, elections, and legislation. It lasted a short time and faded when she journeyed to Europe with a group of friends.

Back at college, she learned that several of her classmates planned to take the LSAT exam for law school. Her competitive nature planted the idea—*If they can do it, so can I.* Her scores sent Beth in search of a suitable institution. Although she enjoyed the Wisconsin campus, Beth wanted no more shivering through cold winters. Her parents lobbied hard for their daughter's return to the "Golden State."

At first, she considered top schools in the San Francisco Bay Area, but she rejected the idea. Too cold and foggy up there. The sunny, temperate climate of San Diego sounded much better, with wonderful beaches and enough distance from West-lake Village to avoid the protective parental umbrella. If she envisioned lounging on the sand near rolling Pacific waves, surrounded by her law books, the image soon evaporated. Law school at the University of San Diego (USD) consumed every minute of the day, and much of the night as well.

Yet, with her high energy, Beth still took the opportunity to work part-time for the U.S. Attorney's Office and later with the San Diego District Attorney's Office.

At the end of her second year at USD, she applied for the L.A. district attorney's summer law clerk program, where I was in charge of hiring. We gave her a one-week training session in courtroom practice and procedure. Beth later said that she always remembered me as being especially tough on her and the other law clerks. I was. I tried to prepare them to think on their feet while unmerciful judges berated them for their failure to understand intricacies of the law. Beth learned that she had to keep standing and arguing in court even under attack from all sides. Some of the trainees wavered under pressure, but Beth seemed to enjoy the challenge. She deflected the slings and arrows with pointed words that rolled off her tongue. I have never seen her at a loss for words, some of them not found in family dictionaries.

That summer we assigned her to the Van Nuys office, where

she handled preliminary hearings. Remarkably, she won all of them. By fall she was hooked on being a prosecutor.

She earned her degree and aced the California Bar exam on the first try. It disappointed her when budget problems for the LADA ruled out new hires. Undiscouraged, Beth submitted her application, and went to work selling fur coats at a Bullock's department store while waiting for an opening with us. When it finally came in 1996, we put her to work prosecuting DUIs and misdemeanors in the small Newhall office. As Beth sharpened her skills, her bosses took notice and moved her to more challenging assignments in Pasadena, Van Nuys, and San Fernando. She was a rising star, and her willingness to tackle hard-core gang trials and other "impossible" cases impressed colleagues and supervisors.

By the time Beth took over the John Racz case, she couldn't recall how many times she had worked in front of juries, but she knew it included prosecuting forty murder defendants. One extremely difficult case had resulted in sending a woman to death row.

At its conclusion, Beth Silverman needed a break and decided to see other parts of the world. She lined up a safari trip to Africa with several friends. As time drew near for departure, all of them except Beth abandoned the safari idea. She refused to be denied the experience and went by herself. Even though she loved it, more world travel took a backseat to her busy work schedule.

Her home is a respite—Beth's only escape from the madness of murder cases. On weekends she recharges her batteries by gardening, finding joy in feeding, pruning, and watering her prized roses. She also lavishes love on her two dogs, Jake and Daisy. It is often said that you can tell a lot about a person from their choice of dogs. Jake is a boisterous, protective golden retriever/German shepherd mix, rescued by Beth from the pound in 2000. She bought Daisy, a mischievous, lovable golden Lab pup, in late 2007. Boisterous, mischievous, noisy, and lovable. No matter what the weather is like, Beth takes them for their daily walks, laughing and struggling as they pull in opposite directions. She understands and empathizes with their contrariness. The dogs are the only thing in Beth's life over which she has no control.

CHAPTER 18

OUT OF
THE PAST

Ronald Bowers:

The past, I realized, would necessarily play a strong part in Beth Silverman's future, particularly as related to pending court actions involving John Racz. Since his wife's body had never been found, and no hard evidence had turned up, serious doubts existed in our downtown offices that a grand jury would issue indictments against Racz. And even if they did, how could a trial jury possibly convict him of murder?

Two major no-body cases, one from the 1950s, and one more recent, might provide some insight and guidance in how to proceed.

The older case occupied headlines across the nation for months, and continued decades afterward. The conviction of L. Ewing Scott for killing his wife in 1955 turned into one of the most notorious and groundbreaking events in criminal justice history.

Back in the late 1960s, I remember hanging out in the DA's coffee-break room up on the old Hall of Justice's fifth floor. By late afternoon, the cubicle usually bustled with prosecutors coming back from court. Someone would inquire how their trials were going, and this always unleashed a torrent of salty language about horrible rulings made by hard-nosed judges. Everyone would shriek with laughter. Another attorney would pipe up and say that the judge had done the same thing to him in a similar case. These old-time lawyers were not a shy lot, and they all tried to outdo one another with exaggerated war stories.

The king of master litigators was J. Miller Leavy, who had joined our office in 1932, at the age of twenty-six. When I worked with him, during his time as the chief of Trials for the DA, I held Leavy in awe. I took every opportunity to watch him in court and learn from his masterful techniques. During proceedings he seemed to be in complete control of everything, even the judge.

Everyone loved listening to his tales. Each morning he brought in bagels and cream cheese, prompting us to rename the coffee room as the "J. Miller Deli." Sometimes, while telling his stories and heating bagels at the same time, he would get distracted and burn them, sending the odor wafting through marble hallways. If you were lucky enough to be in his office during the late afternoon, you would see him open the bottom drawer of his big wooden desk and pull out a bottle of bourbon. In those days, hard liquor and smelly cigars comprised an essential part of veteran prosecutors' lives. Leavy got a kick out of sipping the booze and regaling youngsters like myself with accounts of sending the notorious Barbara Graham to death row. Hollywood later depicted her crime and execution in a classic movie, *I Want to Live*, starring Susan Hayward. In 1948, Leavy had prosecuted the notorious Caryl Chessman, a career criminal known as the "Red

Light Bandit." Even though his crimes consisted of robbery and rape rather than murder, Chessman also was condemned to die. His highly publicized appeals dragged on for years, until 1960, when they finally ended inside San Quentin's apple green gas chamber.

I can still see J. Miller Leavy spinning his yarns, leaning back with one foot on his desk, one hand behind his head and the other lifting his glass of bourbon. He spoke in the silver-tongued style of William Jennings Bryan, with the voice of an evangelist. Leavy's physical presence, unfortunately, didn't match his eloquence. Short at about five-six, his midsection bulged from the consumption of too many bagels. Arched eyebrows made his soft, round face appear always surprised. His full, wavy silver-gray hair, though, would have made movie stars jealous. Leavy's horn-rimmed glasses became his trademark, due to a habit of taking them off and waving them around in trial to punctuate whatever he said.

My favorite episode of Leavy's exploits gave us some ideas on how to approach the John Racz case, since it set a precedent for prosecuting a murder in which the victim's body hadn't been found.

Leonard Ewing Scott, who preferred to use the initial "L." in place of his first name, married Evelyn Throsby, a wealthy socialite, in 1950. Four years younger than his bride, age sixty-three, Scott had been a paint salesman whose income didn't even warrant filing income tax. Evelyn, on the other hand, had grown increasingly rich by the death of three previous affluent and elderly husbands. No Gary Cooper in appearance, Scott still had pleasant features, stood about six feet tall, with a full face, large intense eyes, and left-parted gray hair slicked straight back.

On May 16, 1955, back in Los Angeles, Scott took his wife shopping for a new car and test-drove a top-of-the-line Mercedes Benz. When they returned home, Evelyn realized they were out of tooth powder. (Young people probably laugh at the idea of brushing with powder, but it was common back then, especially for artificial teeth.) L. Ewing Scott drove off to buy some. Later he claimed that he returned within thirty minutes and discovered that his wife had left in her car. He didn't report her missing and didn't make any calls to check on her whereabouts.

When I reviewed the Scott case, I marveled at how it foreshadowed John Racz's reaction to Ann's disappearance.

For eight months, Scott came up with one excuse after another rationalizing Evelyn's extended absence, all the while depleting her assets. On March 8, 1956, Captain Art Hertel and a team of police officers searched the Scott estate in Bel Air. While L. Ewing Scott observed from a balcony, Captain Hertel walked several yards to another section of the yard and stopped close to the incinerator. He dropped to his hands and knees, scraped away some dead leaves, and lifted out a set of dentures. Expanding the search, he uncovered several other items, including some pills, a can of tooth powder, a hairbrush, cigarettes with a long holder, parts of a woman's garter, and a few items of costume jewelry. Moving a few yards farther, he came up with two pairs of glasses, both of them charred from burning.

Evelyn Throsby Scott's dentist verified that the false teeth belonged to her, and another doctor stated that he had written her prescription for the glasses. Just as Ann Racz wouldn't have taken a trip without cosmetics found in her bathroom, Evelyn certainly would not have left her dentures and glasses behind. The cache of her possessions implied that L. Ewing Scott had disposed of them because he knew she was dead.

Investigators found that Scott had canceled a long list of Evelyn's standing appointments, suggesting his knowledge that she wouldn't be coming home. Combined with the other circumstantial evidence, they presented it to the DA with a request to charge L. Ewing Scott with murdering his wife. No, said the DA, at least not without a confession.

In the pre-Miranda era, homicide cops had considerably greater latitude in questioning suspects and trying to squeeze out an admission of guilt. They arrested L. Ewing Scott and grilled him for eighteen hours, but he never broke.

L.A. police chief William Parker stepped into the investigation. He publicly warned Scott not to leave town. Apparently spooked by the chief's involvement, L. Ewing Scott bought a 1953 Ford, using the name Robert Scott, and took off. Scott's flight lasted nearly a year. In April 1957, border agents caught him trying to make it into Canada from Michigan. Extradition eventually returned him to California to face a murder trial.

Prosecutor J. Miller Leavy understood that it represented the greatest challenge of his career. A few bodiless convictions in the state had been achieved when defendants admitted knowledge of the victim's death. But none had been achieved with defendants who maintained that the spouse had voluntarily left, and might return at any time.

The first step, Leavy decided, required convincing a jury that Evelyn's life had, in fact, ended. Then he needed to prove that her husband had killed her. It was a two-step process.

The trial commenced in October 1957, over two years after Evelyn Throsby Scott had vanished. Leavy produced witnesses to show that no one had seen or heard from her in that time, breaking her life patterns of constant social interaction. She had made no financial transactions, purchased nothing, nor did her name appear on any travel manifests. And, certainly, she had no compelling reason to vanish. By all logic, she must be dead.

Leavy next showed jurors that L. Ewing Scott clearly had the motive to murder his wife: greed. He coveted her extensive fortune for himself and demonstrated this by manipulating investments into his name, much of it through forgeries, soon after she disappeared. When he tried to burn her personal possessions, including dentures and glasses, it demonstrated his expectation that she would never return.

The witnesses Leavy paraded in front of the jury may have seemed excessive to some. He called many of Mrs. Scott's friends to report the various and conflicting explanations her husband gave for her disappearance. It became obvious that he had trouble keeping his lies straight. The defendant did not testify. His lawyer, instead, tried to poke holes in Leavy's case, mostly with attempts to create doubt about Evelyn's death. No physical proof had ever emerged to dispute the contention that she might still be living somewhere, having escaped from a husband she feared.

A highlight in the annals of courtroom legends came when the defense argued this issue. The attorney spoke directly to the jury in oratorical style. He turned toward the courtroom entry, pointing his extended finger, and proclaimed that Evelyn "might walk through this courtroom door at any minute." The jurors' heads automatically turned toward the door, perhaps envisioning the stately matron making her grand entrance.

A hush settled over the whole room. The defender's compelling statement played on everyone's desire to avoid convicting an innocent person.

J. Miller Leavy, the master storyteller, knew exactly how to fight back. In his rebuttal, he stood, locked eyes with the jury, and said, "Every head in this courtroom turned toward that door just now—except one—the defendant's!" He had not bothered to look, Leavy declared, "because he knows she's not going to walk through that door. He killed her." Dead silence reigned as the jurors shifted their gaze to L. Ewing Scott.

Whether this dramatic moment really unfolded exactly that way is still argued. No matter. The jury returned with a verdict of guilty. Sentenced to life in prison, L. Ewing Scott served twenty years before being freed at age eighty-one due to failing health. Before his death, he reportedly confessed to a book author of, indeed, killing Evelyn Throsby Scott by striking her on the head with a hard rubber mallet. He told of stuffing her in the trunk of his car, driving to Las Vegas, and burying her on the east side of town. Perhaps her remains are under one of the towering, glittering casinos built in the following decades. Or, as some people professing inside information say, she might be under an on-ramp to the Hollywood Freeway, which was being constructed at the time of Evelyn's murder.

While L. Ewing Scott served his time, he initiated a barrage of appeals. Up to that point, no American appellate court had ever upheld a murder conviction in which the body hadn't been found, unless the defendant had confessed. The California court recognized the tightrope they walked. They certainly did not want to confirm a verdict if the defendant had not committed murder. On the other hand, they realized that justice isn't served if killers can get away with murder by successfully disposing of a body and keeping their mouths shut.

In searching for a precedent to help rule on the L. Ewing Scott appeals, the courts slammed into a brick wall. Nothing could be found in California case, nor in any other state. Willing to dig even deeper, they went all the way Down Under—to Auckland, New Zealand. A newlywed man whose bride had vanished claimed they had taken a cruise on a ship called *The Star of India,* which sank, and she perished. Investigators could find no records of a ship by that name. The suspect changed his story. The marriage, he said, had been a sham, all arranged so she could run away from her parents with another man, who had paid him to lie about the scheme. The lie fooled no one and the suspect was convicted. The appeals court ruled: *There was neither the body nor traces of the body, nor anything in the form of a confession, but in our opinion, that does not exhaust the possibilities. There may be other facts so incriminating and so incapable of any reasonable explanation as to be incompatible with any hypothesis other than murder.*

Hanging their hats on the New Zealand decision, the California Appellate Court upheld L. Ewing Scott's conviction.

I have pondered the facts of this landmark case many times, inspired by my younger-day contacts with J. Miller Leavy, and my ongoing interest in bodyless cases. It contained some powerful guidelines for Beth Silverman to consider in prosecuting John Racz. Without it, I seriously doubt that we would have been able to take the case to a grand jury and obtain an indictment.

CHAPTER 19

"HE WANTED
IT ALL."

Ron Bowers understood that the guilty verdict against L. Ewing Scott paved the way for future successful prosecution of "no body" cases. Yet, another more recent case provided an even better template for use in the case against John Racz.

A Long Beach, California, jury convicted Bruce Koklich in October 2003 for murdering his wife. Jana Koklich, age forty-one, had disappeared on August 20, 2001, and no one had seen her since. The investigating team included Sergeant Dee Scott, of the L.A. Sheriff's Department, who would soon inherit the Racz case.

Just a few months older than Jana, Bruce sought wealth in even greater strides than John Racz had. He married the daughter of California state senator Paul Carpenter in 1990. Jana, an attractive, well-educated, fun-loving blonde, suited Koklich's needs perfectly. They opened a real estate office in northern Long Beach and prospered through her managerial skills and his aggressive salesmanship. By the new millennium's beginning, they had accumulated a net worth of more than $3,000,000 in property and investments, and earned in excess of $250,000 annually. Their comfortable Lakewood home, with a large swimming pool, abutted a golf course.

If Koklich had hoped to gain political leverage by marrying into Senator Carpenter's family, those dreams evaporated not long after the wedding. Convicted of political corruption, Carpenter fled the country in 1994. Taken into custody a year later, he served four years in prison, and upon release, he retired to Texas, where he died of cancer in 2002.

Financial success and a gregarious, attractive wife apparently didn't satisfy all of Koklich's needs. The couple, with no children, developed separate interests over time. She gained a little weight but still enjoyed the company of her female friends, particularly Nini Angelini, the operator of a nearby skin care business. With his soft face, feminine bow-shaped lips, and receding chin, Bruce needed something to recharge his existence and self-esteem. An idea crept into his head, festered, and metastasized.

Jana Koklich and pal Nini scored a couple of tickets to an Eric Clapton concert for Friday night, August 17, 2001, at the Staples Center, near downtown Los Angeles. The spectacular steel-and-glass structure, home of the L.A. Lakers, Kings, and other sports teams, regularly drew huge crowds for spectacular events featuring the most popular entertainers.

At the end of Clapton's performance, the two women headed back to the Koklich home in Lakewood. With Nini driving, they arrived after eleven-thirty and chatted for a few minutes about Jana's appointment the next day for Nini to give her a facial. After saying good night, Jana went inside and flipped the lights on, off, and on again, to signal her friend that all was well.

They would never see each other again.

No one other than Bruce Koklich knows what transpired

that weekend. He told anyone asking that he and Jana had spent a quiet Saturday and Sunday at home.

Acquaintances of Jana knew that punctuality and dependability ranked high in her value system. She never missed appointments or failed to promptly return telephone calls. That's why it surprised friends when she failed to keep her seven o'clock appointment on Saturday morning for her usual physical workout. Her personal trainer called Jana's cell phone at 7:03 A.M. and left a message but never received a response. Completely out of character for Jana.

Nini couldn't believe it when Jana failed to show up on Saturday afternoon for the facial massage they had confirmed the previous night. She, too, called Jana's cell phone and the home number. Neither Bruce nor Jana called back. Jana's father, who lived in Texas, worried when his daughter didn't contact him about a planned trip.

Jana's mother, a Long Beach resident, had been expecting to hear from her that weekend about possibly attending a movie together on Sunday. Her attempts to reach Jana by telephone, like everyone else's, went unanswered and no one replied to the messages she left.

Finally, on Monday morning, after the mother called the Koklich home three times, Bruce responded. He told her that Jana had left for work and should be arriving at the agency in a few minutes. Relieved, but puzzled, the mother wondered why she had heard from Bruce instead of her daughter. Relations between Bruce and his wife's family had been strained, and he seldom had any contact with them.

Nini Angelini also received a message from Bruce on her answering machine. He said that Jana could be reached at home on Monday evening. For some strange reason, he also mentioned his plans to attend a funeral that morning, and that he would be in the office later.

Bruce arrived at the real estate office well before his employees. After completing some computer chores, he left with a friend for the funeral, and returned shortly after eleven o'clock. Clerks and sales representatives all asked him about Jana, alarmed about her absence. Seemingly unworried, Bruce said he would go home and see what might be detaining her. Oddly, he invited one of his staff to accompany him on the short drive. They found the house silent and empty.

Appearing worried, Bruce called Jana's mother and the physical trainer and asked if either of them had seen her. Bruce knew a member of the Long Beach Police Department (LBPD), and called him next for advice on filing a missing person report. A jurisdiction issue arose. The Koklich home stood in sheriff's territory, while the real estate office fell within the LBPD's area. If Jana had been accosted by a car-jacker, it could have been within either agency's purview. The Long Beach police decided to accept Koklich's report.

In the Koklich home, a housekeeper, whom they had em-ployed for nine years, began her chores on Tuesday morn-ing, August 21. Something struck her as weird in the master bedroom. She remembered following her usual routine on the previous Tuesday of making up the king-size master bed with clean, patterned, fitted sheets. Now, though, wrinkled stan-dard-size sheets, much too small, lay on the mattress. Never before had Jana or Bruce changed the bedding. It confused the woman even more when she couldn't find Jana's favorite down pillow. Curious, the housekeeper searched cabinets, the washing machine, and even the trash, but she found no trace of the missing sheets or pillow.

During the next couple of days, Bruce Koklich appeared to be crying when he spoke to a few people about his missing wife, but they all noticed that he shed no tears. It happened again at a press conference on Wednesday to request help from the public in finding Jana, and to release a photograph of her white SUV. Jana's mother stood near Bruce, and to her, his show of emotion appeared feigned. It offended a few of Jana's friends when Bruce made comments suggesting that she had often been irresponsible. One neighbor's anger flared when Bruce commented to her, "You remember when we walked by and waved to you on Saturday or Sunday." It distinctly had not happened, the woman said, and she had a good memory.

Even worse, Bruce asked another of Jana's acquaintances, "How long does it take before a missing person can be declared legally dead?"

A woman living a few miles south of the Koklich agency, in a more dangerous section of Long Beach, happened to be watching television news and saw a report appealing for help in finding Jana Koklich. It showed a photograph of the missing SUV. A short time later, she stepped outside and recognized the vehicle parked at the curb. She told her sister about it and they both had a closer look. Someone had left the SUV's windows wide open, with a purse on the passenger seat, and keys in the ignition. With a cynical snort, the woman said, "Too obvious. Anyone could see it was set up."

The woman's son, though, couldn't resist temptation. After his mother went back inside, he and a pal snatched the purse, rifled through it, and pocketed cash and a cell phone. Leaving credit cards inside the purse, they tossed it onto the roof of a two-story apartment building across the street.

The youth's mother soon spotted the cell phone, persuaded him to tell where he had gotten it, and called her pastor for advice on how to keep her son from facing charges in a possible homicide investigation. In this high-crime-rate neighborhood, the streetwise pastor knew most of the local gangbangers and hoods. He made a few inquiries and learned that another youth had taken a handgun from a door pouch in the SUV. He confiscated it from the boy and contacted the police.

Another witness came forward to report that on Sunday night, August 19, she had been in a crime-ridden neighborhood, near the same area, and had observed something suspicious. A white male, wearing a white dress shirt, had been sitting in a light-colored SUV parked in an alley. Maybe this would not have drawn her attention, except that these streets had been staked out as the exclusive territory of African-American gangs. As the woman drove slowly by the parked SUV, she said, the man quickly started it, peeled out, and accelerated down the street.

A concentrated LBPD dragnet for Jana's missing white SUV produced results one week later. Someone had driven it several blocks from the site where it had been seen at the curb, pulled into a narrow alley, and parked it in a littered single-car garage of an abandoned apartment building. Examination of the vehicle showed that someone had wiped it clean of fingerprints, but dark smears on the rear carpet proved to be bloodstains.

For behaving as a husband consumed with grief and worry about his missing wife, Bruce Koklich wouldn't have won any acting awards. Within days of Jana's disappearance, he flirted with a woman working in his bank by saying, "I think your blouse would look even better if it were off you." In a subsequent clumsy attempt to charm her in a manager's office, he sat on her lap. Not getting the response he hoped for, Koklich finally asked her, point-blank, if she would go out with him to a Britney Spears concert. "Absolutely not," the woman replied.

Another similar effort failed when he asked his travel agent to attend a concert with him. She declined. Koklich tried to sweeten the deal by offering to include dinner at a nice restaurant. She still refused.

Salesmen can't let rejections discourage them. Bruce zeroed in on the attractive granddaughter of an elderly neighbor by putting a note under her windshield wiper, attached to his photo, expressing his interest in meeting her. She didn't bother to respond.

Striking out in Long Beach caused Koklich to extend his search for female company. He targeted an attractive distant relative, age eighteen, who lived in the San Francisco Bay

Area. Megan Thomas (pseudonym) had been experiencing adjustment problems with her family and wanted to get away from home. Calling her directly, Bruce said he needed someone to look after him since his wife's disappearance. He told Megan that she could live rent free in his house, have the use of a car, and he would pay her a fair salary. However, it wouldn't be a good idea to tell her father about it.

Megan waffled for several days before finally agreeing to give it a try. Like a stallion in heat, Koklich raced north on I-5, met her at a prearranged rendezvous site, and brought her back to Lakewood. While the nation still reeled in horror from terrorists hijacking a jetliner on September 11 and crashing into New York's World Trade Center, Koklich had sex with eighteen-year old Megan on his mind.

Perhaps the naïve teenager didn't quite understand the full extent of the deal Bruce offered. When he began making sexual overtures, she evaded them. He rationalized to her that they really were only step-relatives, and had no real blood ties, so that made it okay for them to sleep together. No, she said. Only one motivation had led her to accept his offer—freedom from her restrictive parents. Finally, though, she relented to sharing his bed, but on the condition that there would be no sex involved. It bothered Megan that the master shower door wouldn't close, and he could see her bathing.

Nothing seemed to sway her to give in to Bruce's advances. He told Megan that she could wear any of his missing wife's expensive clothing, even bras and bikinis. She ignored his suggestions to model some of Jana's lingerie.

They attended sporting events and dined out. In one restaurant, the air conditioner sent shivers through Megan, and he draped his coat over her shoulders. She noticed a handgun in one of the pockets.

A September heat wave sent temperatures soaring, and Megan needed something cold to drink while lying out by the pool. Bruce had gone to his office, so she searched the bar and found a drink he had mixed for her the previous day, promising it would really help cool a person down. She took a sip and liked the taste. After downing one glass, Megan felt relaxed, so she drank another one. She had some more, and felt no pain. In fact, she didn't feel anything and passed out.

The next thing Megan knew, she lay flat on her back in a bed upstairs, and her bathing suit had been partially removed. With her mind in a foggy haze, she couldn't figure out where she was or what had happened. She saw Bruce standing in the adjacent room, talking on the phone. He wore only boxer shorts and appeared to be in a state of sexual arousal. When he hung up, he came to her, saying he wanted to finish massaging her.

With her mind beginning to clear, Megan realized that a hell of a lot more had happened than a massage. Her tampon had been removed, and she accused Bruce of molesting her. He denied knowing anything about it. Convinced that he had raped her, Megan managed to climb out of the bed, staggered into another room, and locked the door.

That night, trying to convince her of his innocence, Bruce took Megan to a sports bar. She agreed to go, preferring to be in a crowd rather than alone with him. When they left, he drove fifteen miles to Huntington Beach, telling Megan that he wanted to show her a condo where his good friend lived. The buddy, he told Megan, sometimes had let him use the place to entertain women. Laughing, he smirked, "In my time of grieving, he lets me stay here. Like I'm really grieving."

Back in the Lakewood house, Megan hoped nothing else would happen. Koklich, though, kept pressing. He suggested that if she didn't want to have conventional sex with him, at least she should agree to oral sex. She adamantly refused.

Megan's five-day stay hadn't provided Koklich with the sex kitten he had envisioned, so he told her to get her things together for a trip back to San Francisco. He dumped her off near her parents' home. Megan waited a brief time before

contacting a rape crisis center called Mountain Women's
Resource Center, and reported her belief that she had been
sexually "violated" while unconscious. They notified the
local police.

Through interagency communications, the information
wound up with the LASD detectives who had been investigating the missing person case. Armed with a warrant, they
searched Koklich's home, discovered trace elements of blood
on the master bedroom carpet, and found a box of condoms
next to a container of Megan's tampons under a bathroom
sink, exactly where she had seen them placed. It helped corroborate her statements. To investigators, it became apparent
that Koklich could have disposed of his wife to make way for
younger, sexier companions.

Suspicions had already grown with the discovery of stains
in the rear of Jana's SUV, which proved to be her blood. Little
doubt remained that this missing person case should now be
considered a homicide.

Koklich's bizarre behavior made him a strong suspect. Detectives learned that he had been asking acquaintances if Jana
ever missed appointments, and urging them to say that she
often arrived late or simply skipped scheduled meetings. To
others, he hinted of Jana displaying irresponsible traits. Her
friends, shocked at these allegations, angrily repudiated them.

Piecing together what they knew, detectives worked out the
likely scheme Koklich had planned and executed. He wanted
people to believe that en route to work that Monday morning,
Jana had been a carjack victim. He couldn't have been involved, since he attended a funeral, and he made certain
everyone knew about that.

A witness had seen the SUV parked in the Koklich garage
Saturday and Sunday morning. If he killed her, it could have
happened anytime that weekend. And if he transported her
body in that vehicle for disposal, the trip probably took place
sometime late Sunday night. After dumping her, perhaps

down an old oil well sump, he planted her car in a rough neighborhood, windows open, keys and purse inside, hoping that someone would steal it and become a suspect in Jana's disappearance.

Another neighbor reported hearing loud noises coming from the Koklich residence late on Friday night, August 17. Detectives realized the timing correlated with Jana's arrival home after the Clapton concert.

To file charges against Koklich, the sheriff's team needed more evidence. They launched an intensive search for Jana's body in the oil fields of Long Beach. Innumerable potential hiding places could be found among working and abandoned wells, sumps, culverts, and piles of rusting pipes. As a real estate broker, Koklich knew every piece of property in the region. He and Jana owned twenty-one parcels of land, any one of which might offer a burial site.

Investigators also pursued the other possibility: Jana had walked away from the marriage and started a new life away from her husband. Not very likely, but it must necessarily be explored through checks of financial transactions, travel rosters, hospitals, coroner's offices, jails, interviews with family and friends, and multiple other possibilities. The efforts all ended the same way—no trace of Jana Koklich could be found.

After over five months of probing the mystery, sheriff's detectives took the case to the district attorney. Jana's life had doubtlessly ended and circumstantial evidence pointed to her husband as the killer. Possible motives included a large life-insurance policy. The DA decided to take it to a jury.

As Bruce Koklich prepared to leave his real estate office for lunch at the end of January 2002, officers entered, snapped on handcuffs, and transported him to jail. The arrest took place just one week after Jana's father, Paul Carpenter, died in Texas. In his final weeks of life, he stated that he believed Koklich had murdered his daughter out of greed. "I think she wanted a divorce and rather than split his assets two ways, I think he wanted it all."

As John Racz would do several years later, Bruce Koklich posted a million-dollar bail. Unlike Racz, he posted a reward of $100,000 for information leading to Jana's return.

Now the DA faced the obstacle-filled task of prosecuting a no-body case.

CHAPTER 20

A FATEFUL
LINK

Ronald Bowers:

   The Koklich case came to my attention during the time I worked in the Trial Support Division of the DA's office. This new operation came about back in 1995, when they asked me to create a central location where trial deputies could obtain assistance in making their presentations more persuasive to juries. The O.J. Simpson murder case had a lot to do with recognizing the need for something better. Influenced by the modern reliance on visual media in news and entertainment, today's juries expect to see something similar in trials. They are no longer impressed by an attorney merely standing up and delivering a barrage of words.

   Because I was creator and chief of the Trial Support Division, most of the important cases came across my desk before they went to juries. My duties did not include dictating to prosecutors how to try their cases. I simply made myself available for advice and help in creating visual aids. I was aware of the Koklich matter, but I was not initially involved in the presentation of it.

Bruce Koklich's money allowed him to hire a prominent and skillful defense attorney, which ramped up the need for a heavy hitter for the DA. Eleanor Hunter drew the problematic assignment. The absence of a body weighed heavily on chances for a conviction. Juries must believe—first and foremost—that a murder had been committed.

Certainly, the motive remained nebulous. It appeared that Bruce Koklich wanted to get rid of his wife and replace her with more attractive female companions, or perhaps he feared that she planned to divorce him and take half of their assets. Jana had been making herself over to look slimmer and younger. Did she want to find another man? Life insurance money may have also played a part in his plans.

Detectives had found no evidence to reveal how Jana died. Her bloodstains in the back of the SUV, and a smattering of stains in their master bedroom, offered no inkling. She may have been shot, bludgeoned, or strangled. These gray areas could be perplexing to a jury.

Still, the circumstantial evidence gave powerful inference of her death, and that Koklich had killed her.

Eleanor Hunter took it to trial in February 2002. After laying out the probable motives, she presented a scenario in which Koklich killed his wife in their home, wrapped her body in the missing sheets, put her in the SUV, and dumped her somewhere in the Long Beach oil fields. Witnesses spoke of the defendant's bizarre behavior, pursuit of other women, and inconsistent statements.

The defense worked hard to show that Jana could still be alive. The couple's successful business and good relationship, defenders pointed out, did not support the theory of murder. Koklich took the stand and described their ideal marriage, in which he and Jana had never argued—even though he had been unfaithful at times. He said he had absolutely no reason to hurt her.

Jurors retired and deliberated a full week. Seven of them believed Koklich had killed his wife, but five took the opposite point of view. Judge Robert Higa declared a mistrial on March 25, 2003.

Disappointed, Eleanor Hunter analyzed what had gone wrong and started working on a new approach for the retrial. The defense had hammered away at the motive theories. Eleanor decided that her changed strategy would de-emphasize the financial incentive, and focus instead on educating the jury about the importance of circumstantial evidence. For assistance, she contacted us at the Trial Support Division.

Eleanor had been relying on her oral skills to get her message across to jurors. She did excel in oratory, but I am a strong believer in the use of visual aids. In my opinion, PowerPoint slide show presentations can effectively and rapidly educate juries. The formula consists of four factors: inform, clarify, persuade, and, most of all, make it memorable. I recommended to Eleanor that she take this approach. She agreed, so I drafted a slide show for her consideration. With her input and some modifications, we wound up with an opening statement consisting of forty slides.

The retrial in September featured Eleanor delivering her opening statement with the use of PowerPoint. To eliminate doubt that Jana Koklich had died, Eleanor enumerated a long list of missed appointments and the victim's failure to return any telephone calls—all inconsistent with her life patterns. Slides emphasizing the words "Reliable," "Responsible," and "Dependable" were designed to brand these images into the jurors' minds.

Eleanor's visuals next depicted all of the things this case was *not* about—kidnapping, robbery, burglary, carjacking, heat of passion, or self-defense. She illustrated this with photos showing the house alarm set, doors locked, nothing disturbed, nothing stolen, no sign of forced entry, no carjacking, and the missing SUV. We recognized a certain vulnerability in the carjacking part of it. The defense could suggest that some thug had jumped into the SUV at a stoplight on Jana's way to work, forced her at gunpoint to drive to a secluded spot, killed her, and taken the car. So Eleanor made it clear that the vehicle had been seen in Long Beach with Jana's purse inside, containing cash and credit cards, not the modus operandi (MO) of a carjacker.

More slides conveyed to jurors the importance of the housekeeper's discoveries about the substituted sheets, and that a feather had been found in the SUV consistent with feathers from the missing pillow.

Bruce Koklich's conduct would be a crucial part of Eleanor's prosecution, so she concentrated on hitting the jurors hard with every detail of his activities demonstrating that he had not behaved like a worried or grieving husband. A list appeared on the screen outlining Koklich's refusal to have telephone contact with anyone during the weekend after August 17. He claimed that he had spent Saturday and Sunday relaxing at home with Jana. Eleanor cited evidence that when Jana didn't show up at work on Monday, August 20, Bruce seemed more apathetic than worried. A slide for Tuesday indicated that Koklich went to work, held a press conference, suggested foul play, and told several lies to detectives.

Hunter informed jurors that after Bruce announced Jana's disappearance, he did nothing to help find her or to help the police. He posted no billboards, initially offered no reward, and showed zero interest in seeing where the SUV had been found. He never missed a day of work, started flirting with other women, asked about procedures for declaring someone dead, and started working on his defense as early as August 22.

Jurors seemed particularly attentive to slides about Koklich's experiences with an eighteen-year-old woman who stayed in his home not long after Jana vanished.

Eleanor Hunter's effective use of visual aids impressed reporters. The *Long Beach Press-Telegram,* on September 18, headlined their story: NEW KOKLICH TRIAL GETS HIGH-TECH BEGINNING: PROSECUTORS GIVE MIXED-MEDIA SHOW. The piece noted that the presentation used a mix of photographs, audiotape, video footage, and reproductions of several pieces of evidence: *Deputy District Attorney Eleanor Hunter supplemented her opening statement Wednesday with a slick PowerPoint presentation projected on a courtroom wall.*

As the trial progressed, the prosecutor emphasized behavioral issues and downplayed motive. She highlighted Jana's reliable, predictable patterns, which had suddenly and inexplicably halted.

The defense called witnesses attempting to rationalize Bruce Koklich's conduct. This time Bruce chose not to testify. They tried to cope with evidence that Jana's SUV had been left in a rough neighborhood in an obvious setup, but they couldn't erase the suspicion it placed on Bruce Koklich. Who else would have reason to do that? They also elicited testimony from psychologists suggesting that it's not uncommon for men who have lost spouses to seek new female companionship.

The jury began deliberations on the morning of October 9 and came out with a verdict five hours later. They found Bruce Koklich guilty of second-degree murder. A stunned defense team couldn't believe it.

Judge Philip Hickok delivered the sentence: fifteen years to life in prison.

A feeling of accomplishment permeated the DA's office and we congratulated Eleanor Hunter for a job well done. I personally felt proud of her for showing the flexibility to change her whole strategy and adopt a more visual presentation. Jurors, I strongly believe, appreciate using their eyes as well as their ears to assimilate evidence and information.

In the late summer of 2006, when I stepped into the muck and mire of the John Racz case with Sergeant Dee Scott and Deputy DA Shellie Samuels, I flashed back to the Bruce Koklich trial. The powerful interlocking linkage between them, I felt certain, would provide some insight for proceeding with the pending trial of Racz. In my mind, I began listing the comparisons.

Obviously, the most important connection focused on the missing bodies of Jana Koklich and Ann Racz. This denied us the wealth of evidence that usually springs from autopsies of murder victims. Forensic evidence, or the lack of it, ranked a close second. At least investigators had found smatterings of Jana's blood, whereas not one single element of hard evidence had turned up for the Racz detectives. Strike two!

Money as a motive had to be considered. Both Koklich and Racz had accumulated considerable affluence, and neither man wanted to lose half of it to an estranged wife. We had de-emphasized motive in Koklich's second trial, but we might have to spotlight it in the forthcoming Racz litigation.

Another similarity could be seen in the apathy shown by both men, along with their inconsistent statements or outright lies. This, I thought, could play a big part in prosecuting Racz.

In both cases, the victims had been meticulous, organized, punctual, predictable women who documented their activities. Their sudden unexplained disappearances dramatically broke their patterns of behavior.

Bruce Koklich had made a clumsy attempt to set up Jana's SUV for a thief to take it, and perhaps become a suspect. Racz had planted Ann's minivan in a parking lot.

Both men lied to investigators, with Racz perhaps a little more sophisticated in his statements about seeing Ann twice at restaurants and giving her money, in addition to his insistence that she had gone on an extended trip.

An unusual likeness existed in both Koklich and Racz posting bail, a million dollars for each of them, and remaining free during their trials. This can create a difficult problem for the prosecution. The defendant is able to come and go, alongside the jurors, and even rub elbows with them in hallways and elevators. It is probably much more difficult to convict someone who has parked next to you in the lot and has stood beside you in the cafeteria line.

In musing about these twin cases, I also noted a few differences.

Three children played important parts in the investigation of Racz, while the Koklich marriage produced no offspring.

Koklich was a consummate salesperson, while Racz, in addition to being a teacher, had been a cop, which might have increased his ability to avoid leaving clues.

A huge disparity existed in the amount of time that elapsed between the women vanishing and their husbands being arrested. Jana Koklich had been gone only eighteen months, while Ann Racz hadn't been seen for sixteen years. This made it much easier to infer that Ann's life had ended.

Sexual matters also provided an element of contrast. Bruce Koklich had immediately started hitting on women, and brought a teenage woman to live with him, while John Racz remained discreet. It might have been inferred that Jana, in remaking her image through a surge of physical fitness, weight loss, and regular facials, had interest in other men. With Ann, though, we would have to deal with the fact that she had fallen in love with Bob Russell, exchanged scores of letters, and had sexual liaisons with him.

I firmly believed we could mine the Bruce Koklich case for valuable guidelines in prosecuting John Racz. Still, I recognized obstacles the size of the Sierra Nevada Mountains looming over Beth Silverman and her support team.

CHAPTER 21

GOING
FOR THE
JUGULAR

Beth Silverman could also see a whole series of daunting obstructions in her path.

First she kicked herself for not alleging special circumstance of "lying in wait" when she made her presentation to the grand jury. If the jurists had included that charge in the indictment, Racz would not have been eligible for bail. Prosecuting Racz for murder held enough difficulty without jurors seeing this good-looking, well-dressed man walk about freely, a devoted father chatting with his son and daughters, and going home each night. Sympathy could develop for him as a gentle ex-teacher and cuckolded husband who had been caught up in a nightmare of sad circumstances. Silverman didn't need those images compounding her problems.

Evidentiary issues also bothered Silverman. She appreciated the incredible amount of work performed by Frank Salerno, Louis Danoff, Dee Scott, and Cheryl Comstock, but wondered if some other crucial bit of information might be lingering out there undiscovered. With her usual self-confidence and high-voltage energy, she plunged into the task of personally looking into it.

Conferring with Sergeant Dee Scott, Silverman said she wanted to have a look at every notebook and written report related to the investigation. Scott dug everything out of the files and dumped a mountain of documents of Silverman's desk, some of them dusty and starting to yellow with age.

As Beth Silverman read through the boxes of material, a new image of Ann Racz took form in her mind. The emerging picture clarified Ann's predicament of being stuck in a loveless marriage and surviving only through devotion to her three children. Something else jumped out: an obscure reference to Ann's church activities. She had affiliated herself with two churches in the Presbyterian faith, one in Newhall and one in Santa Clarita. She attended services regularly, contributed her time as a volunteer worker, and eventually became a part-time paid employee. In Newhall, Ann had been a member of the Elizabeth circle, a group of women who met monthly, on Tuesdays, not only for Bible lessons, but also for social and personal discussions. One of the investigators had printed a list, naming each of the members, including Ann's best friend, Dee Ann Wood. It even identified which members had acted as hostess or lesson leader.

A tiny tickle in the back of Silverman's mind set her to wondering. Exactly what had these women talked about, and could any of them—sixteen years later—shed light on circumstances leading to Ann's disappearance? From her own experiences, Silverman knew that women sometimes tend to reveal personal problems to close friends.

Ann had also sought counseling from Pastor Glen Thorp, of the Santa Clarita branch. Silverman wondered if Thorp would be willing to part with anything else other than what he had told detectives.

Sending another request to Dee Scott, Silverman asked for detectives to trace down each of the women named on the list. It wouldn't be easy. Some of them had probably moved out of state, perhaps remarried and taken new names. Still, Silverman had a feeling that she might have her finger on something important.

The search took some time, but Scott's team located six of the Elizabeth circle women, and continued to search for the seventh. This one, married to a law enforcement officer, had moved to the East Coast. Another member said she had been waiting and wondering for years when she would be contacted. In interviewing them, Silverman learned that Ann had said plenty at the last meeting she attended. She had spoken about the pending divorce and her fears of her husband's reactions.

Unwilling to settle for partial success, Silverman pushed detectives to find the seventh Elizabeth circle member. They finally succeeded, and Silverman added her to the list of intimate friends who had heard Ann express fears of retaliation from John Racz.

One of the women put it succinctly. Ann had said, "If I leave my husband, I'm afraid he's going to kill me. And if he does, *you'll never find my body*." These words struck at Beth Silverman's heart. Riveted by the stark prescience Ann had vocalized, Silverman vowed to do everything possible to find justice for this woman whose remains lay out there somewhere in some lonely site, unceremoniously dumped like so much garbage. Elated too, Silverman realized that if a jury could hear from these women in court, it might well carry a lot of weight. Under Evidence Code 1107, which allows information about a spouse's fear of harm from a husband or wife, this testimony should be admissible.

The other Presbyterian Church link, Pastor Glen Thorp, could be a little more thorny. Beth Silverman arranged an appointment to interview him.

Thorp's reluctance manifested itself right away. The pastor didn't think he should reveal what Ann had said in counseling sessions, and he certainly shouldn't testify in court to these private exchanges. The cleric-penitent privilege prevented it, he said.

Silverman knew that California Evidence Code 1030-1034 covered Thorp's concerns. It sets secrecy rules for a member of the clergy who hears "penitential communication." This is a communication made in confidence—with no third party present—to a member of the clergy who is authorized to hear it under the discipline or tenets of the church, denomination, or organization, and "has a duty to keep these communications secret." Thorp expressed his intention to honor that duty.

The code, though, contains a provision that the clergy member "has a privilege to refuse to disclose a penitential communication if he or she claims the privilege." Silverman explained this to Thorp, and spent a good part of the meeting pointing out that he would not violate the privilege if he testified. Thorp argued his understanding that he was prohibited from revealing anything without a waiver from the penitents, Ann or John Racz.

Countering this position, Silverman contended that Ann's presumed death nullified any need for her permission. Trying to clarify the legal aspects to Thorp, Silverman read directly from a law book she had brought with her. No written code prevented him from disclosing in court what Ann had said. Of course, the pastor had the option of declaring the privilege for himself, but Silverman gave him a dozen reasons why he shouldn't. Thorp's refusal, she explained, might prevent a just conclusion to the trial, and deny the moral restitution Ann deserved. His duty, she said, was to Ann Racz, not an ambiguous tenet or code.

Glen Thorp found himself in a difficult position. He simply wanted to do the right thing, not only under the law, but also for his church and congregation. Private counseling sessions are understood by most people to be absolutely confidential. Yet, what is the correct procedure in case the penitent is murdered? Where is the dividing line between morality, legality, trust, and religious convictions?

Silverman's tenacity with Pastor Thorp paid off. He agreed to testify in court, tell the whole truth, and not to claim the confidentiality privilege.

Now Beth Silverman's prosecution of John Racz had been bolstered with two important witnesses who would tell the jury about Ann Racz's fear of being killed if she left her husband. Ann's prediction that her body would never be found would resonate in the courtroom, since it proved to be accurate. It would lend powerful credibility to allegations that John Racz had been the instrument of Ann's death.

Would this be enough, though? Silverman rightfully expected a landslide of arguments from the defense attacking the prosecution's case, shouting that not one scintilla of forensic evidence existed in support of a guilty verdict.

John Racz hired prominent defense attorney Darryl Mounger, based in the San Fernando Valley community of Sherman Oaks. Short and stout, Mounger had been a used-car salesman until he joined the LAPD as an officer in the 1970s. Controversy erupted a few years later. Accused of misdeeds with a female teenager, Mounger subsequently married her. Claiming a "setup," he retired from the force in 1985, earned a law degree, and often defended police officers. Two of his cases lingered for years in headlines.

In 1991, Mounger defended an LAPD sergeant named Stacey Koon who had been accused of excessive brutality. He and three other officers chased African-American Rodney King and stopped him for speeding and running a red light. They ordered King from his vehicle, and while a bystander videotaped the incident, they repeatedly struck him. Television news stations ran the tape ad infinitum, and three of the officers faced felony charges. Exonerated by one jury, Koon was later convicted by a federal court and sent to prison. His appeals went all the way to the U.S. Supreme Court, which ordered a reduced sentence. Released in 1995, he settled a few miles from Valencia, where John Racz lived, and wrote a book about his experiences.

At the notorious trial of O.J. Simpson in 1994, Detective Mark Fuhrman testified. He had been one of the officers who investigated the bloody crime scene where Simpson's wife and her friend had been slaughtered. In court racial issues erupted, and Fuhrman absolutely denied under oath ever using the epithet "nigger." Months afterward, a tape recording surfaced in which Fuhrman repeatedly voiced the repugnant word. The DA's office charged him with perjury. Darryl Mounger represented him in a guilty plea of nolo contendere, no contest. It resulted in Fuhrman serving no jail time, but three years of probation.

As a former deputy sheriff, John Racz felt comfortable with Mounger defending him against murder charges.

Mounger would be joined in court by his colleague Philip Israels, a tall, Lincolnesque attorney with a solid reputation.

Beth Silverman familiarized herself with both defenders.

CHAPTER 22

"HIS GUILT OR INNOCENCE IS BEFORE YOU."

Spanish settlers, including a contingent of Franciscan friars, erected Mission San Fernando Rey de España in 1797. Located in the northwest limits of what is now Los Angeles County, close to the Santa Susanna Mountains, it became one of the first communities in the southland. A cemetery next to the mission is the burial site today of entertainment luminaries Bob Hope, Walter Brennan, Chuck Connors, William Bendix, William Frawley, Ed Begley, George Gobel, and singer Ritchie Valens.

In the present-day city of San Fernando, a tan stucco courthouse featuring old Spanish-style architecture stands a few blocks from downtown's main artery. The four-story structure, topped by a faux bell tower, is accessed through a wide archway with a bridged footpath. Three elevators lift jurors, lawyers, and observers to courtrooms of the Los Angeles Superior Court system. On one end of the third floor, Judge Ronald S. Coen has presided over trials for everything from mayhem to murder. On the other end is the local branch of the district attorney's office. The red-tiled hallway connecting them is lined on either side by six light-oak wooden benches, where witnesses, jurors, or others may sit during recesses.

Judge Coen began his career as a deputy district attorney, from 1973 to 1984. During that time, he and Ron Bowers worked together on a project to write a DA murder manual.

With the broad shoulders and the muscular body of an athlete, Coen continues to radiate authority. Neatly parted, close-cropped graying hair caps his high forehead, and he sometimes glowers over the top of silver-framed glasses. Coen can project a withering scowl or, conversely, a wide, quick friendly grin, and he often does both. His machine-gun speech delivery requires close attention by lawyers or spectators, and drives his court reporter crazy.

As a blue-collar kid, he worked at a McDonald's during his years at Burbank High School and as a mailman while attending California State University at Northridge. His law degree came from California Western School of Law in San Diego, he stated, "because it was three hundred yards from the beach." But just like Beth Silverman and her lost dreams of sun-drenched study, he never once found time to lie on the sand.

Appointed to the bench in 1985, at the age of thirty-seven, Coen soon earned a reputation of firm but fair rulings, and exhibited an encyclopedic knowledge of the law. He has enhanced this with an old-fashioned three-by-five-inch card file system. Everyone who knows Coen is aware of his five black boxes of well-fingered cards containing complex cross-referenced case-law information. Even today, he still adds new entries each week. Lawyers practicing in front of Coen had better learn the futility of objecting wrongfully or mistakenly citing a legal precedent.

* * *

Sixteen years and two months after Ann Racz's moving day, sixty-five citizens summoned to serve their civic duty assembled in Judge Coen's courtroom. On Monday, June 18, 2007, he commenced the selection process to seat a twelve-person jury, and six alternates, who would decide the fate of Ann's husband, John Racz.

At the defense table, flanked by attorneys Darryl Mounger and Philip Israels, defendant John Racz sat dressed in a neat gray suit, white shirt, and gray tie. He appeared at ease and confident.

Sitting among jury candidates in the audience, Joann, Glenn, and Katelin watched the proceedings with butterflies roiling in their stomachs. Emi and Jerry Ryan stood by, hoping that at long last their quest for justice would be answered.

Beth Silverman, dressed in black skirt, white blouse, and high heels, sat next to DDA John Lewin, who had been assigned as her assistant. At forty-three, Lewin had thirteen years of prosecutorial experience. He could easily have been mistaken for a football linebacker with his stocky build and pugnacious features.

Judge Coen spoke to the crowd of prospective jurors. "This is a criminal trial and the case is expected to last about four weeks. We are going to take the first week of July off. I'll tell you what the defendant is charged with, and I'll allow each side to address you in what is known as a mini-opening statement that is limited to five minutes. The defendant is charged with a violation of Penal Code 187, subdivision A, commonly known as murder. He has pled not guilty and the issue of his guilt or innocence is before you." Coen admonished the group that lawyers' comments must not to be considered as evidence.

John Lewin accepted Judge Coen's invitation to go first and gave a five-minute encapsulation of the case. He described Ann Racz, the troubled marriage, and promised that witnesses would tell of her fears. The case, he concluded, would rest on "overwhelming circumstantial evidence."

* * *

For the defense, Philip Israels rose to contradict the prosecution. With his black-framed glasses halfway down his nose, and eyebrows arched in perpetual surprise, Israels referred to notes as he spoke. He laid out an abridged background of John and Ann Racz and her intent to divorce him. She had freedom to travel the world, but she was still unsatisfied. "She told others that she was tired of the responsibilities of raising children. . . ." The defender appeared animated as he detailed Ann's love affair, as evidenced by the 109 love letters she wrote. "John didn't learn about this affair until a year after Ann had left." John had tried to salvage the marriage, he said, and even gave Ann money to travel and think it over.

"We are asking the jury to take a fresh look at this case with a presumption of innocence. The sheriff's investigators had a presumption of guilt. . . . Remember that after sixteen years— after searches for Ann Racz's body, search warrants, surveillance, wiretaps—there is still no body. No crime scene, no murder weapon, no DNA, or any scientific evidence at any time." John Racz, Israels asserted, "is not the person that the prosecution wants you to think he is. We are asking the jury to consider all the evidence and take a fresher look at his case."

One element of the defense strategy had been revealed. They planned to attack Ann's morality and loyalty to her children. This didn't surprise Emi and Jerry Ryan, but it made their skin crawl. They knew that Ann loved all three of her kids more than anything in the world.

Day one of the proceedings came to a close.

The weeding-out process began on Tuesday morning with each side using peremptory challenges. Jury selection can be a long, arduous task, but Judge Coen prodded it effectively and kept it moving.

Most juror candidates would prefer not to land on a protracted murder case. But at least one person on this panel, a retired middle-aged woman, wanted more than anything else to be selected.

No novice to courtroom procedure, Barbara Kaplan had been a judicial assistant, more commonly known as a judge's clerk. She had served on a previous jury in Judge Ronald Coen's court, and when she learned that her panel would hear a high-profile case, she felt that fate had interceded. "I was sitting in the audience, really wanting to be on that jury. They picked the twelve people and were down to selecting alternates, and the judge was going to have only four. Mr. Lewin asked that there be six. The judge said he would think about it and eventually he did allow six. I was meant to be on that jury because I was the last one selected and became alternate number six. And I couldn't be kicked off because both sides had exhausted their peremptory challenges."

The circumstantial evidence, with no discovery of a body, made it even more interesting to Kaplan. "That appealed to me because I really didn't want to sit on a murder case with blood and gore and dead bodies and all that stuff. So this was good, because it was clean."

CHAPTER 23

SHOWTIME

As the gallery filled in Judge Coen's courtroom, speculation ran high. Insiders, veteran court watchers, and journalists knew that the victim's body had never been found, and they wondered exactly how the prosecution could prove charges of murder. It seemed impossible. And what part would the three offspring of John and Ann Racz play? Would they align themselves with their missing mother, or sympathize with their accused father? Would he get on the stand to shout not only his innocence, but also his outrage at being charged with murder after sixteen years?

The mini-opening statements delivered by Lewin and Israels had been for the purpose of outlining the case to prospective jurors. Now, on the first day of summer, Thursday, June 21, 2007, with the selection process completed, the formal trial began. Judge Coen advised the jury of their responsibilities and explained that each side would now present full opening statements.

Trials cannot be conducted to present the information in

chronological or understandable order. So the testimony comes out fragmented, like the pieces of a jigsaw puzzle scattered all over a table. Opening statements are a preview, like the complete picture on the puzzle's box, showing what the image will finally look like when all the pieces are put in place.

Beth Silverman would take the first turn in assembling that picture.

After a couple of introductory comments, Silverman said, "What you are about to see and what you are about to hear is a fairly comprehensive summary of what we expect the evidence to show in this case. Because there is a lot of evidence to cover, our presentation is rather lengthy. Sit back and relax and make yourselves comfortable, and let me take you back sixteen years."

True to her word about "lengthy," Silverman would speak for nearly ninety minutes.

Beginning with Ann Racz's last visit to the Fortuna house on April 22, 1991, Silverman created word pictures of Ann conversing with John from inside her car, then leaving to buy fast food for her kids at McDonald's. "Unfortunately, as you will learn, Ann never made it back to the house. And to this day, her body has never been found. And other than the defendant's false assertions, [she] has not been heard from by a single other person since that day."

Putting the jurors into a time machine, Silverman transported them back to the marriage of two young schoolteachers on July 1, 1972, John's tour as a deputy sheriff, the birth of Joann, their move to Valencia, Glenn's and Katelin's arrival, and John's return to teaching in 1985. Silverman next focused on Ann's love for her children, dedication to church, and community involvement. "She was considered by all who knew her to be highly responsible and very reliable, and the one thing you will hear throughout this trial, over and over again, Ann was extremely well organized in everything she did. She planned everything in advance. She even kept lists of things she did, detailed lists. These character traits and lifestyle attributes will help prove the defendant is the sole person responsible for her disappearance and murder."

Changing the focus of her spotlight to John Racz, Silverman characterized him as "very controlling" and preoccupied with money. She gave examples of avoiding garbage collection fees, tight restrictions for use of air-conditioning, and rules about toilet flushing.

The couple's marriage, she said, "did not remain the pretty picture from their wedding day," and Ann "fell out of love with John." From there the relationship with Bob Russell blossomed through letters and personal contact. Ann's church affiliation, said Silverman, led to her counseling sessions with Pastor Thorp.

Filling out the picture of Ann's life, Silverman spoke of the mother, brothers, and the help she received from her sister, Emi. In telling Emi about plans to divorce John, "Ann said she wanted her children, but she would be willing to share some custody with the defendant." Silverman brought this up to lay groundwork for countering expected accusations by the defense that Ann no longer wanted the kids.

A very close friend of Ann's would testify, said Beth. Dee Ann Wood knew about the missing woman's plans to leave her husband, and she would also describe Ann's dedication to her children, as well as her meticulous organization and planning for everything, with no hint of compulsive behavior.

The jury would hear from Ann's church circle of friends, Silverman pledged. One would recall Ann's stated fears that John would hurt her or the children. Another would tell of a private conversation in which Ann had expressed excitement about future prospects with Bob Russell, but terror of John. When the woman had tried to alleviate the fear, Ann had looked into her eyes and said, "You don't understand. He told me if I ever leave him, he would kill me, and you'll never find my body." None of the circle had ever heard Ann mention anything about planning a trip.

"Pastor Thorp will tell you that a month or two before Ann's disappearance, she confided similar things to him." He would even warn the couple, "Do not see each other alone. Make sure someone else is present."

Ann moved to a condominium in Peachland, said Silverman, and expressed her fears to the managers.

Taking jurors through Ann's moving day, April 18, 1991, Silverman listed the step-by-step events.

John, she said, had returned home to the Fortuna house and found Ann and the kids gone. He later lied to his school principal about making a missing person report to the police. His subsequent statements to detectives were full of inconsistencies, reluctance to cooperate, and no sign of interest in finding his wife, all indicating consciousness of guilt.

In the completely silent courtroom, with every eye focused on her, Beth Silverman led jurors through the final days of Ann's life, then moved on to the key issue of money. Detailing the joint assets, she made it clear that Racz did not want to divide them with his estranged wife. Ann never made it to the May 1991 divorce court hearing, said Silverman, and explained why. "The defendant would kill her three days after being served with the divorce papers."

The bright future Ann Racz expected to share with Bob Russell, said Beth Silverman, had been blotted out. She read aloud the last letter Ann wrote to Russell, full of glowing optimism.

Ann's final day of life came next in Silverman's spellbinding sequence. She spoke of the VCR trade at a Target store, bank transactions, and the purchase of groceries at a Hughes Market for making pizza that evening. In the early afternoon, said Beth, Ann had delivered checks to John on Fortuna Drive, picked up two of her children from school, promised them homemade pizza for dinner, and returned to Fortuna so they could visit their father.

Jurors would hear testimony from a neighbor who witnessed a long conversation between John and Ann while she and the kids sat in her car, said Silverman. And Joann would take the stand to tell about being hungry and her mother leaving to get some food for the kids at McDonald's.

John Racz had told inconsistent stories claiming that he gave her "a large amount of money" in cash over the next couple of days, stated Silverman, and that Ann went on a prolonged vacation to think things over. "The defendant has also alleged that the final time he heard from his wife was on Friday, April twenty-sixth, when she called him from Los Angeles International Airport. Incredibly, according to Racz, Ann did not mention anything about her children's care, their schedules, or leave any information for them to contact her.

"You will hear testimony from all three of the children, sixteen years after their mother's disappearance, now all adults themselves." Among spectators, mental images of three young children now had to be morphed into grown-ups. Silverman's next comment laced the issue with intrigue: "What the content of their testimony will be, however, remains to be seen."

Ann's neighbor, said Silverman, was the last person known to have seen her alive. He would testify about a brief conversation in which Ann had confirmed Joann's intent to babysit for them that night and mentioned going to McDonald's to get something for the kids to eat. Within minutes after she left, the neighbors had seen John speeding by in his car, traveling in the same direction as his wife.

"The evidence will show," Silverman declared, "that at some point after Ann left the residence, the defendant followed and murdered her.

"We are not required under the law to prove . . . the location of the crime or the weapon that was used to commit the murder. What we are required to do, and what we will prove beyond any reasonable doubt, is that Ann ceased to exist on April 22, 1991. We will also prove that she was killed that day by the defendant, and that the alleged communications he asserts they had on Tuesday and Wednesday in person, and on Friday by phone, are fabrications, which did not and could not have occurred," she explained.

Pausing for a breath, and to let her powerful words sink in, Beth Silverman followed it up. "Evidence will be presented that the defendant was gone for a considerable length of time after he left, allegedly to make the less than one-mile drive to McDonald's. The exact duration will not be proven, but the evidence will show that it was long enough for Joann to re-peatedly call her friend that day, worried that neither of her parents had come back home."

The prosecutor next escorted jurors along a path showing strange behavior, questionable assertions, and odd activities by John Racz in the days following Ann's disappearance. She described the alleged visit by Ann on Tuesday, the trumped-up meetings with her at Tips and Carl's Jr., as claimed by John Racz to detectives, including his uncharacteristic generosity in giving her $25,000, and his remarkable story of walking home from hamburger hill while carrying his children's heavy backpacks.

Neighbor Brenda George would testify, Silverman said. The witness had given Katelin a ride home from school on that Tuesday, and had kept her until John came to pick her up at about seven o'clock that night. In addition, she had kept Katelin every day the rest of the week, even though John Racz did not work during that time. What was he doing? Could he have been scouting for a place to bury Ann?

Silverman directed the jury's attention to a PowerPoint slide projected on a large white screen. "This photo depicts the Flyaway parking lot located in Van Nuys, as it existed in 1991. The evidence will show that on April twenty-fifth, at ten-ten A.M., Ann's white minivan entered the parking lot." The projected picture changed to a yellow parking receipt. "We know this information because this ticket, showing the time and date, was later recovered from inside the minivan. The evidence will show that the car was not driven to the Flyaway by Ann Racz. It was instead dropped off by the defendant after her death as part of his plan to cover up the murder and set up a story as to explain her disappearance."

Witnesses Dee Ann Wood and Emi's daughter Kathy would testify that Ann never used the Flyaway lot, said Silverman, and further, both of them had taken her to LAX on several occasions.

More telephone evidence would come into play. "The defendant did not report to work again on Friday. At three-fourteen that afternoon, records show that a collect call lasting four minutes was received at the Racz residence." The defendant later claimed to detectives that the call was from Ann and that she told him her minivan was parked at the Flyaway and she was going away to think about things. "The evidence will show, however, that this call was not made by Ann, that this was a complete and total fabrication, part of the defendant's cover-up to the murder of his wife.

"Detectives were able to trace the number from where the collect call was placed to a pay phone at LAX. The phone was located in a small bank of pay phones inside of Terminal One. Then detectives obtained records for the adjoining phones, and they made a startling discovery. The records for one of the adjacent phones showed two coin calls placed to the defendant's residence. The first one was made at three P.M., fourteen minutes before the collect call. The second call was made seven minutes later. Despite numerous interviews about the one collect call described by the defendant to detectives, claiming that it came from his wife, he never mentioned the first two calls to anyone.

"Why didn't he reveal them? The circumstantial evidence demonstrates that he made the first two calls himself, using coins, and then used a different phone for the collect call. So then you ask, how was the collect call answered if he made the call himself from the airport and no one was at home?

"You will hear from an expert witness that the first two phone calls were definitely answered at the house. Regarding the third call, he will testify that if an outgoing message is left on the answering machine saying that the caller accepts collect calls, it will be placed through without a live person having answered the phone at the receiving end."

The first two calls, Silverman explained, tested the system to make certain the answering machine was functioning. Then the collect call went through as planned, and it would be the only one to show up on Racz's phone bill. "Much like his inconsistencies regarding the details of how much money he gave Ann, and where these exchanges took place, the defendant trips up on details. In a statement to detectives, on May 16, 1991, he said that during the call from Ann at LAX, he could hear the sound of cars in the background. Yet, the phone banks are well inside the terminal, and no automobile traffic can be heard in there, much less through the phone."

By the way, Silverman said, "Detectives Salerno and Danoff checked passenger manifests for the three airlines serving Terminal One at that time, and did not find Ann's name on any of them.

"There are several other problems with the idea that the collect call was made by Ann Racz." According to her family and friends, Ann did not make collect calls. After she moved out on April 18, she used an MCI calling card. "There was no reason for her to change her well-documented pattern of using the MCI card."

Pointing out that Ann called no one else on or after April 22, nor did she have any contact with her family or friends, Silverman said that Racz's claims of her making a collect call were fabrications. His account of going to the Flyaway a couple of hours after the alleged conversation with Ann and moving her car to a shady spot in order to protect a VCR in the back also sounded suspicious.

One of the most important elements of the trial would be to convince jurors that Ann's life had ended. Addressing this, Silverman listed several factors, including Ann's failure to ever return to the condo, as evidenced by the pizza ingredients left on the kitchen counter, failure to reply to notes left by Glenn and Joann, and a complete stoppage of telephone calls and greeting cards to family and friends. Ann had even left several envelopes containing cards, addressed and stamped, on her desk in the condo to be mailed on April 24, according to her calendar notes. "Evidence will show that had she been alive on that date, as the defendant claimed, those cards would have been mailed."

Informing the jury that Sergeant Frank Salerno and Detective Louis Danoff had spent years investigating the case, Beth Silverman referred to the taped interview they had conducted with the defendant. "You will hear more of this interview during the trial, but at this point, I'm going to play an excerpt from it. As you listen, it's important to note not only what the defendant said, and did not say, but the hesitations and qualifications in his answers."

Each juror's face reflected absolute attention to every word of the tape. As soon as it ended, Silverman said, "Some of the most compelling evidence in this case comes from the defendant's own mouth." She placed heavy emphasis on his evasiveness and inconsistent statements. Observers looked forward eagerly to hearing the full tape later on.

"It is important to note," said the prosecutor, "that the defendant's lies will be uncovered, as most lies are, through his mistakes regarding the details. His answers will demonstrate that although the truth should not change over time, remembering lies can be much more problematic. . . . He has been giving different versions of whose idea the trip was, who asked or offered the money, and dollar amounts allegedly given."

Regarding John Racz's claim of meeting Ann two separate times in restaurants and giving her a total of $25,000, said Beth Silverman, his long history of extreme frugality had raised questions about this sudden generosity. "The defendant was much too concerned and preoccupied with his money to ever have given his wife these funds, whether it was eight thousand or twenty-five thousand, to take a vacation. He also has gone back and forth as to where he met Ann to give her the money. He told Ann's sister, Emi, on May third, that he met Ann at Tips Restaurant, on April twenty-third. He told Pastor Thorp, on May fourth, just the next day, that he met Ann at Jack in the Box, on April twenty-third, and Tips the following day. And the defendant told Detectives Danoff and Salerno, on May sixteenth, that he met Ann at a Carl's Jr. on April twenty-third. His changing of the location from Tips to Jack in the Box to Carl's Jr. will demonstrate the falsity of his story."

Silverman made it clear that John Racz had never filed a missing person report. That duty had fallen to Pastor Thorp at Emi's urging. Jurors would never know how hard she had worked in convincing him to testify. "He will tell you that he went to the defendant's house to see what was going on. During their discussion in the garage, the defendant flew into a rage. He made statements such as 'How dare Ann leave me and file for divorce.' He was in such a rage that Pastor Thorp, as you will hear, feared for his own life."

An example of John Racz's apathetic behavior and odd treatment of Ann's sister came next from the prosecutor. "Emi flew from her home in Arizona after Ann failed to visit their elderly mother as planned, on May twentieth, and drove to the Fortuna residence. She will testify that in conversation with the defendant he was completely unconcerned about Ann, saying that she was on a trip. He refused to provide any details of his last conversation with his wife. Emi will tell you that he was more concerned about himself. Rather than express any concern about Ann, he complained about the difficulties of taking the kids to school and still getting to work on time."

The DDA pledged that financial records would show that Ann had made no transactions in the sixteen years since she vanished.

Yet more oddities in John Racz's statements to detectives came under Silverman's scathing commentary. "When Ann left, the defendant said he felt he would be watching the kids two to three weeks, but did not explain how he came to this conclusion." Despite Ann's history of exemplary care and planning for the children, she departed without any arrangements for their clothing, school supplies, upcoming activities, or day care while Racz worked. And he said something to the kids "which is inconsistent with his version of Ann merely taking a vacation. He told his children, 'If Mom doesn't come back, we'll buy new clothes.' And in another revealing comment, he admitted that while urging Ann not to leave him, he told her he would commit suicide if she didn't come back."

The black-and-gold ring Ann bought in Hawaii finally came under the DDA's scrutiny. "In another example of how the little details are the ones that often trip criminals up, the defendant made a mistake when talking about Ann's new Hawaiian wedding ring, telling detectives she was wearing it the day she disappeared. The evidence, however, will demonstrate that's impossible, because Ann's sister, Emi, will testify that, to this day, she still has the ring." Emi had produced a photograph taken by her husband. It depicted her seated in a wooden chair, holding in her left hand a small roll of white paper with the ring circling it. She also held a copy of *The Arizona Republic* newspaper to her chest, dated long after Ann had vanished. This proved that Ann had not worn the ring, as claimed by John Racz.

After a lunch break, Beth Silverman resumed her opening statements with reference to a calendar that had been taken from the Fortuna residence during a search. Racz had tried to obliterate an entry for April 18, 1991. "That's the day Ann moved out. An expert was able to restore the original entry that the defendant had tried to destroy. It said, 'Hell Day.'"

The defendant, Silverman said, continued to insist that Ann was still alive. "The evidence, however, will demonstrate beyond any reasonable doubt that Ann Racz is dead, and she was murdered by that man more than sixteen years ago." Silverman pointed an accusing finger at John Racz. "The evidence will further show that any argument to the contrary is not just unreasonable, but is beyond all notions of common sense and logic. . . . Ann was a dedicated mother. The thought that she would abandon her beloved children is insulting. For the defendant's statement to be true, this [woman] has voluntarily absented herself from every important event and milestone in her family's life. From soccer games to her mother's funeral. From high-school graduations to the birth of her granddaughter.

"Circumstantial cases are like puzzles. And although we start today with a blank puzzle—at the end of this case, you will have more than enough pieces to find the defendant guilty of the murder of Ann Racz.

"Thank you, ladies and gentlemen, for your time and attention."

Beth Silverman's impassioned speech sounded convincing to observers. No one could guess how it impacted jurors. Everyone in the gallery looked forward eagerly to hearing how the defense would counter the state's ninety-minute indictment of John Racz.

CHAPTER 24

ON THE DEFENSE

The shorter, older of two attorneys at the defense table stood at Judge Coen's invitation, approached the lectern, and said, "Thank you, ladies and gentlemen. I'm Darryl Mounger. . . . What my job is, is to try to tell you what the evidence is from the other side of the pancake. If you have a pancake, there are two sides." Quizzical looks appeared in the gallery.

"We have told you from the very beginning that Ann Racz is a woman in conflict. What I'm going to do is take you back to the 1991 statements, because the statements are going to change over time. The issue here is whether or not she left on her own, or whether or not—you know. When she talked to Reverend Thorp at the church for two years, she made it clear she was an unhappy woman. She was unhappy with the day-to-day things. She wanted more out of life. She wanted to have time to get away, because even the children were a problem.

"Certainly, when she was talking to her best friend, Dee Ann Wood, [who] will tell you, if she remembers correctly, it wasn't an unhappy situation. It was that she fell out of love.

And she also made the comment 'Maybe I should let the kids go to John.'"

Mounger indicated another witness would quote Ann, saying, "I'm tired of the responsibility of having the children." He continued to chop away at her reputation. "This you are going to hear . . . from all of her friends and the people she knew, but the letters that she wrote to her boyfriend will tell you her state of mind, what she was thinking. Her own words are the defense in this case.

"In those letters, she maybe talked about the kids, but she will tell you what she is thinking in those letters. She is very clear . . . saying, 'Trips like these tend to spoil me. No cooking, no cleaning, no kids to haul around. No volunteer work. Nobody to rely upon me. But trips like this are very expensive, so I guess I'll go back to the routine.'

"But of all the statements . . . the most important ones come from her own fourteen-year-old daughter." A few people in the gallery glanced at one another, curious about what Joann might have said to elicit this shocker, but Mounger left it hanging unexplained.

"What you are here for is evidence and facts. And I want to talk to you about the facts of what happened here, and what the 1991 statements were. We heard that Dee Ann Wood was [Ann's] best girlfriend. And you heard when she moved out of the apartment on the eighteenth of April, Dee Ann Wood came and picked her up at the shopping center and took her back to the apartment because she didn't want anyone to know she was there." Observers assumed Mounger misspoke when he said "moved out of the apartment." Ann had moved out of the Fortuna house.

"Dee Ann came back on the nineteenth [and] dropped her off in the morning so she could use her car. Her best friend, who is supposed to know where she is everywhere, doesn't call her on the nineteenth, that day. Doesn't call her on Saturday, the twentieth. Doesn't call her on Sunday, the twenty-first.

Doesn't call her on the twenty-second. So that's strange that she would suddenly end contact with her best friend. All those days that are so important to her when she is first on her own."

Puzzled expressions appeared in the gallery. Was Dee Ann Wood on trial for neglecting her friend? Just what did this have to do with the charges against John Racz?

Mounger made a welcome transition. "But we do find out certain things. We find postmarks on her letters. As much as the words are important, the postmarks are important. Because on the nineteenth, it showed that it came from San Diego. So she did get this. But the postmarks I'm going to talk to you about— all of these postmarks—come from Europe. They come from Germany. They come from France. They come from Japan, Hawaii."

Ears picked up. Did Mounger have postmarked letters to solve the mystery of Ann's location? If that's where observers thought Mounger headed, disillusionment erased it. The letters had all been mailed during her previous travels.

The defender simply wanted to attack the image of his client as a penny-pincher. "Obviously, she is the housekeeper, a mother, but the guy who works, the cheap one, the one that doesn't want to have the electricity burning, and the water used unnecessarily, he's the one paying for the trips, of course. And he's saying in his letters to her—we have those letters that were read to you here by the prosecutor—he's saying, 'I'll do whatever you want. I'll let you do whatever you want.' That's what he's been doing for two years. That's what the evidence is going to show you.

"You will be dealing with a lot of words and a lot of conduct. I'm going to ask you to look at the conduct. It's as important as the words. Throughout the year, what he did not know is she was going to get a divorce, not telling him about it. . . . The boyfriend knows about it, that she is unhappy. [John] doesn't know that she's getting a divorce. The pastor doesn't know she's getting a divorce. Not everybody knows what's going on with Ann Racz."

More muffled grunts sounded among the audience. Pastor Thorp, they had heard, knew of Ann's plans to end the marriage.

Next focusing on Ann's finances, Mounger said that the condo rental agreement she had filled out differed from divorce documents in terms of her monthly income. Another disparity, Mounger said, showed up in the allegation that she never made collect telephone calls. "If you look at her letters, one says in part, 'From calling you every two weeks, to once a week, to twice a week now, and if I don't control my urges, it would cost both of us, especially you with my collect calls.' So this woman has made collect calls when she wants to or has a desire to. In fact, she does have a calling card with a PIN number, but don't think she can't make collect calls.

"The call on April twenty-sixth, they are trying to say there was an answer[ing] machine. Of course, her own words will tell you there is no answer[ing] machine. She says in the letter, 'We don't have an answering machine. If you call, no one will answer, so just call back again.' That's from her words.

"They are going to bring in somebody that retired in 1998, to say maybe John went out and bought a machine for one day and took it back and returned it, because a detective never saw an answering machine."

The move to Peachland, said Mounger, contradicted allegations of her deep fears. "If she was afraid, she would not have rented an apartment a mile away. . . . And the evidence is clear when she [sought] a divorce, her lawyer could have gotten her a restraining order, but he didn't do that. The evidence will show you there was things in conduct that are inconsistent with total fear."

Focusing on "the most important day," Mounger recapitulated every step Ann took on April 22, 1991—from the bank withdrawals to her final visit at the Fortuna house. "She goes to the house at three-thirty. She's in the car, he's standing outside.

That's what the people said across the street. Mr. Pedersen said thirty to sixty minutes. Glenn Racz said thirty minutes. Let's give them the benefit of the doubt and make it four o'clock, in the garage, when Joann comes out and says, 'When are we leaving?' Like a teenager, she wants to do what she wants to do. She's told to go back in the house. She says, 'I'm hungry.' Her mother says she'll go to McDonald's. There's some more conversation. A few minutes later, Dad comes in the house and says, 'You know what, I'll go to McDonald's.'

"When she leaves, she stops down the street and talks to Tom Deardorff. Tom will come in here and tell you she was chitchatting, in a good frame of mind, nothing wrong. She didn't seem like she was scared or nervous. And then she left.

"I believe the evidence is she went from there to the community center and picked up her youngest daughter, Katelin, from a Brownie meeting. . . ." Mounger described Ann's meeting with another Brownie father, Doug Krantz, who told her that the kids had arrived from their field trip, but had gone bowling.

Over at the prosecution table, Beth Silverman made rapid entries on a yellow legal pad. Her first witness, Carol Kuwata, would testify to picking up Katelin and bringing her home. Either Mounger had his sequence of events confused, or he had found something to dispute Kuwata's statements.

Mounger continued: "What we do know is that Katelin came home from bowling. Only seven years old, she couldn't tell you what time she came home, but she came home with Carol Kuwata." Mounger now seemed to have recovered from his error.

"Mrs. Kuwata says, 'I got her home about five o'clock.' When Katelin comes home, her original statement to the detectives was 'I was upset because I didn't live there anymore.' Her original statement was 'When I looked in the window, I saw my dad, and my brother, and I saw my sister.' Fifteen and a half years later, she testified to the grand jury, [saying], 'I looked in the window, I saw my brother and my sister and some neighborhood kids. My dad and my mom wasn't home.'"

Glenn Racz originally spoke of going in the house and playing Nintendo, stated Mounger, and said back then he didn't know how long his dad had been gone to McDonald's. To the grand jury, he testified, "My dad took an hour to come home."

"Times have changed and something has happened and the question should be why and when. If you take the general statements, Dad is home, what happens afterward?" Joann, Mounger said, told detectives that she ate that night at a restaurant called Vincenzo's. And John Racz told detectives of eating there. "When detectives seized all the evidence from the house, they saw a credit card bill from Vincenzo's."

Heartbeats sped up in the gallery. Had Mounger stumbled on something that would significantly narrow the time frame of John's opportunity to kill Ann? Mounger punctured expectations with nothing more than a question. "Did anybody go to Vincenzo's and find out what time they got there?" Maybe he planned to deliver the blow through actual testimony or by introducing a timed receipt during the trial, and not spoil it in these opening statements.

Darting away from it, Mounger returned to what appeared to be his most crucial evidence, the letters Ann had written to Bob Russell. "I can add one more thing. The only postmark in those one hundred nine letters that said Marina del Rey, P.M., it was postmarked on that day." Listeners assumed he meant April 22, although he didn't spell it out. "I think we are going to have an expert in here and he'll tell you what the postal service is like and how they can get a postmark from Marina del Rey, when that was the main post office, before they had a Santa Clarita office. And the mail all goes to Van Nuys."

One cynic thought, *Oh, that makes it crystal clear.* The garbled comment probably confused more than one person.

"Then the evidence is the next day, on the twenty-third,

that John cashed the eighty-nine hundred dollars, and he told the police, 'I met Ann at Carl's Jr.' He said the next day, 'I went and borrowed seventeen thousand dollars.' And they proved that one. He borrowed seventeen thousand against a CD. And he said they went to Tips.

"Ladies and gentlemen, they are going to have evidence saying they couldn't find anybody from Carl's Jr. or Tips who saw them together. But they are also going to put on evidence that they never saw anybody at McDonald's when one of them went to McDonald's."

The cynic conceded this point. Absence of eyewitnesses is like a negative positive. Just because no one could testify to seeing a person at a specific location does not prove the person was not there. And the fact that Racz had brought back cold french fries in a McDonald's bag certainly infers he had been in the fast-food restaurant at least for a short time. Yet, none of the employees could recall seeing him there.

"There are a lot of things that are missing. But if you look at the time frame for the twenty-second, that's the critical day. This is when it had to happen.

"I know, I can't argue with you whether or not John is cheap or whether he wants to conserve water. But I can argue with you about the facts. And the facts show it didn't happen that day."

Did Mounger's comments mean "it" happened another day? Nah!

"You are also going to hear from somebody at the Department of Airports. In 1991, it's not like after September eleventh. You could have gotten on airplanes, you didn't need identification. You just got a ticket and a boarding pass. But they didn't call the numbers. When they got that little piece of paper that had the airplane numbers on it, they had airplane numbers for other airlines that were not in Terminal One. There is not going to be any evidence about those airplanes."

Back to the letters again, Mounger asserted that Detective

Louis Danoff, during a visit to the Fortuna house, had shown Joann the final letter Ann wrote to Bob Russell. Mounger quoted Joann's alleged response: "My mother would never write that. That's not my mother's writing."

With a new vitriol in his voice, Mounger said, "It's the way they have done this investigation throughout the time. Showing a sixteen-year-old girl, who was fifteen at the time, personal letters of her mother's. Well, you can determine the facts." The issue of who showed the letters to whom would cause controversy.

"Now I want to tell you the last thing in here is that I can't compete with the technology, and neither can Mr. Israels. This is not about technology. It's about the facts you hear from the witness stand, it's about the evidence, you see. It's not about the fluff, it's not about anything else. It's about the truth, and that's what we are trying to get to.

"I'm trying to be very short with this, because I think you are all tired of hearing all this stuff. I'm sure you are ready to hear the evidence and get this case going. I'm sure I'm going to get yelled at because I didn't say some things my co-counsel wanted me to. But I think if you look at the facts and look at the day that's important, because I think the twenty-second is the important time, they are going to have to show he had the opportunity. There is no opportunity. They have told you not to speculate, not to guess, but only to follow the law and the facts. And the facts go for John Racz.

"Thank you."

Darryl Mounger had probably accurately expressed the jury's readiness to move on and hear some evidence. Judge Coen apparently shared the same desire. He refused Mounger's request for a short break and ordered the prosecution to call their first witness.

CHAPTER 25

THRUST
AND PARRY

Judge Coen's clerk asked Carol Ann Kuwata to raise her right hand and "solemnly state" she would "tell the truth, the whole truth, and nothing but the truth, so help you God." Kuwata affirmed her oath and took a seat in the witness chair.

Answering questions from Beth Silverman, Kuwata told of her assignment as transportation chairman for the Brownie troop in which Katelin and Kuwata's daughter were members. She knew Ann from Brownie meetings and school activities, and as a mutual soccer mom.

On Monday, April 22, 1991, she said, she had transported four of the young girls to a bowling alley from the school, and then later to their homes. Asked what time she had delivered Katelin to the Fortuna house, Kuwata answered, "I would say, to my recollection, close to five o'clock." But after reviewing notes from a 1991 police interview, she thought it closer to four o'clock.

Philip Israels, conducting the cross-examination, guided

her through a reconstruction of the timing, from picking up kids at school to delivering them to their homes. At the Fortuna house, Kuwata said, she thought the garage door was down. The defense attorney established that she did not know whether or not Ann's car could have been inside.

On redirect examination, Beth Silverman asked, when a child waved to signify someone at home, did it automatically mean the presence of a parent? Kuwata said no, it simply meant someone responsible was at home, and not an empty house.

Carol Kuwata stepped down to be replaced by Douglas Krantz. He told of Ann's participation in a YMCA program to teach kids to swim. The last time he ever saw Ann, Krantz recalled, took place on a Monday when he informed her in the Valencia Hills clubhouse parking lot that Katelin and her Brownie group had gone on a bowling excursion.

Cynthia Alarcon, the final witness for that Thursday, had been the leader of Katelin's Brownie troop in 1991. Before Beth Silverman could ask more questions, Judge Coen announced the adjournment until the following morning.

Judge Coen started court promptly on Friday morning, June 22, and thanked everyone for being punctual. "Usually, about this time, I'm apologizing for a late start. I can do a really good tap dance."

Maybe he meant on the chests of anyone daring to be late. Alternate juror Barbara Kaplan would later say about the judge, "He's known for being tough. He had those jurors—oh, my God—did he have them scared. They were terribly afraid of being late. If he said ten-thirty, you were in there at ten-thirty. The jurors were really, 'Watch out for the judge.' You know, I have a lot of respect for the way he runs his court. Because seldom did he keep us late. I've seen a lot of courts, even the one I worked in, where we would run over and the jurors would be sitting outside for a long time waiting to come in. That hardly ever happened to us. He's got his own sense of humor and that laugh. He didn't keep us waiting and he ran a good court."

Coen instructed Cynthia Alarcon to resume her seat in the witness chair and advised that she was still under oath. Beth Silverman, aiming at cementing the time frames for April 22, 1991, drew from the witness that Katelin's bowling excursion on that day ended at about 3:30 P.M., and that Ann Racz always told friends in advance about going on trips. About Ann's character, Alarcon said, "She was very organized . . . and she always had her hair done nice and was always put together, makeup on."

"Did she ever wear the same thing twice, two days in a row?"

"Not that I remember."

On cross-examination, Darryl Mounger tossed several general questions, then inquired about John's participation with Katelin in the Brownie activities. "Didn't you tell the sheriff's [department] that John was excluded because the other parents didn't trust him?"

Alarcon grimaced, and said, "They didn't feel comfortable with him. I wouldn't say that they didn't want him there. They didn't feel comfortable." Mounger's cross-exam lasted another ten minutes.

After the midmorning break, Lois Becker, Glenn's teacher in 1991, testified. She recalled Ann's participation in the PTA and intense dedication to her children's education. Ann, she said, had dropped by on April 22 to report a change of address, and to be certain the move and separation from her husband didn't disrupt Glenn's class work. Ann made no mention of a pending trip, and confirmed her plans to attend an open house on April 23.

Another teacher, Dorrie Dean, followed Becker in the witness chair. Katelin had been in her second-grade class at Wiley

Canyon Elementary School. Dean told jurors that Ann Racz had been in her classroom at least every other week. In a private conference on March 16, 1991, Ann had told her of the separation and pending move. She shared this information so Dean could watch out for any changes in Katelin's progress. In addition, Ann spoke to the teacher about fearfulness in regard to what her husband might do when he learned of the move and divorce. Like Becker, Dean couldn't believe it when Ann failed to attend open house on April 23.

In contrast to Ann's interactive participation in Katelin's education, Dean said, she saw very little interest from John Racz.

Beth Silverman asked, "If Ann Racz was going to go away and take a vacation, would you have expected her to let you know?"

"Absolutely," the teacher replied.

Darryl Mounger's cross-examination revealed nothing new.

Informed trial observers had been looking forward to hearing what Pastor Glenn Thorp would say in testimony. Would he claim confidentiality, or would he answer questions with the "whole" truth? Thorp took the stand before noon.

He told Beth Silverman that he met Ann Racz in 1989 when he formed a new church. Using the present tense, he described her as "a very lovely, caring woman who really loved life, loved her children, loved faith, was a giving person. . . . She was very well organized, with her life pretty well planned. She watched over her children."

The marital discord came to Thorp's attention in 1990 through counseling sessions with Ann. "She was concerned about her marriage. She felt she was being suffocated and controlled. She was looking at other options in her life." According to Thorp, he had tried to rehabilitate her relationship with John. Silverman asked for details about Ann's dissatisfaction. Thorp replied, "She felt that she was being controlled by her husband and being forced to do things she didn't want to do." That included their sex life, he said.

"Did she also express to you that she was fearful?"

"Yes. She said that when she talked about leaving, her husband would threaten her and say, 'I'll come find you wherever you are and I'll stop you from leaving.'"

"Did she also confide in you that she had begun a new relationship with another man?"

Thorp hesitated a moment, and answered, "She told me about a friend that she had, that she had met a couple of times. And that's all I really knew at the time." Silverman pressed for more, and Thorp said, "She told me the relationship was intensifying. I don't think she ever used the word 'love.' I kept telling her, over and over again, to be careful and to remember that she was married."

Silverman wanted the jury to understand the issue of privacy between counselors and clients. "Do you believe in the duty as a minister, as a counselor, as a pastor, that it's your responsibility to keep confidences of your congregation?"

"Absolutely."

"Do you also balance that with other concerns?"

"Yeah. I definitely do that. But at the time, I would say that confidentiality was the number one issue in my life."

Moving away from that theme, Silverman drew from Thorp information that Ann had always advised him in advance before traveling anywhere, including her destination and how long she would be gone. Often she had sent him postcards. She had mentioned nothing about a trip in April 1991, and he hadn't heard from her since.

In regard to the divorce, Thorp said he understood Ann's intentions to keep physical custody of the children, but she would agree to visitation arrangements. The pastor readily talked about counseling sessions with both Ann and John. John, he said, was a very controlling person who wanted to stop her from leaving, and the guns he kept in their home had worried Ann. Thorp quoted John saying, "I'm going to stop you, whatever it's going to take."

Beth drove home the point with her next question, "Did Ann confide in you that her husband had threatened to kill her if she left?"

"Yes."

Thorp told of plans made on Sunday, April 21, the day before Ann vanished, to have weekly meetings with the couple. Hoping to salvage their marriage, he set the next session for April 25. But when she drove him home on that Sunday night, it turned out to be the last time he would ever see or hear from Ann Racz.

Beth Silverman's questioning of Pastor Thorp used the remainder of the court's shortened day, until Judge Coen announced at noon they would be in recess until Monday morning at nine-thirty.

Settling again into the witness chair, on June 25, Pastor Thorp answered Silverman's direct-examination questions, and told jurors of his extreme surprise when John Racz called him on the day there were supposed to meet, to say that Ann wouldn't be able to make it. The defendant came to the meeting by himself, Thorp said, and "was seemingly sweaty. He had some scratches on his face. Also one on his right hand. They looked fairly new."

"Do you recall describing them to detectives as fingernail scratches?" Silverman inquired.

"I said that could be a possibility, yes. . . . As time went on and it was obvious that Ann was not coming back, I started to get a sick-in-the-stomach feeling and began to reflect on some of those things and thought they may have been significant. I called the detectives."

His concern about Ann, said the pastor, deepened further

by a call from Dee Ann Wood, plus subsequent telephone conversations with Emi Ryan and Bob Russell finally drove Thorp to make a missing person report. The next day, May 2, Thorp told the jury, he drove to the Fortuna house and talked with John Racz.

As jurors watched intensely, Silverman inquired, "Did you ask the defendant questions with respect to the last time he saw Ann Racz?"

"I did. He said that they had gotten into a pretty strong argument and it was not a pleasant sight. He said it took place in the driveway of their home." Reporters and insiders realized that this conflicted sharply with other accounts by the defendant in which he repeatedly claimed to have last seen Ann in a restaurant when he gave her money. Thorp continued, "He became angry. In fact, at one point, I would call it almost rage. . . . It was like 'How dare she leave me.' And 'How dare she, you know, even think about anything other than being with me. . . .' His face was red. The enlarged blood vessels in his neck . . . clenched fists."

"Did he seem at all concerned for Ann?"

"He seemed to be more concerned, in my opinion, for himself."

"During this time when you said the defendant became almost enraged, were you at all concerned for your own safety?"

"Yes. And as a matter of fact, we met in their garage and the garage door was open. I felt comforted that people could see what was going on."

"When you saw this anger, were you able to connect that with the intimidation that Ann Racz had spoken to you about?"

"Absolutely."

When the defense team raised objections, spectators soon saw Beth Silverman's adept way of handling these obstacles and turning them to her advantage. Her mastery of the law and ability to think on her feet gained respect from veteran trial watchers.

She asked the witness about seeing Racz at a school sporting event. Thorp said he tried to learn more about Ann's disappearance. Racz, he said, talked about meeting Ann at a Jack in the Box, giving her money, and suggesting she get away and think things over. A second meeting had taken place at Tips, with yet another gift of money.

Earlier in her questioning of Thorp, Silverman had skirted the issue of confidentiality and the decision facing the pastor to speak out or remain silent. Now she revisited it. Beth asked, "When you first spoke to detectives back in 1991, did you have some concerns with respect to divulging certain information?"

"Yes, I did. Because part of the responsibility of a pastor is confidentiality with their members. And I did not want to divulge anything that had been told to me in private."

"At some point in time as this trial approached, did you make a decision to divulge those confidences?"

"I did," Thorp said, and asserted that it was the first time in his career he had even considered such a thing.

"Given what you have told us so far, why is it that you have decided to be forthcoming with respect to the things that Ann Racz and John Racz told you?"

"Because I understand that once a person is dead, the confidentiality ceases."

Philip Israels conducted the cross-examination. Beginning with Thorp's credentials as a counselor, the defender decided to attack the characterization of his client as controlling. He asked, "You knew about the trips Ann had taken? You knew that she had gone in 1989 without John and the family to Europe and Russia?" Thorp said he knew. "Now, would that indicate to you that a spouse who would let his wife . . . go on a trip like that, would that indicate he was controlling or not controlling?"

Thorp replied, "I would say neither one. He allowed her to

have freedom. . . . I wouldn't say it was anything more than he gave her permission to do it."

Israels made another thrust. "All right. How about in 1990, you heard about the reunion that she went to, didn't you?" The pastor said he couldn't recall it. "Okay," said Israels, "let's just imagine for a moment that she went to a reunion. . . . A person goes to a reunion, but when her spouse wants to go along, she says, 'No, you stay home and take care of the kids. . . .' The question would be, in that situation . . . would you describe the spouse that stayed home as controlling or not controlling?"

Thorp shot back, "I don't think that has anything to do with it, honestly."

Undiscouraged, Israels cited Ann's busy schedule of school activities, involvement in church functions, homeowners' association duties, and asked, "So the person who does all those things outside the home, would that indicate that she was being controlled?"

"I think it was her way of trying to find independence," Thorp answered. "Trying to discover what she wanted to do, apart from when her husband wasn't around the house."

"Would you also say that was true about her Monday Flowers business?"

"Same answer."

"Okay, but a spouse, again, who would let his wife have a business like this, which really made no money at all, would you say that showed he was controlling?"

"I don't think it's relevant."

Thorp gave none of the replies the defense apparently hoped for, yet they may have scored points anyway. Their objective—to plant the seed of reasonable doubt in jurors' minds—might have made some headway, despite admonitions that questions are not evidence, only the answers are.

Israels inquired if Thorp knew of any abuse in the marriage.

"What I knew of was not physical abuse," he answered.

Zeroing in on Thorp's earlier vague allusions to Bob Russell,

Israels asked if Ann was being less than honest with Thorp about the romance. He answered, "It wasn't a matter of she trying to keep something from me. She told [me] she had met Bob a couple of times, and that was all. Later on, I learned more."

"Did she tell you she was having sex with him?"

"No."

Turning the page again, Israels inquired, "Did she ever say to you that she was willing to leave the two older kids with John and just take the younger child?" Thorp said no and Israels let it drop. He wanted to go back to one of the main planks of the defense platform. "Let me ask you, did the prosecution or law enforcement ever let you read the letters she wrote to Bob Russell?"

"I have never read anything."

The next two dozen questions bounced around like a pinball, touching on previous subjects. Israel wanted to know more about Thorp's change of view regarding confidentiality and pushed him to tell names of people with whom he had consulted on the issue. The pastor finally revealed that he had asked Beth Silverman if confidentiality legally extended beyond a person's death. He had received the advice that it no longer applied in that case.

Finally, the defense attorney said, "I have no further questions."

On redirect Beth Silverman laid a brief foundation about people who sometimes say things offhandedly, during moments of frustration, that they really don't mean. She asked, "Do women often mention something like that to you in counseling? Do they come to you and say, 'You know what, I'm tired. And sometimes I have these moments where I'd like to— I don't know—cash in my motherhood card and take a break for five minutes?'"

"Yes."

"And these women at the same time, is that somehow inconsistent with being a good mother and loving their children?"

"Not at all."

The clock ticked close to twelve, and Judge Coen called for a lunch break.

With jurors rested from the morning's onslaught of information, Beth Silverman continued her redirect exam of Dr. Thorp at 1:30 P.M. Many of her questions sought his opinion about conditions that would have changed any of his testimony. If, hypothetically, he knew that Ann had met Bob Russell numerous times, or if she had sexual intercourse with him at any time, would that have changed his testimony? To each inquiry, he answered no.

The prosecutor also managed to bring out a new fact. "Do you recall taking notes with respect to the April twenty-fifth meeting you had with the defendant?"

"Yes."

"Do you recall what—if anything—he told you that you actually wrote down in your notes?"

"That Ann had left and wasn't coming back." Observers felt as if a low-voltage shock had rippled through the room.

Israels's cross-exam appeared to aim at Thorp's honesty, but made little headway. The witness said, "I've tried to tell the truth as best I recall it. I've tried to be an honest witness and that's all I have tried to do." When excused, Pastor Thorp walked out of the courtroom, with an expression of relief on his face.

CHAPTER 26

INTIMATE MATTERS

When Ann moved out on April 18, she employed a local company to help. Beth Silverman summoned Robert Green, the owner, to testify. Before dispatching his two employees, Green said, he had informed them of the need to complete the job as fast as possible. He hadn't personally been present at the Fortuna house on that day, but he heard from his men what had happened.

That evening, and in the following days, the witness recalled, Mr. Racz had called him several times, wanting to know Ann's address, but he refused to divulge it. "It wasn't a very nice conversation, because he was very upset." Green maintained a policy of never revealing a customer's new location, especially in cases of marital discord, which occurred frequently. "These days," he stated, "I don't think I could be in business if it wasn't for divorces." His full testimony took no more than ten minutes.

Brenda George, the Raczes' neighbor from whom John had

borrowed children's clothing after Ann left, came next. She told Beth Silverman that she and Ann had been very good friends, but Ann hadn't told her in advance of plans to move out. She telephoned soon afterward to let her know, and to say that she was afraid of her husband. During a visit to the Peachland condo, a couple of days later, Ann had asked her not to tell John of the location. "She was frightened, but also resolute."

On the following Sunday, April 21, said Brenda, she had seen Ann park in the Fortuna driveway and have a conversation with John, who stood outside the minivan. Its brakelights remained lit the whole time. About eight o'clock that evening, Ann arrived again, and the scene repeated itself.

The witness told Silverman that it took several days after April 22 before she learned of Ann's unexplained absence. Brenda said she spoke to John often that week and complied with his request for her to pick up his children from school every day. She had also allowed John to borrow her own kids' clothing for them. On Tuesday, April 23, Brenda recalled, John had telephoned in the early afternoon to say he would be a little late coming home. It puzzled her, because she knew he had taken the remainder of that week off from work. He didn't show up until seven o'clock that night.

Not until that Friday did Brenda realize Ann had disappeared. Telephone conversations with Emi Ryan and Dee Ann Wood, said Brenda, sent them all into a frenzy of calling everyone they knew to seek information about Ann. And Brenda drew the duty of asking John Racz what he knew about it. She made the call that night, expressed her worry, and heard his brief comments about Ann being safe. The witness quoted John's statement "When I think that she may not come back, it makes me want to cry."

The jury had heard repeated allusions to Ann's travels, but Brenda gave them information for the first time about John's trips. "He would go and visit his family in New Jersey."

"Would he travel alone?"

"Yes."

Judge Coen announced the evening recess with an order for jurors and the witness to return on the following morning, Tuesday, June 26.

With Brenda George again in the witness chair, Philip Israels asked, "Would it be a fair statement—from the very beginning, you were suspicious of John in where Ann had gone?" No, said Brenda. The defense inquired about Ann's travels, then asked if she knew that each of John's trips to New Jersey had lasted no longer than a week, but she had no idea.

"You knew that Ann had a lover?"

"I knew that she had a boyfriend, but I'm not actually clear if I knew it before her disappearance or after."

Israels wanted to know if Brenda could imagine Ann ever indicating weariness of raising children and that she might just leave the older kids with John and take the younger one. The witness replied that "she and I did everything with our children."

Beth Silverman took over again and asked about moms sometimes complaining about kids. Brenda said, "Many mothers of young children say, 'This is it, I'm going in the bathroom and closing the door for the whole day.' And it's all in jest, but we all understand. It's very difficult to raise small children. So when people say something like that, it's not necessarily a serious threat."

Israels objected to her answer and asked the judge to strike it, but he had not voiced his objection properly. Judge Coen ruled, "Hearing no grounds, it's denied."

Trying to make up lost ground, Israels shouted, "Relevance."

"Too late, Counsel," Coen stated.

Brenda's comments would probably go a long way in nullifying defense suggestions that Ann had hinted of wanting to get away from child-rearing responsibilities. She stepped down.

The next two witnesses, Jessica Priddy and Jacqueline Leonard, worked for banks around Valencia in 1991, and testified about investments, accounts, and transactions conducted by John and Ann Racz. They confirmed withdrawals Ann had made from certificates of deposit and deposits she had made to her Monday Flowers business checking account. Also, they verified a loan John Racz had obtained. One of the witnesses said that John had not been an easy customer to deal with. "He would come in at closing time and demand that we open the door and let him conduct his business. It was easier for us to let him in, let him conduct his business, and let him go. But he would take such a long time. I mean, it was just one thing after another. . . . You know, we wanted to go home. We had our families."

The same witness recalled that Racz, sometime after April 22, groused about his wife, saying, "What a bitch." He had also asked, "Do you know what it's like being married to a bitch?"

On cross, Darryl Mounger brought out detective's notes, observing that no such comment had been mentioned to them, but the witness said that it happened after she had spoken to the investigator. Mounger also tried to smooth over the alleged behavior of his client in demanding service at closing time. The defense asked if other clients came in late too. "No," said the witness. "He was the only one, then we had to listen to his mouth." Mounger objected and Judge Coen ordered the comment to be stricken. But in the old courtroom cliché, it's hard to un-ring a bell, and the jury had definitely heard this one chime loud and clear.

References had been made in opening statements to the Presbyterian Church women's circle to which Ann had belonged. Now the jury would hear for the first time from one of those women. Roberta Bailey took the oath and said she had first joined the group on April 16, 1991. At that meeting, she recalled hearing Ann Racz speak. "She was afraid and asking us to pray for her strength and safety. She was a little concerned about what the next couple of weeks would bring. She was afraid of her husband, afraid of what he might do. But she had finally decided that she needed to leave him for her safety."

No, said Bailey to Beth's next question, Ann had not mentioned any plans for taking a vacation, or for abandoning her children.

Defender Israels's questions established that the witness could recall hearing Ann frankly telling of her troubles, but she couldn't remember hearing anything about her having a lover. Nor could Bailey recall Ann specifically saying that John was going to follow her and kill her.

After a brief sidebar discussion, the prosecution called Compton School District principal Peter Danna, now retired, as their next witness. He told of receiving a phone call from John Racz, who worked for him then, on the afternoon of April 18, 1991, to report that his wife and children had left him. Racz had requested some time off to deal with it. Then he had asked, "Do you think I'm the kind of guy who would be violent? Do you think I'm a mean person? Do you think I'm the kind of person who would hurt somebody?" Danna had answered no to all three questions, and granted John permission to be away from the job.

Racz didn't return to work until April 29. On his first day back, Danna noticed a scratch mark on John's neck, which might have been made by a raking fingernail. Also, Danna heard Racz claim that he had made a missing person report about his wife.

To the prosecutors, this exhibited a direct lie told by John Racz, and they hoped it registered with the jury.

The defense got Danna to say that the scratches he observed on Racz's neck, on April 29, could have been only two or three days old, meaning they might have been inflicted after Ann vanished.

Cheryl Freet, who with her husband had owned and managed the Peachland condominium rented by Ann Racz, came next. She said that Ann had specifically asked never to call her at the Fortuna house. Messages could be left with her niece Kathy Ryan. Freet said that she and her husband had left a note for Ann on the night of April 22 regarding some repairs they planned to do in the condo. Ann never replied to it.

Another court day had reached its closing time, and Judge Coen called for the evening recess.

On Wednesday, June 27, 2007, the jury waited in the hall while all four lawyers met with Judge Coen to discuss the 109 letters Ann Racz had written to Bob Russell. Darryl Mounger indicated he wanted to introduce all of them into evidence. Coen said he would read them during the day's lunch break and make a ruling.

Back in session, the prosecution called Patricia Fulton, another member of the church circle, who said that on April 16, 1991, Ann Racz had been the designated leader for that particular meeting. She had chosen the discussion topic "Taking Risks." Ann told the group that she had made a very risky decision, to leave her husband, John, and to take her children with her. The women learned about the condo, Ann's moving day, and her filing for divorce. And they heard Ann express her fears.

Fulton told the jury that Ann always got rides to the airport from friends or relatives, and never used a public facility, such as the Flyaway. And Ann advised her friends in advance of the exact time frames she planned to travel. In that April meeting, she said nothing about any upcoming trip.

The defense asked if the circle had talked about Ann's boyfriend or possible solutions to her problems other than divorce. The witness said many topics had been discussed briefly.

After lunch, before allowing the jury to be reseated, Coen held a conference with all four lawyers to discuss whether or not Ann Racz's 109 letters to Bob Russell should be admitted into evidence. The defense fought hard to have every letter allowed, but Silverman saw no legal reason for admitting them. Coen, at last, suggested a compromise allowing limited segments into play. They reached no agreement, and Judge Coen, leaning toward excluding them all, said he would decide later.

Theresa Thomas, a librarian from Hart High School, stepped from the gallery up to the witness chair. The school was named after silent-film star William S. Hart, hero of countless Westerns, who had lived in Santa Clarita, where his hilltop home, now a museum surrounded by a large park, stood less than a mile away.

Thomas testified that Ann Racz had been a regular volunteer worker in her library, and that Joann Racz had attended the school. Knowing that Theresa had gone through a divorce, Ann had confided all about her unhappy marriage and consulted with her about divorcing John. "I gave her advice about planning ahead so there would not be an uproar, only a smooth transition," Thomas said. She had also suggested that Ann prepare things to be moved in advance, and carry it out while her husband was gone. The whole blueprint for Ann's moving day had been inspired by Theresa Thomas.

Silverman asked, "Did she tell you about the fears she had?"

"She told me she was afraid of her husband, that he had threatened to kill her if she ever tried to leave. And I know people say crazy things when they go through a divorce. I said, 'Ann, don't take that for real. People just go crazy during a divorce.' And she said, 'But he has a gun.' And that's when I realized she was really afraid. I wish I had taken it more seriously."

It had stunned Theresa Thomas when Ann didn't show up for an open house at the end of April. The witness said she had the greatest respect for Ann's dedication as a responsible parent who would never abandon her children.

After a brief cross-examination, Theresa Thomas stepped down.

Mohammad Islam, from Bangladesh, raised his hand to take the oath and divulged his job as parking supervisor at Van Nuys Flyaway. In faltering English, he said, "People leave their car to the parking lot and take the Flyaway bus, go to the LAX airport." John Lewin struggled with syntax in asking questions of the witness, but finally had Islam identify the yellow parking ticket found in Ann's car, issued April 25, 1991, at ten o'clock in the morning. "Customer pull that ticket from machine, gate open automatically, customer get in, and the gate close." The machine, he said, is called a "spitter." The witness verified that no trees or buildings in the lot in 1991 existed to provide shady parking.

Having trouble establishing his point, Lewin made a request of Judge Coen. "I would like the court to take judicial notice of the fact that the sun moves over the course of a parking lot in a day, and that, therefore, as a matter of accurate determination from scientific reading, that the sun cannot and does not stay in one direct location throughout the day." Observers wondered if legalities could get any sillier.

The judge said, "I can take judicial notice the sun rises in the east and sets in the west. That's as far as that goes." His tongue appeared to be solidly lodged in his cheek.

Darryl Mounger got agreement from Islam that some customers park large vehicles, like motor homes, in the lot for long terms. These might provide temporary shade.

After Islam left, Coen gave the jurors a fifteen-minute break at the prosecution's request for another conference. Once again, they had a complex, heated discussion of the letters Ann had written to Bob Russell. The judge made one modification in his ruling that most of the letters would be inadmissible. The final letter, written by Ann on April 21, would be allowed.

A quiet buzz rippled through the audience when Beth Silverman called her next witness, Bob Russell. He spoke of knowing Ann since their high-school days, during which they dated a few times, then lost contact as they went on with their separate lives. After they reconnected in 1989, when he sent her a Christmas card, the relationship grew again, mostly through letters and phone calls. Russell told the whole story, including his understanding of her unhappiness with John Racz, and their meetings in the Bay Area, San Diego, and Valencia. They had plans to spend the future together, he said.

Russell knew about Ann's move to the condo, he testified, and her plans to stay there at least six months or until the divorce became final. With her financial settlement, Russell said, and proceeds from his own house he planned to sell, they looked forward to acquiring a home large enough to accommodate her three children and his one daughter.

His voice cracking, Russell spoke of a telephone conversation with Ann on Friday, April 19, and said, "She was exuberant." She called again—for the final time—on Sunday, and seemed both happy and content with her move to the condo. Using tissues, the witness dabbed at his moist eyes.

"Did she ever mention at that point in time that she was thinking about taking any sort of trip or vacation?" Silverman asked.

"No, not at all." But they did plan a small trip of their own. "We were going to Disneyland for my daughter's fifth birthday. And I asked her to bring Katelin and her other two children."

Russell had even made airline and hotel reservations for June 2. Of course, Ann had been missing nearly six weeks by that time.

Ann's final letter, dated April 21, but postmarked April 22, reached Russell after she disappeared. Silverman handed it to the witness and asked him to read it aloud. He complied. As soon as he finished, Judge Coen called for the evening recess, and ordered resumption of the trial on the next day.

Russell settled into the chair, again, Thursday morning. To Silverman's questions, he spoke of receiving no more phone calls or letters from Ann after the one dated April 21, although he had sent several to her pleading for a response from her as soon as possible. Within a few days, Dee Ann Wood telephoned and informed Russell that no one had heard from Ann since April 22. "That's when I realized the worst, in my mind," he said. Eventually Detectives Danoff and Salerno flew up north, interviewed him, and, with his permission, took the 109 letters she had written.

"Subsequently, did you tell law enforcement that you became fearful for your own life?" Silverman asked. Yes, Russell answered, and it lasted for a long period of time.

In her questioning, Silverman read aloud small portions of a few more letters—as allowed by Judge Coen to show Ann's state of mind, specific future intentions, and actions in accordance with that intent. He prohibited all other content of the private correspondence.

Cross-examining, Philip Israels brought up Russell's documented statements to investigators. He acknowledged having expressed at one time some concerns about taking responsibility for all three of Ann's children. Probing a little deeper, the defender asked, "You knew that John and Ann were still having sex?" Both Silverman and Lewin raised objections, and the judge sustained them. However, he allowed the next question, "Isn't it true you told Detective Danoff and Detective Salerno that you started having sex with her the second time you guys got together?"

Russell said, "I'm trying to recall. I might have said that. Yes."

To the proposition that one of the detectives had persuaded Russell of John Racz's guilt in murdering Ann, Russell replied, "No, he didn't convince me. To tell the truth, I was suspicious before that."

Perhaps unhappy with that bit of information, Israels returned to several questions about the sexual relationship. Judge Coen sustained objections to an inquiry about being able to see the Valencia hotel, where Ann and Bob had spent one night, from the Racz residence. But did that image brand itself in jurors' minds?

Handing Russell the envelope in which Ann's last letter had been sent, Israels asked him to read the date and postmark. The witness complied, saying, "The twenty-second of April, 'ninety-one," and "Marina del Rey."

Judge Coen interjected, "This witness can't testify where this item was posted from." That information would have to come from an expert on the matter.

Still intent on airing the intimate matters, Israels asked a series of questions about the meeting between Ann and Bob on Thanksgiving, 1990, in San Diego. Objections filled the air again. Israels inquired, "Did you tell your daughter when [Ann] came to visit you in Northern California that she was a married woman?"

Without a word from the prosecutors, Judge Coen snapped, "Sustained."

Unfazed, Israels continued. "You knew . . . when you met Ann at the [hotel in Valencia] that her husband didn't know about it?"

Objection! Sustained.

"Do you remember taking her to your parents' home?" Yes.

"Did you tell your parents this was your lover?"

Objection. Sustained.

"Did you know whether or not Ann told her husband about your affair with her?"

Sustained!

"Wasn't there a certain deception going on?"

Objection! Sustained.

Russell admitted that he sent mail to Ann via her Monday Flowers mailbox. "That way John wouldn't know about the correspondence. Isn't that correct?" Israels asked.

Objection. Sustained.

"Did Ann ever tell you she was pregnant?"

The prosecution objected again, on the grounds of relevancy, and asked Judge Coen if they could approach the bench. Silverman whispered at the sidebar, "I think we have crossed a line . . . given there is no evidence to support it."

Lewin added, "To stand up and ask an inflammatory question like this, with the years of experience Mr. Israels has, without having cleared it with the court, not only shows disrespect I think to counsel and myself, but disrespects the court. And it is improper."

Turning to the defender, Coen asked, "What is the relevance?"

Israels explained, "The relevance is his state of mind. After she told him of the pregnancy, he stopped writing her . . . for several weeks."

"There was never a pregnancy," Beth protested.

Arguing his point, Israels said, "We are at a disadvantage here. He would not cooperate with our investigator. How are we supposed to find these things out?"

Fiery in her contempt, Silverman said, "That doesn't mean it's a free-for-all in front of the jury."

Judge Coen, voice calm, said, "I understand. Sustained on those grounds."

One of the jurors spoke aloud. "Your Honor, I apologize for the interruption, I have a question on the multiple letters read by the prosecution not being entered—"

Coen instantly interrupted. "Excuse me. You are not allowed to ask questions. I know what I'm doing." The blushing juror replied, "Understood. Thank you."

The room-rocking turbulence settled down. But after a few minutes of peace, Israels's interrogation raised more objections.

"Do you remember telling the investigators in 1991 that you at first thought Ann seemed a little obsessive?"

Objection. Sustained.

At one point in his queries, Israels referred to Sergeant Dee Scott as "Miss Scott," and Detective Danoff as "Louis Danoff." John Lewin took exception. "I'm going to object to the reference to Detective Danoff. Mrs. Scott is not Miss Scott. It's Detective Sergeant Scott. Louis Danoff is Detective Danoff."

Without betraying any impatience in his voice, if he felt it, Coen replied, "I will allow counsel to call the witnesses whatever he wishes."

Regarding any fear Bob Russell may have felt, Israels asked, "John never harassed you, did he?"

No, Russell said. Nor had John Racz ever contacted, accosted, or harmed him in any way.

On redirect Beth Silverman established a level of clarification about allegations that Ann might have agreed to let John Racz keep the two older children. Russell agreed that she had been adamant in her wish to keep custody of all three children and would fight for that.

After a few more queries from both sides, and several more objections, Bob Russell appeared relieved when Judge Coen said, "Thank you, sir. You are excused."

CHAPTER 27

"SHE WAS IMMACULATE."

The next two witnesses spent only a short time testifying. Joanne Yokote, Ann's cousin who lived in Hawaii, told jurors that none of the large network of relatives in Hilo and Honolulu had heard from Ann since she vanished. Had she taken refuge on the Islands, they certainly would have known about it and shared the information.

Next, Donna Bruhn, Glenn Racz's fifth-grade teacher spoke of Ann's dedicated participation in school activities, and said that Ann's children ranked at the very top of the mother's priorities. She had sought out Bruhn, a single mom, to ask what it was like to be in that role. They had conversed about it only a week or two before Ann vanished. On that occasion, Bruhn said, she had dropped off some material at the Fortuna house. Ann had a special talent for calligraphy, which she often used on diplomas and awards, and this is what took Bruhn to her friend's home. Their exchange and conversation took place on the front sidewalk.

"As far as I could determine, she was uncomfortable. She was looking around," said Bruhn. They planned to have lunch together to chat more about single parenthood, but it never took place.

The defense had no questions.

Pam Cottrel, a science teacher and member of the church's Elizabeth circle, replaced Bruhn in the witness chair. As other friends had, Cottrel lauded Ann's dependability, love for her children, and interest in their education. The witness also complimented Ann's appearance. "She always had her makeup and hair perfect. Everything was coordinated." And she never wore the same clothing day after day.

Asked about the group's meeting on April 16, Cottrel said that Ann had been designated to lead it that day. "She apologized to us and said that other things had happened in her life and she didn't have the lesson prepared. She was making a major decision in her life. . . . She was going to seek a divorce from her husband."

Silverman asked about Ann's demeanor that day. The witness replied, "I observed that she was nervous. When she would speak about her husband, her eyes would get kind of big. She was a little pale and seemed unsettled about this momentous thing. . . . She was very afraid."

Did she indicate what she feared?

"She said she was afraid her husband was going to kill her."

Asked if Ann had offered any details, Cottrel said, "She was worried about guns in the household, and was afraid he was going to shoot her or the children once this divorce situation came to light." Cottrel had been reluctant to see Ann's point of view at the time, she said. "I was on [the] rifle team for the University of Toledo. My husband was on the Ohio

Pistol Team. We are both competition shooters, grew up with guns in the household, and I took offense that she would say because we had guns in the house, that he might hurt her. I argued with her about that."

How did Ann respond to that?

"She said he would sit in a dark room and tell her he was planning something. He was planning the perfect crime and she felt—"

Philip Israels jumped up. "Objection, Your Honor. Motion to strike. May we approach?" At sidebar, in the usual sotto voce conversation, he complained that the defense had never received discovery on this subject.

Beth Silverman contradicted him.

Questioning of the witness resumed, and Cottrel said that Ann thought John was planning to murder her. . . . She wanted to get herself and her children away from what she considered a threatening situation. And she wanted custody of the kids.

"Did Ann Racz discuss with you his temper?" Silverman asked.

"She said he had a violent temper. That's why she felt when she let him know she was divorcing him, that he would become violent."

"Did you also note what was going on in the area near Carl's Jr. and McDonald's?"

"Quite a bit of construction. Houses and condos in various stages. And a lot of earth being moved—a lot of concrete being poured." During the initial investigation, she had brought this to the attention of Sergeant Salerno and Detective Danoff, on the possibility that it might help lead to finding Ann. After that, Cottrel lost track of the case when she moved to Ohio with her military pilot husband.

Recounting how Ann had spelled out her fears and John's evils, Israels asked Cottrel why she hadn't called the police when she heard of this. The witness explained that she had been only one of several women in that room, and felt like she was on the periphery. However, she had "touched base" before leaving town.

Among all of Ann's relatives and friends, three women knew her most intimately: her sister, Emi, Emi's daughter Kathy Gettman, and Dee Ann Wood. Observers waited eagerly to hear from them.

Kathy walked through the barrier gate next, and swore to tell the truth. Answering Beth Silverman, she said that she and her aunt Ann had been exceptionally close, and she had lived in the Fortuna house spare bedroom for three months, in 1988. During that time, she said, she observed the relationship between Ann and John. "It did not appear to be a loving couple, like I have seen exhibited with other married people." They seemed "distant." She characterized John as "controlling, wanting things done his way. He was the one who set the rules." Kathy gave jurors examples of John's parsimonious methods in use of toilets, air-conditioning, and trash disposal. She said Ann had to beg for extra money to buy special food for holidays. John would sneak out extra portions from buffet restaurants, and even brought plates home.

"Paper plates?"

"No. The ceramic plates."

More confirmation came from Kathy about Ann's devotion to her children, meticulous organization, and dependability. Kathy also let jurors know that Ann would never have traveled without certain cosmetic items, changes of clothing, and her curling iron, nor had she ever traveled alone. Someone always provided her aunt with transportation to the airport, said the trembling niece, and Ann had never used the Flyaway parking facility. One other assertion by Kathy lent to the growing mountain of evidence that Ann's life had ended—she never failed to send birthday cards to all members of her family.

The court day closed with Kathy still on the stand, and Judge Coen ordered her to return on Friday, June 29.

Before testimony resumed the next morning, Judge Coen informed jurors they would have a full week off. "We will next be in session on July ninth. So, if I order you back on Monday, please remind me."

Beth Silverman continued her interrogation of Kathy Gettman, bringing out evidence found inside the condo that Ann had planned on returning the evening of Monday, April 22, 1991, to prepare pizza for her kids, and to continue the daily routine matters of her life.

Asked by Silverman if John Racz ever did anything to help find Ann, Kathy replied, "Not that I had ever seen. In fact, I asked him why doesn't he call the sheriff's department more often, or call at all to check what was going on? He said he didn't have time."

An incident in late December 1991 stuck with Kathy. With Emi, she had entered Racz's house to pick up the kids, and noticed a birthday card on the fireplace mantel. Kathy read handwritten words on it saying, *For my husband.* They both examined it closer, saw the signature *Ann,* but realized that it bore no resemblance to Ann Racz's neat handwriting. John's birthday was in October. Why it had been placed there remained a mystery.

Cross-examination by Israels established that Kathy felt suspicious of Racz soon after Ann vanished. The defender moved on to Ann's travels without her husband, but objections, all sustained, prevented her answers about who paid for the trips. To many of his questions, Kathy seemed combative and said she couldn't remember. She did recall driving by the Flyaway several times to see if Ann's car remained there. Israels asked if a car parked next to a large vehicle sometimes had shade. Wrinkling her face, Kathy said, "Yeah, that would be the general thing that would happen with the sun moving."

As he had with other witnesses, Israels brought up Ann's liaison with Bob Russell. "Did you know they had a sexual relationship?"

"No."

"Did you know she was making phone calls to this friend from your house?"

"Yes."

"You knew that this was something she was keeping from John?"

"Yes."

On a roll, Israel elicited answers indicating that numerous people knew of the pending divorce, but John didn't. From there he tackled the issue of physical abuse. "You never heard from Ann that John had hit her?"

"Hit her? No. Broke his arm hitting something? Yes."

Judge Coen called for a lunch break. When court resumed, the prosecution offered a stipulation, agreed to by the defense, that Ann Racz's Monday Flowers bank account, containing $3,628.48, had been abandoned and never collected. Several jurors made entries in their notebooks.

Trying to establish that Racz's money-saving measures in use of water and electricity may have been nothing more than conscientious conservation efforts, Israels quizzed Kathy repeatedly, but made little headway, mostly due to sustained objections.

Beth Silverman took over on redirect. Emphasizing that Kathy and Emi had worked closely with investigators in the hunt for Ann, Silverman asked, "At any point in time . . . did the defendant ever accompany the search parties?"

"No."

After a few more inquiries by Beth, and no further questions by the defense, Kathy Gettman was allowed to rejoin observers in the gallery.

Thomas Deardorff, who lived in the third house down Fortuna Drive from the Racz home, stepped up to take the oath. With the bearing of an executive, and a confident look in his light-colored eyes, he looked too young to have lived there twenty-nine years and to be the father of an adult daughter. Deardorff described the neighborhood, the casual relationship with Racz, and said that Joann sometimes babysat for his daughter back in 1991. The witness knew Ann well enough to testify about her stellar involvement in school activities, church, and conscientious care of her children.

On the afternoon of April 22, while washing one of his restored cars, he had noticed Ann driving away from the Racz house, waved her down, and asked if Joann still planned to babysit that night. Ann had said, "No problem, she will be there." Then Ann said she had to go get the kids something to eat.

"After Ann left, do you recall making another observation?"

"Yes. I was still working in the driveway, and very shortly after she left, John drove down the street." He appeared to be following her. Deardorff said he continued working on his car at least an hour, and during that time, he never saw John return. Jurors again made entries in their notebooks.

Darryl Mounger conducted the cross-exam, and began by trying to cast doubt on the idea that John had been following Ann that day. The witness said he usually waves as neighbors pass by, and they wave back, including John. "But he didn't wave to me that day."

It didn't work either to suggest the witness might not have

noticed if John returned before an hour passed. "There was other people driving around, but I didn't see John, or Ann."

"Do you remember when you were first asked about this, how long it took for John to start following down the street, or leave to go down the street? Do you recall saying five to seven minutes?"

"I don't remember that, but that's what I've been told I said. But it wasn't that long, I'm sure." Mounger pointed out that Deardorff had told the grand jury it might have been three to five minutes, but he still insisted it wasn't even that long. The defense concluded by asking, "If you are leaving three to five minutes behind someone, you are not following them, right?"

Deardorff agreed. It remained to be seen if jurors did.

Larry Baker, Ann's divorce attorney, came next. He told Beth Silverman that Ann Racz, as his client, wished to dissolve the marriage, live temporarily in Peachland, then resettle somewhere with Bob Russell, with custody of her three children. And she had expressed fears of retaliation by John Racz, not necessarily for divorcing him, but as a result of being forced to divide all assets and for losing custody of the kids.

The witness confirmed Ann's fear that her husband would not let her leave. Because he heard nothing more from her after April 22, Baker tried to contact Ann several times, with no response. "Was she somewhat flaky, disorganized?" Silverman asked.

"Oh, God, no! No. She was immaculate. That's the first thought that came to my mind every time I think about her. She was immaculate. She would joke. She was very upbeat about what her future held for her."

On that note, Judge Coen called for adjournment, which would last a full week. Court would be in session again on

July 9. "Have a good Fourth of July, have a good week off, and I'll see you back here on the ninth."

Jurors appeared refreshed and alert when they settled into their chairs on Monday morning, July 9. One of the alternates, Barbara Kaplan, wore her usual smile and still hoped she might become a part of the primary twelve, who would render the final verdict.

Witness Larry Baker resumed the stand, and Beth Silverman, who had worked every minute while others rested, continued her direct examination. The witness had also spent some time with the case, reviewing transcripts from the grand jury indictment. It helped refresh his memory of talking to Ann Racz for the last time on April 19, 1991.

Recapping some of his earlier testimony, Silverman affirmed Baker's opinion that Ann would never have abandoned her children.

Philip Israels began his interrogation by establishing that no record existed of John Racz physically assaulting his wife or directly threatening to do so. And no requests had ever been made to obtain a restraining order against him.

"Did she tell you that she and John were having normal sexual relations right up to the last date?"

Silverman instantly objected and Judge Coen sustained it, but Israels asked to approach for a sidebar conference. These are usually whispered so jurors cannot hear the discussion. Israels began, "Your Honor, isn't it relevant that she should be telling—"

Silverman, known for sometimes being a bit noisy, said, "Maybe we can go outside if he's going to talk this loud."

Judge Coen, always cool, advised the defender, "The microphone is right here."

Beginning again, Israels said, "Isn't it relevant that she is telling all her friends at the church circle how abusive he is, and all of these threats and all of these things, and yet she's telling her attorney they are having normal sexual relations up to the very last moment, right up to the very last day before she goes to her attorney? Isn't there something inconsistent about that? It goes to our whole theory that this is a woman in conflict, that she is telling one thing to one person, and something else to somebody else."

With his usual dignity, Coen said, "The ruling stands."

Silverman spoke up. "Your Honor, just for the record—"

"There is no reason to respond," the judge advised.

Even feistier than usual, Silverman continued. "Well, I want it on the record. If they want to get into this whole issue, we have a bunch of witnesses who can testify she was talking about being forced to have sex every night. If they want to open the door."

"The word is 'normal sexual relations,' and that's what he (Baker) told Salerno and Danoff. It's in the notes," Israels countered.

In his most paternal manner, Judge Coen said, "As I stated, the ruling stands."

The lawyers retreated to their stations, and Israels addressed the witness, asking a series of questions having nothing to do with sex, but marriage counseling instead. More objections came, and he finally sat down.

Another very close friend of Ann Racz's, and a member of the church circle, became the next witness. Judy Carter, a tall, comely woman, told Beth Silverman that she had worked in 1991 as church secretary for Pastor Thorp in the Santa Clarita Presbyterian Church, but she attended meetings with Ann at the Newhall branch. Ann had worked alongside Judy in Thorp's office, at first as a volunteer, then later as a part-time employee.

Ann had confided in her about the marital problems and confessed to being afraid of John, Carter said. "She was quite fearful of him." Her fright, said Carter, may have stemmed from an
incident in which John lost his temper at her and broke his hand
against a door or a wall. Carter had also heard from Ann about
Bob Russell, and Ann gave her his telephone number to let Bob
know if anything happened to her. Carter said she had been at
the church circle meeting and heard what Ann had told the other
members. Like so many other witnesses, Carter felt that Ann's
primary interest revolved around her children.

Raising many of the same points he had emphasized throughout the trial, Israels added a new one: "Didn't she indicate she
was planning on leaving him in the summer of 1990, but she did
not want to mess up her European trip?"

"Yes."

In redirect, Silverman seized the subject of trips, using it
to obtain acknowledgments from Carter of Ann's meticulous
planning, of telling all of her friends in advance, and frequently sending cards or letters while traveling.

Sometimes in trials, the planned order of witness appearances must be modified to accommodate their need to travel
long distances. At the conclusion of Judy Carter's testimony,
with permission from prosecutors, the defense inserted their
first witness. Robin Dorr, Ann's travel agent, now living in
Illinois, had been contacted by a private detective investigating for the defense, and she had flown to California to testify.
Ostensibly, she had seen Ann at the travel agency in Valencia
after April 22, 1991. A storm of objections citing hearsay and
other procedural issues disjointed the questioning by Israels.
The witness seemed to be tying her sighting of Ann to a day
that a photocopy machine malfunctioned in the agency office,
April 23. However, she had difficulty stating with certainty
when the machine had been broken.

If Ann's visit to a travel agent, on or about the time she vanished, suggested to jurors that she really might have taken an extended trip, the prosecution undermined that with another admission from the witness. Ann had dropped in that day not to book a flight. Instead, she had heard about a contest advertised by a major airline and wanted a list of cities it served. Further, in cross-examination, the prosecutor asked, "When you were referring to April 23, 1991, isn't it true that appears to be *not* the day you were saying Ann came in, but the day of the contest drawing?"

"According to the notes I just saw today, yes."

Delivering one more crushing blow, the prosecutor asked Dorr to read aloud from notes made by Frank Salerno when he interviewed her. In a soft voice, Dorr read, "Missing person came in regarding [the airline] at end of March or first part of April."

The gambit had crashed and burned. The best Israels could do in resurrecting it consisted of asking the witness, "The point is, you really don't know when she came in?"

"Right," Dorr said, and stepped down soon afterward.

To clarify any possible confusion about notes detectives had made while interviewing Robin Dorr, the prosecution called Louis Danoff, now retired six years, to the stand. John Lewin referred to a blue-covered notebook containing Danoff's writing. He asked, "Is it fair to say if they were assigning penmanship grades, [you would get] probably not an A or a B?"

"I was going to be a doctor," Danoff quipped. For use in court, he had transcribed the scribbling into typewritten pages, and Danoff read aloud from them. His information confirmed that Ann Racz had asked the travel agent for a list of the airline's destinations so she could choose a city if she won a drawing to be held on April 23, 1991.

Danoff spent only a short time testifying, but he would return later in the trial.

First, though, a witness everyone had been waiting for came forward.

CHAPTER 28

"IS THIS HARD FOR YOU TO SAY?"

Every spectator had been eagerly waiting to hear from the three Racz children, all adults now. Their attention spiked when Joann, just five days short of turning thirty-one, took the witness chair. Having been summoned by the prosecution, it appeared that Joann would be testifying against her own father.

Under Silverman's questioning, Joann began by asserting that she still loved her dad. After identifying numerous photos of her extended family, Joann affirmed her parents' absence of affection for one another, their frequent arguments, her father's control of the money, and his "heavy" temper. She spoke hesitatingly, as if reluctant to criticize him. Pain appeared in her expression as she recalled moving to Peachland, the pending divorce, and the need to keep it all secret. Joann's stress grew more intense with mention of Ann's fear of retaliations from John. "She didn't want me to say anything, because if my dad found out, he might do something."

Joann's emotional struggle showed in her soft, wavering voice, frequent requests for Beth Silverman to repeat the questions, and stumbles in recounting the events from April 18, moving day, to April 22. Stress dimmed some of her recollections. By reviewing investigators' interview notes, she told of being picked up from school on that fateful Monday and going to the Fortuna house. En route, her mother had promised home-prepared pizza for dinner. Ann had not spoken of any planned trips.

Reciting her memories of that day, Joann said she went into the house to watch Glenn play Nintendo, while her mother stayed in the car for a conversation with her father, who stood at the driver's window. "I came out to the garage and I asked, 'When are we eating?'"

"Did you tell your parents you were hungry?"

"Yes. My mother said she would go get McDonald's." Joann recalled going back inside, after which, "My dad comes in and says that he will go get us food." But Joann did not have a "clear recollection" of how much time passed before he returned, only that he brought back "ice-cold" food. She did remember speaking by phone to her girlfriends.

Judge Coen shattered the courtroom tension when he announced the evening recess, and said they would skip Tuesday. Court would again be in session on Wednesday, July 11.

As ordered, everyone found their places on Wednesday morning, and Joann continued answering Silverman's questions, arriving again at the point where John Racz had brought back cold McDonald's food. Joann repeated that she fully expected her mother to return that day, take the kids to the condo, and have a pizza dinner, instead of disappearing into an invisible, silent vacuum.

Silverman cited a list of Ann's responsibilities and obtained Joann's agreement that it would be completely out of character for her to suddenly discontinue them. Ann's unprecedented failure to return had plunged Joann into a vortex of anxiety and worry, Joann told the court. Questions she had asked her father went unanswered or received repetitious, shallow replies about her going away on a trip to think. Desperate, she had called relatives and Ann's friends to seek help or information, but those efforts yielded nothing. With her girlfriends, Joann had stopped by the condo several times to see if her mother had been there, perhaps to pick up some of her clothing.

The frustration, Joann said, turned to anger. Within the first few days, she left sarcastic notes in the condo for her mother, if she came back. In one, Joann wrote, *All my stuff is gone. Believe me, this is not my home. It never will be.* Another said, *Dad is who I'm going to live with because at least he tells me where he's going to be. He loves me unlike some mean people I know.*

Turning toward the jurors, Joann explained, "I felt like she didn't tell me what was happening and I wanted to get her attention." Observers realized that it also represented conflicting emotions and pitiful hope—by a young girl—that the abandonment wasn't real, that her mother would return. Joann had ended the note, *Well, I'm doing okay I guess. Just whenever you want to come back for me.*

Airing the bitter messages for jurors might also have been a clever strategy by Beth Silverman. Knowing the defense would eagerly bring them out, the prosecutor beat them to the punch.

Silverman asked, "Do you still love your mom?"

"Yes, of course."

"Has there ever been a day that's gone by in the last sixteen years that you haven't thought about your mom?"

"I think about her all the time."

By the middle of May 1991, Joann said, her hopes about her mother had dimmed. She told the jury about talking to Detective Sally Fynan. "We had a conversation and I said that she must be dead. . . . I just naturally thought something tragic had happened."

Silverman switched gears to deal with Darryl Mounger's opening statements regarding John Racz allegedly making a call from LAX to his own answering machine; he had declared that no answering device had been found in the Racz home. Silverman asked, "Do you recall when you moved out [to Peachland], did the Fortuna house have an answering machine?"

"Yes," said Joann. Nearly all of the jurors could be seen making entries in their notebooks.

Moving quickly past it, Silverman inquired, "Did your father ever express any concern as to where your mother was?"

Joann minced no words. "He did not express any kind of concern. He never talked about where she was staying, where she went on a trip."

"When your father has told you that your mother didn't just leave him, but that she also left you and your brother and your sister, did you ever have a response to that?"

"Yes. I would say right back that she left *him* and she did not leave us." It had infuriated Joann when, during an argument with her father, he had called Ann a "bitch" and a "whore." She recalled another hurtful incident. "During a fight we were having in the garage one evening, there was a piece of art my mom had made. And during a very intense moment, he spit on her artwork."

Racz had told Joann that he spoke to Ann on April 26, and Joann had demanded to know what her mother said. But his only answer had been "None of your business."

To Silverman's inquiry, Joann said she had moved out of the Fortuna residence eight years earlier, at age twenty-two, but she had subsequently stayed there a few times, for short terms.

Spectators had wondered if Beth Silverman would bring up Bob Russell, knowing full well that if she didn't, the defense probably would. Silverman asked, and Joann recalled that her mother had a friend named Bob. "I remember she took one trip up north to visit her friend. She took Katelin." About her father's reaction to it, Joann said, "He was jealous."

In another father-daughter dispute, Joann recalled, he had said terrible things. Silverman referred her to a written report and asked if it refreshed Joann's memory of exactly what had been said. Yes, she replied, but fell silent. "Is this hard for you to say?" Beth asked.

"Yes," said Joann.

"Does it upset you?" Yes.

Charging to the rescue, Silverman quoted from the question-answer transcript, spitting out the harsh words with no hesitation. "Have you told the detectives that your father only says bad things about your mother, that she is out there fucking around while he is there for you?"

Giving Joann a moment to think about it, Silverman asked, "Is that a statement your father has made before?"

"Yes."

Closing her direct exam by screening a picture of Joann's daughter, Kayla, born in May 2001, Beth asked if Ann would have deliberately missed her first granddaughter's birth.

"No," said Joann. "I am one hundred percent sure of that."

Before starting the cross-exam, the defense gave way to the prosecution's request to put on another witness from another state. Retired sheriff's sergeant John View came forward and raised his right hand.

View said he had retired in 2002. He and Detective Sally Fynan had been the initial missing persons investigators searching for Ann Racz. And he had once worked at the same substation as John Racz. Through the prosecutor's interrogation, View took jurors through the first few weeks of the perplexing hunt for Ann. The court's time ran out, though, and View would have to stay in San Fernando one more night.

* * *

On Thursday morning, July 12, he continued his step-by-step description of the investigation, including reading aloud from his report of sixteen years ago detailing an interview with John Racz. Jurors heard several references to the defendant's odd and evasive behavior. In May 1991, he and Fynan turned the missing person case over to homicide. Sergeant Salerno and Detective Danoff took it over.

After lunch the lawyers finally allowed John View to step down and return to his life of retirement. Joann Racz sat on the witness chair's front edge again to face cross-examination. Darryl Mounger wished her an early happy birthday. Among a barrage of questions about her friends and family life, he asked Joann if she had liked her father in 1991. She said she had.

The defender wanted to challenge some time frames established by prosecutors for the afternoon of April 22, 1991. Joann had testified that she usually got out of school at 2:30 P.M., but Mounger produced a class schedule indicating her last-period art class ended at 2:55 P.M. With a map of Hart High School, he asked her to trace the steps, with estimated time, it would take to meet her mother in the parking area. Joann couldn't recall exactly.

Mounger got to the point and asked if she and her mother had actually reached the Fortuna house at about three-thirty in the afternoon. Joann said it could have been that early, but she refused to agree that her mother had left for McDonald's at 3:45 P.M. Nor could she estimate how much time had elapsed before her father departed. The defense attorney asked, "Your father came back a short period of time later with cold food. Is that correct?"

"Yes," Joann replied. Her interpretation of a short period of time remained unclear. The whole case could hinge on it, since the defendant stood accused of killing Ann Racz during that window of opportunity.

"Do you remember how long it was before he came back?" Joann couldn't recall, but she said she might have estimated to detectives a period of twenty minutes. Mounger inquired if it could have been five minutes. Joann didn't think so. Showing an investigator's report to her, he asked if it changed her memory.

Joann agreed that it helped, but she referred to another sentence in the report in which she had said, "I am uncertain how long he was gone."

Moving on to other topics, Mounger touched on Racz providing meals for the children and taking care of them during Ann's previous trips. Joann explained that in a couple of cases, she had stayed with a neighbor. Mounger brought up the answering machine issue again, but Joann couldn't recall when it had been acquired.

The defense drew agreement from Joann that she had sometimes told friends she believed her father killed her mother, and had at one time called Detective Danoff to ask that he arrest him. To Mounger, she rationalized that she had probably just been behaving like a temperamental teenager.

"If you believed those things," said Mounger, "and tried to get him arrested, I'm just curious why you stayed with him at the house?"

Joann's answer touched hearts in the audience. "This is a very, very difficult situation that I was in. It was not an everyday situation. I had to work the best with what was dealt to me." She added, "There were times that I was living in fear."

As soon as Mounger finished with the witness, Beth Silverman established that Joann had not looked at a watch or clock on April 22 during any of the events in question. Thus, any estimates of time she had given to detectives had been based only on wild guesses.

Silverman also brought out through Joann that Racz had hired lawyers as early as 1991, and that she was "forced" to go with her father to meet Darryl Mounger soon afterward. In a 1996 conference with him, she had asked Detective Comstock to accompany her, and Comstock had. At that session, Silverman asked, "Was it suggested to you that your mother is alive and had abandoned you?"

"Yes."

Another court day came to a close. Joann would return the following morning to complete her testimony.

If anyone felt superstitious about coming to court on Friday the thirteenth, it did not faze Judge Coen. He had no time for petty silliness.

Maybe bad luck struck Joann, though, because she showed up a little late. To fill in the time, prosecutors questioned a retired neighbor of Racz's, Don Pedersen. First, though, in a brief hearing out of the jury's presence, John Lewin said that Pedersen's testimony would indicate that Katelin had told him about visiting a lake with her father, at which no hiking or fishing took place. Instead, she and John had sat and looked at the lake. Lewin hoped it would suggest to jurors that Racz might have disposed of Ann's body there. Judge Coen would have none of it, and stated that the prejudicial effect far outweighed any probative value.

Another issue popped up. One of the jurors had a scheduled vacation and needed to be replaced. That left five alternates.

Donald Pedersen, his face weather-beaten and his hair thinned from nearly eight decades in the sun, took the oath and gripped both armrests as he eased into the chair. If his muscles had aged, his mind had not. Speaking in confident, articulate terms, he said that he lived directly across the street from John Racz. Ann, he said, was a "sensational" mother. She had once taken a trip with John and left the Pedersens in charge of the children. He recalled that Ann had called every night to check on them.

In his testimony, Pedersen said the appearance of a moving van on April 18, 1991, had amazed him. A few days later, he had observed Ann's car, nosed into the garage, while she sat inside and John stood at the driver's side. After nearly a half hour, the kids had climbed out and entered the house. They kept talking approximately another twenty-five minutes. After that, the witness said, Ann left and stopped down the street to speak to another neighbor. A few minutes later, John backed his car out in a hurry and followed Ann.

Israels's cross-exam brought a vociferous series of objections, mostly sustained. At a sidebar conference, Judge Coen lectured the defender about procedural matters, and added, "I'm sure you are not doing this intentionally—you are making faces when I make a ruling. Don't do that again." Israels apologized.

Interrogation suggesting that Ann had been eager to shed the responsibilities of raising children also fell flat.

Another question asked the witness to rank the "impossibility" of Ann abandoning her kids, using a scale of one hundred as the lowest possibility and zero as highly probable. Pedersen barked, "One hundred and twenty."

He left the stand with head held high and a new bounce to his step.

Joann Racz didn't look nearly as enthusiastic when she sat down to deal with a third day of emotional grilling. Beth Silverman tried to be gentle with inquiries about Joann submitting DNA samples in case her mother's skeletal remains ever turned up. Also asking about Joann's 1996 meeting with defense counsel, Silverman said, "Did they talk to you about what could happen if your father was convicted?"

"Yes."

"Did they attempt to make you feel that you should testify a certain way based on that?"

"There is not any way they or anybody would be able to sway me in any direction of how I should testify. Because I want to use what I remember, and I feel like I know my mom and I want to be able to do what's right without anybody else's opinion or request." She loved her mother, and at that very moment, Joann said, she wore a necklace and ring that had belonged to Ann.

Asked if, despite the hurtful events, she still also loved her father, Joann said, "Yes." She had come to grips with her difficult position in which telling the truth might be harmful to him.

Referring to a 1991 meeting with Joann and her father, Darryl Mounger asked, "Was that the time your father *forced* you to come to my house?" She said it was. "And when he *forced* you, did he tie you up?"

Sarcasm tinged Joann's voice. "No, he did not tie me up."

"How did he force you to come?"

"I remember just saying I don't want to go." She explained that as a young teenager, she had no other choice, though.

After raising a few more points framed to suggest that he had not tried to influence Joann, Mounger said, "Thank you. No further questions."

Joann exhaled a giant sigh of relief when Coen said, "You can stand down."

Following a lunch break, Ann's best friend, Dee Ann Wood, accepted the mantle of witness for the prosecution. She spoke of their long relationship in which they knew intimate details of each other's lives, and she educated the jury about the church circle. Ann's main interest, said Dee Ann, had focused on her children, as indicated by the majority of her activities relating to them. Dee Ann had never met Bob Russell, but she knew all about his role with Ann. She also knew that Ann had started thinking about leaving her husband long before Russell came into the picture.

To establish once more that John Racz could have placed a collect call from LAX to his own residence with no one there to receive it, Silverman asked if Dee Ann had ever seen an answering machine in the house while visiting Ann. "Yes," said the witness.

Dee Ann Wood's clear recollections of Ann, spoken with passion and a sense of humor, painted a detailed picture of the missing woman's activities, fears, loves, and plans for the future. The jurors perhaps could now see her as a real person, not just a mythical object of legal wrangling. Maybe they could even see a clearer image of what happened in the final weeks of her life.

They heard Dee Ann say, "She would have told me if she was taking a trip. She had just moved with her kids and was trying to get them adjusted. Her focus was to make sure they were settled with this whole new situation."

About Ann's car being left at the Flyaway, Dee Ann said, "That was the most baffling thing. When I read that her car was found there, I knew immediately something was wrong. I was always the one who took them to the airport. Once, when I couldn't, I offered to take her to the Flyaway. She said no, she would call someone else, because she preferred to go right to the airport. She would never use Flyaway."

When Dee Ann had finally heard, on April 28, about Ann's unexplained absence, she called Bob Russell. "I said, 'Is she with you? Tell me, is she with you?' And he was shocked. 'No, I have not heard from her.' He was very worried."

Conversely, John Racz, said Dee Ann, showed no emotion about his wife being missing.

Philip Israels asked, on cross-exam, how long the answering machine had been in Racz's home, but Dee Ann did not know. Through Dee Ann, he also reestablished that the defendant had never struck his wife. Regarding the portrayal of John Racz as a controlling spouse, the defender asked about activities the two women had shared, such as going to movies, church circle meetings, swimming together, and separate commitments by Ann to her Monday Flowers business and volunteering at school. Dee Ann confirmed these independent functions. She also agreed that John and her own husband sometimes babysat while the wives attended movies. The concept of John Racz as a dictatorial controller may have been diminished in jurors' minds.

Dwelling for a short time on whether Dee Ann knew of sexual intimacy between Ann and Bob Russell, Israels let it slide after a short recess. Following the break, he focused on the sexual relationship between Ann and her husband, and referred to an investigator's document suggesting that it had been "normal." But Dee Ann recalled Ann's whispered accusation that John had forced her to have sex every night, soon after she hinted of her desire to leave him.

The defense wondered why Ann had moved to Peachland on April 18, instead of waiting until the school semester ended, when she could have put a greater distance between John and herself. Dee Ann couldn't lend anything new to that quandary.

As soon as Beth Silverman began redirect, she took Dee Ann back to the document referring to "normal" sex relations between Ann and John, and she asked her to read the next few sentences aloud. They stated: *John made [Ann] have sex every night and she hated it. He insisted that she awaken him if she came to bed after he did. This was going on since she told him she wanted to leave.* Along with Dee Ann's confirming statements about John's tight control of money and household issues, the forced sex may have resurrected jurors' image of the defendant as a controlling person.

The defense waived the opportunity for recross, and Judge Coen declared the court in recess until Monday.

Glenn Racz, the only son of John and Ann, would be the first witness that morning. His surprising allegiance and anger would shatter expectations.

CHAPTER 29

A MATTER
OF TIME

The first business on Monday morning, July 16, dealt with disturbing news. While jurors waited in the hall, lawyers presented a problem to Judge Coen. Detective Sally Fynan, now retired, had been scheduled to testify, but severe illness would apparently prevent it.

In a remarkable twist, the defense had planned to summon her. Philip Israels stated, "She was to be our first witness. . . . She may be the most critical witness in this case." Coen called the issue "premature" and said they should consider various options later.

With the jurors in place, John Lewin called Glenn Racz to the witness stand. If from all the previous testimony spectators had mentally pictured an immature boy, they were in for a shock. A handsome, married adult, now twenty-seven, educated in mechanical engineering at the prestigious University of California, Santa Barbara, stepped forward.

Lewin asked, "Is it difficult for you to be called to testify against your father in this case?"

Obviously nervous, Glenn said, "Yes." He spoke of the current relationship with his dad. "We are good friends, try to hang out a few times every month and spend time together." He admitted that he would have to think about each question from the prosecution to weigh how it would affect the outcome of this trial.

Asked to recall the relationship with his mom, Glenn said, "I knew her, I guess as well as any [young] boy would know his mom. Yeah. We didn't get deep about any personal stuff."

Observers could sense something cold about the answer.

Several witnesses had described Ann's total devotion to her children. Lewin asked, "Do you believe that you and your sisters were the center of her life at that point in time?"

"No." A wave of surprise rippled through the gallery.

Now the prosecutor opened the curtain on a predetermined strategy. He would need to impeach his own witness by showing that Glenn had completely changed his attitude about Ann since testifying to the grand jury. Something had turned him against his mother, and prosecutors suspected he had been embittered by a stack of love letters Ann had written to Bob Russell, some of which contained specific sexuality.

"Have you been honest when you talked to investigators or the grand jury in the past?"

"Yes."

Lewin referred to a detective's report from 2006 quoting Glenn as saying, "She was a real good mother. She was as close as I could imagine her being, you know, with an eleven-year-old boy."

The prosecutor asked, "Do you recall saying that?" Glenn seemed reluctant in answering that he did. Lewin requested an explanation of his changed attitude.

Glenn disclosed, "I feel like she put her own desires—

when she was with this other man, she put herself ahead of us. Certain things like that."

"So it's fair to say you have some hurt feelings, you are upset with your mom regarding the affair with Bob Russell?"

"Yes . . . she did certain things very good and was great on things with my school and socially. However, there's another side with her adulterous affair that makes her not perfect."

In an attempt to circumvent Glenn's bitterness over Ann's love for another man, Lewin asked him to leapfrog backward over it, and express how he viewed his mother before learning about Bob Russell. But Glenn wouldn't use any adjectives about her other than "good."

At one point, the attorney asked, "Do you consider yourself to be an unbiased witness?"

"I think that's impossible," Glenn admitted.

Producing a recording of Glenn's words in a 2006 interview, Lewin played segments of it for the jury. They heard effusive compliments about love and admiration. The prosecutor stopped intermittently for corroboration from Glenn, but he relied heavily on memory failure. This prompted Lewin to ask, "Is your memory worse between 2006 and 2007 regarding what happened and how your mom felt about you?"

Unwilling to bend, Glenn replied, "Probably the longer the time from 1991, the worse it gets." Asked why his remarks about Ann did not agree with the recorded ones, Glenn explained, "I think since the 2006 interview and now, I've been shown things that are—instead of just on one side, like saying my dad did it . . . I'm shown the other side of the story a little bit. That has made me . . . think it might not just be—put other ideas out there that I didn't know about before."

Just as his sister Joann had struggled with conflicting emotions, Glenn was obviously torn with divided loyalties. He seemed to have ropes tied to each wrist, pulling him in both directions at once, and succeeding only in severing his heart.

Joann's words had seemed to lean in favor of her mother,

while Glenn's view of Ann had apparently been eroded, placing him in his father's corner.

Lewin wanted to know if the "other ideas" he had mentioned came after discussion with John Racz's lawyers. "Yeah," said Glenn. "They've showed me the evidence from other things that I didn't know about." At Lewin's objection, Judge Coen struck the explanatory sentence.

Relying on his oft-used scale of zero to one hundred, Lewin asked Glenn to rate his mother as an "involved parent." The son gave her "about a ninety-five." But to Lewin's inquiry why not one hundred, he said simply, "I don't know."

Ticking off a long list of educational-support activities, Lewin got agreement from Glenn that his mother had participated in them, but Glenn said he couldn't recall any details.

"Was she the type of mom who would leave you without notice, who would just disappear?"

"I don't know." But to the grand jury, he had given an unqualified "No" answer.

Referring to transcripts of the October 2006 hearings, Lewin led Glenn through numerous other examples showing changed responses. Rationalizing his altered responses, Glenn said, "I feel like I've learned more about the other side of the case since then." He continued to hedge his answers, often claiming faded memory.

"When did you learn about your mother's affair with Bob Russell?" Lewin inquired.

"At least over a year ago," Glenn replied.

His answer confused observers. If he had known of it before the grand jury hearing, why the changed attitude now? "I think it was from the letters more than just an affair. But after seeing some of her heart poured out in some of those letters to this guy, it seemed like, wow, she was putting her love affair of this guy before us. That's why I changed my mind," Glenn explained.

"Who showed you those letters?"

"Darryl and Phil." Mounger and Israels.

Even though Glenn's comments seemed to be mired in anger, he denied it. About the affair, he said, "I feel that it wasn't right. I'm not angry at her." Glenn even went so far as to say he had forgiven his mother, partly motivated by his Christian beliefs.

Lewin asked, "Even if your father killed your mother, isn't it true that as a Christian, you have forgiven him?"

"Yes."

An observer mused about the interesting concept. Forgiveness for adultery, but tinged with bitterness; forgiveness for possible murder while remaining "good friends" with the accused perpetrator. Sometimes logic is inexplicable.

It took a dozen or more questions, with reminders from the grand jury transcript, for Glenn to finally give a qualified opinion that his mother had been fearful of John in April 1991.

After a long lunch break, Glenn Racz continued his trend of noncommittal answers to John Lewin. Repeatedly he asserted that reviewing transcripts of his grand jury testimony or interviews with detectives did not refresh his memory. Glenn finally did agree that his mother probably would not have gone on an extended trip without saying good-bye, and that he would have expected some contact from her. Yet, on Lewin's scale, he could only say he was 80 percent certain of last seeing her on April 22, 1991, before she drove away from the Fortuna house. And he had no recollection of anything else that day. Several times Glenn alluded to being influenced by what other people said, rather than his own independent memory.

Showing him a segment of grand jury testimony that said, *"I remember besides playing with my sister, just looking outside in the garage every once in a while and my mom was still there talking to my dad,"* Lewin asked Glenn if he recalled that. "I recall saying it," Glenn replied.

"So you recall saying it, but you just don't actually recall that it happened?" Glenn again made reference to a "jumbled puzzle" he had assembled in his mind from various sources.

Lewin snapped, "Mr. Racz, who could possibly give you information about what you saw involving your parents in that garage other than yourself?"

Faltering, Glenn regurgitated the question, then mumbled, "Nobody. Only from my memory."

Like a linebacker who had intercepted a pass, Lewin ran hard. Reminding the witness that he had sworn an oath, he asked, "As you sit here, is it more important to tell the truth, or is it more important for you to make sure you don't say anything that hurts your dad?"

Glenn replied, "It's more important for me to tell the truth." Still, when reminded that he had told the grand jury of seeing his mother and father talk for about an hour, Glenn now said he had no memory of how long they spoke. Nor could he recall any other specifics.

The prosecution at last scored with an admission from Glenn that the grand jury testimony had included recollection of his father leaving the house and returning "eventually." Lewin asked, "When you used the word 'eventually,' you were referring to him being gone a long time. Is that correct?"

"Yes."

Glenn received a temporary respite from the grilling when Lewin asked Judge Coen's permission to put another witness on the stand for a short time.

Kristin Best, one of Joann's close friends in 1991, came forward. Beth Silverman first extracted from Kristin laudatory descriptions of Ann Racz's organization and involvement in her children's lives. Kristin had lived near the Peachland condo, and had heard a conversation between her mother and Ann in which Ann had expressed fear of John Racz. After that, Kristin's mother had forbidden her to go to the Fortuna house again.

The witness clearly remembered having telephone

conversations with Joann on April 22. "Her mom dropped the kids off at the [Fortuna] house. . . . She was supposed to go to Mc-Donald's to get food for the children." Instead, Kristin recalled, Joann's dad came in and said, "Your mom is not going to get the food. She is leaving. I'm going to get you guys McDonald's. I'll be right back."

After they hung up, said Kristin, Joann called again several times to say her parents had not returned. She sounded "in fear." At last, in a final telephone call, Joann told Kristin that her father had shown up with "freezing cold" food. Doing her best to estimate the time elapsed before Mr. Racz returned, Kristin said, "Two, two and a half hours."

On cross-exam, Philip Israels wanted to know if, in subsequent years, Joann had ever asked Kristin for help. No, Kristin replied, tears beginning to spill down her cheeks. After a fifteen-minute recess, she recalled that Joann had once said she needed help getting to the bottom of the mystery of her mother's absence. Kristin had asked, "Joann, do you really feel your dad did this?"

"Yeah, I really do," Joann had replied.

Regarding the length of time John Racz had been gone after leaving the Fortuna house, Kristin told Israels that, according to Joann, it was dark outside when he returned. Spectators realized that sunset in April is a little after seven o'clock. If he had left at four, that gave him three hours to do whatever he did. They wondered why Israels drew this information from the witness.

The prosecution, satisfied with Kristin's answers, declined asking anything else.

Glenn Racz's memory hadn't improved when he resumed testimony. He said he had no recollection of how long his father had been gone on April 22. At the grand jury, he had said "More than minutes. A few hours."

Lewin asked, "When you said that, you believed it to be true. Is that correct?" Yes, Glenn replied, but he now had no memory of the time elapsed.

"What's the next thing you remember about your dad that evening?"

"I don't remember anything." About his sixth-grade graduation two months later, he did recall that his mother hadn't attended, but he couldn't say whether or not his father had.

Another long litany of questions met with more malfunctioning memory. Lewin said, "Do you think your mom is still on a trip or vacation?" No.

"Do you think your mom is alive?"

"I think it's possible." This—despite the fact Ann had not attended his graduations, his wedding, or any other important event.

"Mr. Racz, you don't want to know what happened in this case, do you?"

"I do want to know, yes."

"Then why haven't you asked your father?"

"I have asked him if he did murder my mother."

Perhaps not wanting to hear Glenn's version of how John Racz had answered that question, Lewin changed the subject. "Have you asked him specifically where she went on vacation?" Glenn couldn't recall, but he acknowledged that his father had been evasive about it.

The witness would have until the next day, Tuesday, to think about his testimony, since Judge Coen called for the evening recess.

Before calling the jury in on July 17, Judge Coen assembled the lawyers to iron out a big problem. Several jurors, prior to being caught up in the Racz trial, had scheduled and paid for summer vacations in advance. Coen didn't want to force cancellations, nor risk a mistrial from losing jurors, so with counsels' agreement, he decided to suspend the trial between July 30 and Monday, August 13.

John Lewin had been given time off on Tuesday morning, so Beth Silverman called five other brief witnesses to prevent wasting time. Cheryl Jensen, a former librarian at Wiley Canyon Elementary School, came first. She informed jurors of her close friendship with Ann, who had worked as a volunteer in the library. Ann had confided to her all about the marital problems and planned divorce.

In Jensen's testimony, she reconfirmed what early witnesses had said about Ann's dependability, devotion to her kids, Bob Russell, and the absurdity of the notion that she would leave on an unannounced trip and never again contact family or friends. Certainly not for a paltry $25,000.

Something new came from Cheryl. In late March 1991, the witness stated, "she came into my office, crying and hysterical. She said John had been cleaning his guns, or had the guns out, and threatened, 'If you leave me, I will kill you.'" Later, Cheryl said, "John informed me that Ann was forbidden to see me or associate with me, because I was going through a divorce and he felt that I was coaching her."

On cross, Israels probed most of these assertions, then threw in a question that startled everyone. "Did she ever tell you that she got turned on when John would get adult videos?"

Beth Silverman's mouth flew open. "I'm going to object. That assumes facts not in evidence."

"Sustained."

Another acquaintance and fellow church member of the Racz family succeeded Jensen. Roma Prior, now eighty-four and a widow, had arranged meal deliveries for John and the kids by other women in the congregation soon after Ann vanished. On Monday, April 29, she had invited the Raczes over for dinner.

Beth Silverman expected Roma to testify that John had made a claim, while eating in her home, that Ann had called him the previous day, April 28. Unfortunately, the elderly woman's memory had long since faded away, making her unable to provide any useful information, so Judge Coen excused her.

One-half of the legendary detective team strode forward again. Some people seem to command a room when they enter, and Louis Danoff filled that role as well as anyone. Reminded that he was still under oath, he relaxed in the witness chair, crossing his legs.

Beth Silverman needed Danoff to fill in the blanks left by Roma Prior's exhausted memory. He verified conducting an interview with her on May 29, 1991. Frank Salerno had been there too, and both men took notes. Danoff pulled his powder blue notebook from a coat pocket. At Silverman's direction, he read aloud from it.

According to the notes, Roma had attended church in the early afternoon of Sunday, April 28, and saw John Racz there. She had invited John Racz and the children over for dinner on Monday evening, April 29. While dining, John mentioned that Ann had called him on the previous day, Sunday, in the early afternoon. He said he asked her to come back home, and that she wouldn't tell him where she was.

Observers caught the drift. If John had been in church early Sunday afternoon, how could Ann have called him? Mounger was unable, on cross-exam, to dislodge this impression.

Louis Danoff stepped down, knowing that it probably would not be his last turn.

In her clarion voice, Beth Silverman announced, "The people call Christina Bibel." In the gallery, a few whispers commented about the perfect name.

As other witnesses had, Bibel spoke in glowing terms of Ann's qualities, especially her unselfish zeal for her children. And her friend had not said anything about going on a trip in the near future.

Bibel told the jury that she had sat next to Ann Racz at the April 16 meeting of their group and that Ann appeared "very frightened." Asked to expound, the witness said, "She was fearful for her life, that her husband would try to do something."

"Did she communicate what that threat was?"

"Yes." After the meeting, in a personal conversation, "she said that her husband was going to kill her if she would ever leave him."

Ann had spoken of her friendship with "a gentleman up north," the witness said, along with something else. According to Bibel, Ann had confided to her that John Racz knew all about the relationship too.

"I was trying to ascertain if she really did believe that John was capable of killing her. And I asked her several times, 'Are you sure that he is capable of this?' She looked at me with such fear in her eyes and she said, 'He told me that he would kill me.'"

If that happens, Ann had reportedly said, "You'll never find my body."

When Philip Israels took over the witness, he couldn't resist an urge. "Ms. Bibel, has anyone ever told you that you have a great name for a church group?"

"Yes."

Referring to detective's notes, Israels charged that Bibel had never told investigators of Racz's alleged threat to kill Ann. "The first time you mentioned that John would kill her was in an interview on June 12 of this year, 2007, with Ms. Silverman. . . . Is that correct?"

"That's correct."

"Did you know that Ann's friend was actually her lover?"

"She never did tell me that [he] was her lover. I just assumed it."

When Beth Silverman took over again, the witness reconfirmed telling detectives that Ann feared for her life, and that she planned to keep her kids.

After Christina Bibel's testimony, Silverman called one more witness before summoning Glenn Racz back to the stand. Theresa Minch, a fellow member of Pastor Thorp's congregation, added to the growing list of friends who could recall Ann's fear of being "hurt or killed" if she left John Racz. Ann knew the witness had gone through a divorce and consulted her about the process, since both of them had been married to men with law enforcement experience.

On cross-exam Minch told Israels that Ann had said her husband did not know about "the boyfriend."

If Glenn Racz dreaded facing more questions on the witness stand, he showed no signs of it when taking the chair again. John Lewin resumed the direct examination, and found that Glenn's memory hadn't improved with the long rest.

Joann, he admitted, often asked their father what had happened to their mom, but Glenn couldn't remember telling the grand jury that the conversations about her often "raised sparks."

"What was your father's reaction when Joann would bring up your mom?"

"I remember . . . it was emotional, where he would cry."

After more "I don't remember" replies from Glenn, Lewin asked the judge, at sidebar, for an official finding "that the witness has been deliberately evasive during his answers."

Judge Coen proclaimed to jurors, "I find that the witness is being inconsistent in his statements, and . . . is feigning lack of recollection."

Glenn Racz maintained his distance. The witness's carefully worded responses indicated that references to a detective's notes or recordings only helped him remember saying certain things, but didn't help with recollection of the actual events. He continued to deny intentionally avoiding giving answers that might damage his father's case.

In regard to his feelings after Ann disappeared, Glenn danced around the question but said, "I definitely remember missing her and wanting my mom back." But he rationalized most of his vague responses by saying that he had heard conflicting and varying information, for sixteen years, from a variety of sources. These, he explained, confused him and made the truth elusive.

On the question of his father's possible involvement in Ann's fate, Glenn had once said, "I'm not going to pass judgment." He might not even accept a confession or a jury's verdict of guilty. Lewin asked, "That's what you said, correct?"

"Well," said Glenn, "I also said until I'm convinced. And . . . just because if a jury would find him guilty, that doesn't automatically mean that I'm convinced in my heart. . . ."

Would this be true even if his father admitted doing it ? Glenn remained equivocal, still saying he would have to be convinced.

"Mr. Racz . . . are you a biased witness?"

"Yes."

"Very biased to support your father, correct?"

"I try not to be biased at all, but I'm human, so I'm biased. I don't know."

"Who are you biased toward?"

"Well, I mean, I'm sitting on that side of the courtroom, so on the side I'm sitting, behind my dad, so . . ."

Lewin brought up the issue of grieving for his mother. Glenn replied that he might have those feelings, "a little bit. But mostly, I feel like I don't have closure on my mother dying. It seems like to grieve, you have to fully have closure. You have to know she is dead."

Still hammering away, Lewin at last drew affirmation from Glenn that suspicions about his father had been in his mind. And he admitted that he had attended very few of the annual memorials for his mother.

"As you sit here, isn't it true that you hope, Mr. Racz, more than anything, that the jury will acquit your father?"

"Yes." Still, Glenn later qualified that answer with expressions of hope that justice would be done for his mother.

Conducting the cross-exam, Darryl Mounger called attention to Glenn's many meetings with detectives to discuss the mystery of his mother's disappearance. The defense attorney also managed to slightly dent the estimate that John had been gone "a few hours" when he left on the afternoon of April 22, 1991.

The court's day ended, and Glenn Racz stepped down.

Still under oath, he resumed his cross-exam testimony on Wednesday morning, July 18. Mounger brought up the subject of letters Ann had written to Bob Russell. Glen admitted that their content altered his opinion about her devotion to the kids. "Do you believe that your mother could have left you?"

"Yes."

Regarding the portrayal of John Racz as "tight with money," Mounger asked if the father had paid for Glenn's college education, music lessons, trip to Europe, and other expenses. Glenn said he had.

"As you sit here today . . . do you believe your father killed your mother?"

"No."

* * *

Lewin, on redirect, ran into another memory failure. He did get a pointed answer to one question. "Over the years, is it fair to say that your dad would make disparaging comments about your mom?"

"Yes."

"What would he say?"

"I remember one time he said that maybe she is out there with another guy, f-ing another guy. I remember that."

"He didn't use the word 'f-ing,' correct? He used the full word."

"Yes, the full word. . . . He was crying when he said it." At first, Glenn modified the comment by saying his father had been "angry" at the time, but then he changed it to "sad." Lewin challenged the change, suggesting that Glenn had tried to cover up a word that might be incriminating. This, Lewin suggested, showed the ability to remember specific details. The witness didn't respond.

At the end of Glenn Racz's testimony, his inner conflicts had been exposed to the scrutiny of not only the jury, but to the spectators and news media reporters. Glenn's loyalty to his father could be understood to a certain degree, even though some might accuse him of shading the truth. Others might find insight to inner rage over his mother's conduct with another man.

One of the jurors, Barbara Kaplan, later expressed her own thoughts: "It bothered me a lot when we discovered the children were shown the love letters, Ann to Bob Russell. I found that very disturbing. You can understand why they, especially the son, testified as he did. Boys often put their mothers on a pedestal. That's the way the mother is supposed to be. What Glenn said on the stand, in essence, was that he didn't know who his mother was. When he read those letters, he was no longer sure that he was important to her. He wasn't so sure that she was such a good mother, that he didn't really know her. That shows the selfishness of John Racz. He should never have allowed those letters to be seen by his kids.

"If the defense attorney gave them to the kids to read, with John's permission, that shows me a very selfish, self-centered person who would think, 'I'll do whatever I can do to save my skin.' Showing those letters to the children changed their testimony. Also, I think it scarred them. I think it changed their whole idea of what kind of a woman she was. Because here she's writing these love letters that I guess were very specific. Those letters were not meant for the kids to see, ever. Ann would not have wanted them to see the letters.

"It really made me angry. Angry with the attorneys and with John Racz. I'll say it to anyone, and maybe somewhere along the way the message will get to those children. I ask them not to condemn their mother for what she did, for having a lover while still married to their father. Because she, in her mind, had already divorced that man a couple of years before she even left him. She was no longer in love with him. This other man came along who treated her kindly. She was vulnerable. Those children haven't lived enough life to understand. I hope they will change their minds as they get older. As they live life and become a little bit more liberal in their thoughts. Because they should not condemn their mother or let it change their opinion of her, and they should have been happy that she found a little bit of happiness before she died. I have tears when I think of those children. What happened to them was not fair. They should love their mother the way they knew her."

CHAPTER 30

THE HUMAN CRY

Retired sergeant Frank Salerno, the partner in a legendary pairing of investigators, looked comfortable in the witness chair, having occupied hundreds of them during his thirty-two-year career.

To Beth Silverman's first question, Salerno revealed that his retirement from the LASD did not mean he had gone fishing. On the contrary, he gave his profession as a "private investigator."

During the next few hours, Salerno spoke of a protocol he had developed and taught regarding homicide cases in which no body had been found, and how he applied it in the Racz investigation. Jurors and spectators were treated to a narrative that might equal a crime movie directed by Martin Scorsese. The witness took them through interviews with a smart, evasive suspect, endless searches through mountains, digging in deserts, crawling into a bootlegger's cave, and exploring rugged canyons, where actual movies had been filmed. He offered insight into dealing with brokenhearted relatives. And he detailed grisly discoveries of human remains cast aside by savage killers.

The other side of detective work also came out through Salerno's testimony—hundreds of phone calls, the dull examination of bank records, airline manifests, telephone bills, repeated visits to a shadeless parking area, and a multitude of plodding, hard work. The search and mystery dragged through weeks, then months, and years. Yet, two homicide cops stuck it out with dogged determination. It disappointed Frank Salerno that no forensic evidence ever turned up.

Mostly, they had dealt with a myriad of inconsistent statements, evasion, and outright lies from John Racz.

Salerno's testimony lasted the rest of that Wednesday and all day Thursday, July 19. He got a short break when a crime lab expert took the stand for a few minutes to verify that an entry on a wall calendar in the Racz home, for April 18, 1991, had been modified. The original words, he said, were "Hell Day."

After resting over the weekend, Salerno faced a final blitzkrieg of questions. First, though, on that Monday morning, July 23, Judge Coen announced the loss of another juror, who had taken sick. By lottery one of the four alternates would become a regular. Among the three remaining alternates, Barbara Kaplan kept her fingers crossed, hoping to be promoted to serve with the twelve triers of fact.

Fortunately for Salerno, the great bulk of his testimony came from questioning by Beth Silverman, simply because she needed his narrative to lay out investigation facts to the jury.

After lunch the detective caught another break when the prosecution put a telephone company expert on the stand. Jeff Bertrand, an area manager, Asset Protection, said, "I do investigations. Thefts against our property, internal matters, and anything that would affect the assets of AT and T." His previous twenty-six years with LAPD, after which he retired in 1998 as a lieutenant, had gained him training in bunko schemes. Bertrand had gained expertise in coin-operated telephones, the generation of phone bills, and placement of collect calls.

With Lewin posing hypotheticals, Bertrand established the possibility that someone had placed three telephone calls to the Racz number on Fortuna Drive, from pay telephones at Terminal One, LAX, on April 26, 1991. The first two, at 3:00 and 3:07 P.M., lasted fifty-one and forty-three seconds, respectively. The third call, at 3:14 P.M., lasted four minutes, and was billed as a collect call.

Did that last one mean that someone was necessarily at the house to accept the collect call charges? Not if there was an answering machine, said Bertrand.

According to the expert, "In those days it was very routine for law enforcement units, who are constantly receiving calls, to do it through an answering machine announcing, 'Operator, we accept collect calls.'" It didn't escape observers that John Racz had been a sergeant in law enforcement with office duties at the Malibu substation.

In Lewin's hypothetical, a person could have made the first call, left a message on the machine, made the second call and used a code to make certain the message had been recorded. The third call could be made on a collect basis, and it would be recorded on the receiving number's bill. Bertrand agreed that the whole scenario would work.

Israels established that the phone company wouldn't necessarily know if a subscriber had connected an answering machine to his line. And he set his own hypothetical about someone using coins to make calls, runs out of change, and makes the third call collect. Bertrand said it could happen.

The jury would have to decide which one they believed, and if it fit into the matrix of other facts.

* * *

Replacing the telephone man, Frank Salerno spent some time explaining the videotaped interview he and Louis Danoff had conducted with John Racz on June 28, 1991. He finished the day with comments about what officers found with a search warrant at the Fortuna house on July 5, which included phone bills and a calendar Racz snatched from an evidence collection bag and defaced the date of April 18.

Salerno spent the entire court day testifying on Tuesday, July 24, and occupied the stand another hour on Wednesday morning. Drained, he finally stepped down.

His old partner, Louis Danoff, filled the chair once more. The detective had worked alongside Salerno until his colleague's departure in August 1993, then continued investigating the Racz case with the help of a new teammate. Danoff accepted the golden umbrella, and retired on March 30, 2001. But he kept probing the mystery of Ann Racz as a dollar-per-year volunteer.

Danoff told Beth Silverman that the lack of physical evidence certainly did not signify that no crime had been committed. And the passage of so much time had strengthened it.

"Why?"

"Because, after five years, you might have doubts whether Ann is just missing or is deceased. After sixteen years, I think it becomes pretty easy to believe that Ann Racz is dead."

His face turning gentle, Danoff commented about one of Ann's children. "I have been in touch with Joann over all these years. Joann was the first one to put in the human cry that her mother is missing. Over these years—and it took a long time to get her trust—Joann has said to me that she believes her father killed her mother, and she has confronted him on numerous occasions in which he never answers her."

* * *

The prosecution next called Joji Yoshiyama, Ann's brother. Ann, he said, had told him of her plans to end the marriage, and at one point asked Joji if she might be able to stay with him in Gardena for a while if necessary. She had been exceptionally loving and close with her family. "I remember when my dad was ill, she always came to visit him with the children. She would never have abandoned them."

John Lewin brought up the meeting Joji, his brother, Takeo, and sister Emi had with John Racz on the second anniversary of Ann's disappearance. With the court's permission, he asked Joji to read aloud the document he had written afterward. Toward the end of the memoir, Lewin stopped Joji to ask, "Did John appear to be more concerned about the fact that his wife was missing or more concerned about what people might be saying about him?" Before Joji could answer, Judge Coen sustained an objection from Israels.

Joji's written statement about John's deliberate answers and "thinking before answering" brought another objection, but Coen overruled that one.

Israels worked on cross-exam to show that anyone might have memory loss, as John had professed, two years after an event, even a traumatic one. He asked, "Did you know your sister had a lover?" but a sustained objection made it moot.

Joji Yoshiyama's written record of a long-ago conversation had hinted of evasion or lies by the defendant, but only the jury could decide which it was.

Sergeant Delores Scott stepped from the gallery to the witness stand after Yoshiyama's exit. She told Beth Silverman she had taken on the cold case of Ann Racz in 2005. It had consumed a considerable amount of time to review stacks of previous records before she regenerated the investigation. Detective

Cheryl Comstock partnered with her, beginning in the middle of 2006. Numerous discoveries of human remains in the region had not led to any new facts about Ann Racz. Interviews with a variety of people, including Pastor Thorp, Kristin Best, Bob Russell, and John Racz, had reconfirmed known inconsistencies, and spotlighted some additional ones.

Scott described the arrest of John Racz at LAX on October 21, 2006.

After a lengthy cross-examination, Philip Israels asked, "In all of the investigation that you have done in this case, have you ever found any physical evidence that linked John Racz to any harm done to Ann Racz?"

Scott said, "What do you mean by physical evidence?" She made reference to countless pages of investigative information.

"So you've got documents, you've got papers, right? Do you have any physical evidence, scientific evidence?"

"No scientific evidence. No."

"Of any kind?"

"No."

"I have no further questions," said the defense attorney.

Emiko Ryan, now age seventy, came forward with a spry step, looking determined.

Beth Silverman announced, "Your Honor, for the record, this will be our last witness. I thought you were going to be happy." Judge Coen smiled.

The witness acknowledged numerous conversations with her "baby" sister in which they discussed the unhappy marriage and plans to dissolve it, but Ann had never even hinted of giving up her children.

Silverman brought up the black-and-gold ring Ann had

bought in Hawaii. Emi said that Ann had given it to her aunt Kay, who lived in Hawaii, to take back to the jeweler for sizing.

The final conversation between Emi and Ann, said the witness, took place by telephone on April 21, at three-thirty in the afternoon. According to an MCI phone card bill, it had originated from a pay phone in Newhall, connected to Emi's number in Mesa, Arizona, and lasted thirty-two minutes. Beth Silverman emphasized that Ann had not made a collect call. According to Emi, Ann had sounded "happy and relieved" about moving from the Fortuna house. She had not mentioned anything about a forthcoming trip, but she looked forward to visiting their mother on April 24.

Beth's questions allowed Emi to pour out her heartfelt stress and pain from learning about Ann's disappearance and from the long years of searching for her. The witness described several conversations with John Racz in which he changed his story or cloaked it with evasion. But one thing stood out. Racz had spoken of seeing Ann at the Tips restaurant on hamburger hill, and John said that he noticed Ann was wearing the black-and-gold Hawaiian ring. Emi knew this could not be true.

Time had run out again, and Judge Coen called for the evening recess.

On Friday morning, July 27, Emi Ryan continued her testimony. She told of cleaning out the Peachland condo in preparation for vacating it and finding about $120 in cash. Ann certainly would not have left it there, had she taken a trip.

Another odd comment came from John Racz, said Emi, during a conversation in late May, when Ann had been missing about one month. According to the witness, John said that Ann had no longer wanted to wear her original wedding ring nor to sleep with him. Why? "He told me that he thought Ann was a lesbian."

A few times, Emi said, she had even accompanied Louis Danoff on a canyon search for Ann. John Racz never had. Also, Emi and her husband, Jerry, had posted rewards for information leading to Ann, something else John Racz had never done.

Emi's nephew Glenn had made an interesting comment while visiting her in Arizona, the witness recalled. He volunteered, "My father said that maybe Mom is in heaven."

Joji Yoshiyama, in his previous day's testimony, had read aloud his notes from a meeting with Racz in April 1993. Emi had also written her recollection of that conversation. Silverman asked her to read it aloud to the jury.

In Emi's memoir, she noted John's version of April 22, 1991: *Kids came inside, all three. Said kids wanted to eat hamburgers for snacks. So either him or Ann took orders and Ann was going to McDonald's to get them. Said she came to the garage door and Glenn came to her and said goodbye and kissed her. John said Ann left and never came back. So he went to look for her later.*

Observers recognized discrepancies in relation to what had been aired in the trial. All three kids had not been there when Ann left, only Glenn and Katelin. It seemed doubtful that Glenn had said good-bye and kissed his mother. And John's version of leaving "later to look for her" didn't fit.

Emi read a notation about John telling Joji that it was the last time he saw Ann. The story later changed to seeing her at Tips to give her money.

The biggest confrontation between Emi and John had taken place on January 19, 1995, in which Racz accused Ann of being somewhere and having sex, and Emi repeatedly slapped him. Beth Silverman asked about that incident and Emi provided all of the details, in specific language.

Winding up, Silverman queried Emi about the likelihood of Ann abandoning her children, failing ever to contact her family again, and missing every important anniversary, birthday, funeral, or celebration among her relatives. Emi said that behavior was beyond any possibility.

As a final point, the prosecutor asked Emi to show Ann's Hawaiian ring to the jurors. Her aunt Kay had given it to Emi. Withdrawing a red satin bag from her purse, Emi carefully unsheathed a black-and-gold ring and held it up. Silence filled the courtroom.

Philip Israels invoked the possibility that memories can fade over so many years, and gently applied it to what his client might have said to the three siblings in 1993. Next he brought up sex, and asked if Ann had discussed any sexual relationships with Emi. No, said the witness. Had she read the letters between Emi and Bob Russell? No, said Emi, she regarded them as private.

Objections from the prosecution deflated several of Israels's questions. Regarding the 1995 confrontation between Emi and John in his garage, when she slapped him, Israels asked if John had pushed or hit her. No, she replied, he kept his hands in his pockets the whole time.

Beth Silverman clarified, on recross, that Emi had slapped him about ten times in response, each time, for his saying that Ann was "out there fucking." Yes, said Emi, that led to each slap.

Israels finalized the testimony by asking if anything had been found when Emi joined Louis Danoff in one of the canyon search expeditions. No, Emi replied.

Alternate juror Barbara Kaplan finally got her wish before court went into recess for two weeks. One of the twelve regulars told Judge Coen that she would prefer not to cancel vacation plans, and he excused her. By lottery, Kaplan's name came

CHAPTER 31

INNOCENT ARMOR

Monday morning, August 13, dawned with the threat of breaking heat records. In Judge Coen's courtroom, the prosecution formally rested its case. Now the defense would call witnesses for the purpose of persuading jurors that John Racz did not murder his wife.

Due to severe illness, Detective Sally Fynan had not been expected to testify, but she had recently recovered enough to show up in court.

At the defense table, Darryl Mounger did not appear to be very well himself, and Philip Israels stood to question the witness. Now retired, Fynan recalled being assigned to the missing person case of Ann Racz at the beginning of May 1991, with her supervisor, Sergeant John View.

Israels began with the events of April 22, 1991, establishing through the witness that Joann had asked for something to eat, and that when Katelin arrived home from a Brownie meeting, she recalled her father being there. Pastor Thorp, she stated, had never said anything about John Racz threatening or abusing Ann, nor had he mentioned anything to her about seeing scratches on Racz. Fynan disclosed that Emi Ryan, when interviewed, had said she didn't know if John had been physically abusive.

With the prosecution now in the role of conducting cross-examination, Fynan spoke of her first conversation, by telephone, with John Racz, about two weeks after Ann vanished. "I certainly remember it well because it was a very odd conversation. He was almost jovial. He did not appear to be worried. He went on about how she called, they exchanged money. She called two or three times after April twenty-second. It was just the strangest conversation I ever had with anybody."

Another inconsistency in Racz's stories came from Fynan. She recalled him saying that when Ann made the collect call on April 26, she did it "as she was taking a shuttle" to LAX "from the Flyaway lot."

To clarify it, the prosecutor asked, "Is it your understanding that the defendant was telling you that she was saying to him on the twenty-sixth, 'I will be taking a shuttle to the airport' and that when the call was placed, she was not at LAX at the time?"

"Oh, absolutely. She was at the Flyaway." Fynan had recorded it in her notes.

Taking the witness again, Israels wanted to know why she might have expected the defendant to be worried about his wife if he knew that she had filed for divorce and believed that she had gone on a trip to think things over. Fynan said she didn't accept that he believed Ann had gone on a trip.

Additional contentious questions and objections took up the rest of the morning.

At the lunch break, a journalist left the gallery and walked downtown to buy some film. When he returned, he rode up in the elevator with John Racz and a defense investigator, who asked the writer if he was a doctor—a witness the defense expected. Replying in the negative, the writer chatted briefly and gave each of the men a business card.

After a bailiff called order in the court, Judge Coen announced that Fynan's testimony would be interrupted temporarily to make way for another witness. A diminutive man with a mustache, glasses, and wearing a blazer, despite the heat, came forward. Dr. Edwin C. Krupp said, "I'm an astronomer and director of the Griffith Observatory in Los Angeles." Classic movie buffs, especially Joji Yoshiyama, would probably recall scenes filmed at that observatory for the 1955 film *Rebel Without a Cause,* starring James Dean.

Dr. Krupp told Darryl Mounger that he had researched, at the defense's request, what time darkness had set in on April 22, 1991. Speaking about "evening civil twilight" as the time the "disk of the sun is six degrees below the ideal flat horizon," Dr. Krupp said, "The time of sunset [on that date] was seven thirty-one P.M., and the end of evening civil twilight, which would mark darkness, was seven fifty-seven P.M."

"What time would it actually be dark, when that evening glow is gone?"

"Astronomers calculate darkness for any given night at the end of evening astronomical twilight. That corresponds to the period when the sun is eighteen degrees below the ideal flat horizon." On the date in question, in Valencia, "that time was nine oh-one P.M."

Who would have known?

Apparently, the defense hoped to erase the impact of testimony from Kristin Best. In telephone conversations with Joann, during the wait for John Racz to return home that evening, she had heard Joann say it was dark when her father came in.

John Lewin apparently didn't care to dispute the testimony. To observers, it appeared to verify that if Racz had left his house at four o'clock, and returned after seven-thirty, in the darkness, he had plenty of time to carry out the crime. Instead, Lewin wanted to know how much Dr. Krupp charged for his expert testimony. The witness said, "Four hundred dollars per hour."

With that, Sally Fynan returned, perhaps wondering why her testimony would earn zero dollars.

Israels took Fynan back to the statement she cited from Racz in which he said the collect call from Ann came from the Flyaway. He made no dent in it.

Taking another tack, Israels asked if Fynan recalled hearing a statement from any of the three children about John telling them how long he had been gone on the trip to McDonald's. She didn't. Israels returned to what seemed to be his favorite topic, inquiring how many of the people she interviewed knew that Ann was having an affair. At sidebar Judge Coen ruled the question was cumulative, and the waste of time outweighed the probative value.

In rapid fire, the defender cited a number of things Fynan had never found: a crime scene, a murder weapon, physical evidence of a crime, scientific evidence of a crime, witness to a crime, an answering machine at the Fortuna home, or scratches on Racz. She had to agree with all of them.

Looking triumphant, Israels sat down.

Louis Danoff, by now familiar to court watchers, strode to the stand once more. Mounger, perhaps a little friskier from the headway his co-counsel had made, asked, "Am I going to call you Detective, Mister, or Uncle Louie?"

"Whatever you want," Danoff said, grunting.

Suggesting that the investigators had been primarily interested in building a time frame that would give Racz the window of opportunity to kill Ann, the defender asked about some things the investigators did not do. Stoic and literal, Danoff said they were simply collecting information at that point.

With agreement from the detective that he had participated in hundreds of murder investigations, Mounger wanted to know how many of the victims had been killed by police choke holds. His inquiry created a grim picture in the minds of observers, and possibly jurors. The defendant had been trained in that technique of restraint. Had he used it on Ann to squeeze the very life out of her? Mounger asked a series of questions regarding details of how it is applied, leaving a few spectators to wonder why.

Seemingly satisfied, Mounger leaped on the issue of the answering machine, hammering at the idea that no one had decisively confirmed its existence in John Racz's home.

He ended the session with a list of things detectives did not find: Ann's purse, telephone book, glasses, and jewelry, including two pendants she often wore on gold chains, one a sheriff's star and the other a sapphire.

Louis Danoff finally completed his duties of sixteen years on the Ann Racz case. He stepped down, but he would be there for the grand finale.

At the afternoon break, the journalist sat scribbling notes, and felt someone touch his shoulder. John Racz stood there, extending his hand. The two men shook hands, then parted, leaving the journalist scratching his head in puzzlement.

Two of John Racz's offspring had testified in the prosecution's case-in-chief, but the third, Katelin, had been conspicuously left out. Philip Israels called her to the stand to be questioned for the defense.

Witnesses are often asked right away about their professions, but Israels skipped that part for Katelin. Insiders knew she had dabbled at several jobs. For a while, she had worked in a pet-grooming shop, and more recently had tried the exotic nightclub entertainment industry. Whispered conversations shared rumors that she now lived with her father, who had paid her to resign from her work and accompany him to court every day.

Slim and attractive, with long, dark hair and brown eyes, Katelin, barely audible, took the oath to tell the whole truth, then demurely seated herself. Israels began by reminding her that she had made statements in 1991 as a child, and more recently to the grand jury.

Taking her back to April 22, 1991, Israels tried to deal with conflicts in those statements, but he struggled against a dozen sustained objections. He found a foothold by asking Katelin if she had ever had conversations with her sister about what had happened in 1991. It surprised observers to hear her say no, they never talked about it.

"Do you remember having an answering machine back in 1991 at the Fortuna address?"

"No." She thought they hadn't installed one until 1997.

"Does your father sometimes get scratches from gardening?"

"Yes."

Katelin said she could not remember whether or not her father had been at the house when she arrived on April 22, 1991. Israels turned her over to the prosecution.

John Lewin asked if she considered herself unbiased. Katelin said she did, but divulged being very close to her dad. Asked where she currently resided, she said "Newhall" and claimed she hadn't lived with her father for about five years.

"Does your dad provide you with any financial support?"

"I don't understand the question."

"Does your dad give you money still?"

"No."

"What is the last time your dad gave you money?"

Contradicting her last answer, she said, "He gave me a check last month. It was [for] fifteen hundred dollars." Katelin denied any other monetary gifts since she had left home.

"Did you ask him for any money last month?"

"He compensated me, because I quit my job so I could be here." She agreed that John Racz basically was paying her to be in court, and she had not missed any days. Still, she regarded herself as unbiased.

Memories of her mother, said Katelin, came in fragments. "I remember specific things, that's all." But the witness affirmed traits mentioned by Lewin, such as dedicated, loving, affectionate, meticulous, involved in school activities, helpful with homework, and communicative with her kids. "She was a soccer mom too."

"Did she make a big deal out of your birthdays and holidays?"

"I don't remember." Lewin reminded Katelin that in testimony to the grand jury nine months ago, she stated that Ann did make a big deal out of birthdays. But now she answered, "I don't remember ever having a big birthday bash. It would be just the family, and that's it."

"Can you imagine your mom taking an extended vacation and not saying good-bye?"

"I don't know." To another similar question about the possibility that her mother had abandoned her, Katelin answered that it could have happened. Prodded a little more, though, she reverted to "I don't know."

Apparently weary of the topic, or perhaps frustrated with the vague answers, Lewin moved on to Katelin's father, only to hear a repetitious shield of "I don't remember." Her previous testimony seemed to have changed or fled her mind. She rationalized the differences by saying she had, at the grand jury, "felt obligated to fit the pieces in with what I didn't know." Those pieces, Katelin claimed, came from conversations with relatives. So, to her, the truth had taken on a new meaning. Giving the witness an opportunity to account for her evasiveness, Lewin asked, "Has anything happened to you physically in terms of a significant head trauma or anything like that between the grand jury and your testimony today?"

Using her own interpretation of head trauma, Katelin replied, "Yes. I have read the letters that my mom [wrote] to Bob Russell." "Darryl" had given them to her.

Juror Barbara Kaplan could be seen rapidly writing in her notebook. The letters, she thought, had wreaked their havoc.

For Lewin, the young woman presented a formidable challenge. She spoke in a soft, childlike voice, but she wrapped herself in armor more impenetrable than steel. Often requiring him to repeat his questions, and chanting, "I don't know," Katelin managed to avoid any statement damaging to her father. Yet, asked if that was her intent, she denied it.

The prosecutor inquired, "Do you view yourself as part of your father's defense team?"

With all the demure innocence she could muster, Katelin said she was nothing more than "a witness."

Regarding Ann's devotion to the children, Katelin gave a more definitive comment. "When my mom was writing the letters to Robert Russell, when did she have time to do that if she was so dedicated? How could she have time to write over one hundred letters in a year?"

"Does that mean she didn't love you?"

"It means she wasn't honest and she could have been into other things that she wasn't honest about either."

Katelin danced away from most of Lewin's question with the agility of an Olympic ice-skater, but she did say that if her father had committed the murder, he should be found guilty.

This youngest offspring of Ann and John Racz's engendered the same compassion that had been felt for Glenn and Joann. Katelin had endured unimaginable anguish in losing her mother, and seeing her father charged with killing her. Spectators could see through the veneer of her rationalizations and evasions. The scars would no doubt remain with her forever.

She stepped down at last, and gave her father a weak smile.

The next witness, a female friend of the defendant, had moved into a home on Fortuna Drive in 1997. She had read a news report describing the testimony of another neighbor, Thomas Deardorff, and contacted the defense team to volunteer her opinion that he had not been truthful. On the stand, under Israels's questioning, the woman said she walked her dog daily, and had discovered that, while standing in front of the home Deardorff had occupied in 1991, it would be impossible to see anything going on at the Racz residence. Curvature of the street would prevent it. So she wanted to contradict Deardorff's comments about seeing the moving van, and about John Racz leaving to follow Ann on that fateful day.

Cross-examination resulted in her admission to being a "very close" friend of Racz's, and she did not believe that he murdered his wife. The witness also did not know whether trees or shrubs currently on the street had existed in 1991, nor did she know where Mr. Deardorff had stood when he made his observations. Jurors would have to decide if her contribution carried any weight.

Another brief defense witness took the oath from her wheelchair, due to a broken ankle, and remained in it to testify. Ann Racz, she said, had written newsletters for a homeowners' association managed by the witness. She told Israels about a newspaper article telling of Ann's disappearance on April 22,

1991. "I thought that was not possible because I remember seeing her at the intersection of Wiley and Lyons after that date."

Muffled whispers rippled through the gallery.

The witness believed the sighting had occurred on April 25. She had been driving her car, making a left, late at that intersection, and spotted Ann coming from the opposite direction, making a right turn. They had acknowledged each other. The woman made a police report one month later after seeing the news article.

On cross-examination, she could not identify Ann's white minivan from a photograph, but was "eighty percent certain" that she had recognized Ann Racz. And her certainty of the date stood at about 80 percent. In the police report, she had expressed a possibility of children being in Ann's car and had said the event "could have been six weeks ago, I'm not sure." That would have made the sighting well before April 22.

Philip Israels told Judge Coen that he had only one more witness, but the person couldn't come to court until the next day, Wednesday. To save time, Coen allowed the prosecution to put on the first of only two rebuttal witnesses, even though the defense hadn't yet officially rested its case.

Frank Salerno rose to take his final turn at bat. Beth Silverman asked him if, on May 29, 1991, he had interviewed the woman who had just finished testifying. Salerno said yes, and he had taken notes of it. "Eventually she gave me a date of April twenty-fifth, but she wasn't certain." The woman had related it to a day she left early from work. "She went on to say it might have been as long as six weeks before our conversation." She had also expressed certainty about seeing kids in the car.

Through Salerno, Beth Silverman struck another blow at the woman's story. Ann's car had been parked in the Flyaway lot on April 25, 1991, as verified by a yellow parking receipt found inside it. She could not have been driving it at the in-

tersection of Wiley and Lyons. If that witness had truly seen
Ann, it must have been six weeks before her report, or approximately April 17, the day before she moved to Peachland.

Frank Salerno left the witness chair, having completed his
last official act on a case he had inherited more than sixteen
years ago.

Detective Cheryl Comstock took the oath and faced Beth
Silverman. A veteran with three decades of police experience,
she had partnered with Sergeant Dee Scott as the most recent
sleuths on the Ann Racz case. Silverman questioned her
about their conversations with Katelin, beginning on June 9,
2006. Comstock declared that Katelin's demeanor had been
"dramatically" different from how she behaved while testifying. At that time, Katelin had been friendly, but from the
opening day of the trial, she had been "distant" and defensive,
barely acknowledging Comstock's "hellos to her."

In addition, said the witness, Katelin's accounts of her
mother had definitely changed. Initially she "absolutely did
not believe her mother had abandoned her."

Did you ask her why she changed beliefs?

"She told me that she had several meetings with her father's
attorney, Mr. Mounger, which took place at his home, and
that . . . Mr. Mounger had, in fact, told her that her mother had
abandoned them."

In a May 7, 2007, interview with Katelin, said Comstock,
"there was a lot of defiance and restiveness in trying to draw out
information from her. Completely different from my first contact with her." The same thing had happened with Glenn Racz.

Katelin's testimony had included cynical comments about her
mother's devotion. "She told us that she remembered her mother
to be devoted to not only her, but Joann too," Comstock said.

"Did she tell you she had numerous conversations with her
father about the case?"

"Yes."

Beth inquired about one of the early, friendly interviews. "Did you ask her if the idea that her mother had abandoned her was sad for her to think about?"

"I did. And she responded, 'Yes, but it's sadder to think that my father slaughtered my mother.'"

Sounding tense, defender Israels cross-examined. "Were you aware that in 1991, she said that when she got home from the Brownies meeting, her father was there with Glenn and Joann?"

Comstock said she wasn't there at the time, but she had read the documentation.

"Okay," said Israels, and made a quantum leap in subject matter. "You describe yourself as a fact finder. Did you ever go to the L.A. airport to make a determination on whether or not there were surveillance cameras there in 1991?"

"No, sir, I did not."

Israels also wanted to know if Comstock had gone to Katelin's school to check records of what time she got out on April 22, 1991. And Glenn's school. And Joann's school.

Back to Katelin, he asked if Comstock had ever let her read 109 letters in reference to this case. "No," she replied, "I would never have done that, sir."

Israels also seized the opportunity to inquire if a crime scene, murder weapon, any physical evidence, scientific evidence, or witnesses to a crime had ever been discovered.

"No, sir."

When Silverman took over again, she asked, "Detective, the fact that you never found a crime scene, does that indicate to you no homicide took place?"

"Absolutely not."

"Does that indicate that Ann Racz is still alive?" Silverman ran through each of the hurdles erected by the defender. Comstock kicked at all of them.

Regarding the letters, Comstock expressed the same thing that juror Barbara Kaplan would later say. "Those were personal letters meant for those individuals and no one else's eyes."

A slip of paper had been discovered in the condo on which Ann had printed several area code (800) numbers of airlines, and the defenders had hinted it could relate to Ann's plans to take a trip in April 1991. Silverman asked Comstock to read a portion of Ann's letter to Russell, dated July 3, 1990. It suggested that Ann had prepared her list, then tried to find cheap airfare to visit Russell.

At the end of Detective Comstock's testimony, observers looked toward the defense table. Would John Racz get up and tell what happened in his own words? It didn't happen. He chose to remain mute.

That left only one witness to be heard from, on the next day.

The morning of Wednesday, August 15, brought more record temperatures outside, making Judge Coen's courtroom a welcome, air-conditioned respite. The case's final witness seated himself.

Stephen Yee had spent eighteen years as a manager at Los Angeles International Airport, including 1991. Philip Israels asked him if surveillance cameras had been in place at that time. Yes, said Yee. In the terminals' "holding areas, right before you get to the airplane takeoff areas. They were for skyjacking, not terrorism." Tapes had been kept on record for six months, then burned, unless a law enforcement agency asked to borrow them. Other cameras screened license plate numbers of vehicles leaving the central parking area.

Israels asked the witness, if the sheriff's office had called to request use of those videos, "would you have cooperated with law enforcement?"

"Yes."

If observers expected dazzling fireworks as a climax to the

defense's case, they saw something more like a wet firecracker that fizzled and never exploded. Israels turned the witness over to Beth Silverman.

She said, "We don't have any cross, Your Honor."

Israels announced, "The defense rests."

"That's it. It's over," Judge Coen informed the jury. He ordered them to return on the following day to hear the lawyers deliver arguments, summarizing their cases.

This phase is eagerly anticipated by journalists and veteran court observers. It ties up all the loose strings. It's like Charlie Chan calling everyone into a drawing room and telling how he solved the case. The opening statements predict how the puzzle pieces should be assembled, while the final arguments present the final picture with all interlocking pieces in place.

Unless some of the pieces are missing!

CHAPTER 32

No Surrender

<u>Ronald Bowers:</u>

I have known Beth for quite a while, and admired the way she handled the heavy workload. But the Racz case changed her routine entirely. Because the trial landed in Judge Coen's San Fernando courtroom, it forced her to work temporarily out of the DA's office in that building. When she travels, she brings a truckload of boxes and files, which requires expanded working space. In San Fernando, she declared eminent domain over the law library, stacked cartons to the ceiling, and covered every square inch of its long conference table with documents. Her idea of winning is knowing every detail about the crime and all the witnesses.

One of the ways Beth makes herself at home is by toasting her bagels every morning in the lunchroom. Reminded me of my hero when I first started, J. Miller Leavy. But he never donned bright fuzzy pink slippers, like those Beth brought from home. She isn't self-conscious about her appearance while working in the privacy of the office. Her thinking is that she'd rather be comfortable. When it's showtime, though, she puts on her high heels and prances into the courtroom.

During a two-week break in the Racz trial, Beth returned to our downtown quarters.

I had been working on several cases with other deputies and one for Beth scheduled to start after completion of the current trial. In her usual frenzy of energy, she dropped in to see me about it, and breezed right out of my office again, saying she needed to bring other items of evidence for discussion. She left me hanging. I knew that she had just started to think about the final phase in the Racz trial, and I assumed she might have it all lined up. When she didn't return to my office, I turned my attention back to my computer files on a different murder. I don't know how much time had passed when I heard her unmistakable voice bellowing at a fever pitch. With no intention of eavesdropping, I could tell she was on the telephone and that she seemed to be in a predicament with a slide show she needed for the Racz closing argument.

Even after she hung up, I could hear her groaning about it. I decided to go see if I could help her. At the door to Beth's room, I tentatively glanced in and could see her eyes glazed over as she stared toward a blackboard. On it she had printed a list of numerous cases assigned to her, all pending action. She seemed mesmerized by it, and I could see that she had calendared more murder cases than anyone else in the Major Crimes Division. I seldom ever saw Beth wearing this type of gloomy expression. In my kindest voice, I asked if she had found the material she needed.

Her head turned toward me and she said in a remarkably quiet voice, "Ron, I sure could use some help with my Racz argument." Beth explained the problem to me. The law clerk assigned to help with her PowerPoint hadn't completed it due to other commitments. She acknowledged that the trial had consumed so much time, it had ruined her opportunity to assemble her ideas in a logical order. Raising a yellow legal pad into my line of vision, Beth thumbed through more than twenty pages of notes.

I knew how hard Beth had worked on the case and that she needed someone to lend a helping hand. I said, "Okay, let's see what we can do." At my request, she agreed to take the next thirty minutes and create a list of the key ideas she wanted to present.

She looked up and asked, "Ron, are you sure this is what I need to do?" In the most authoritative voice I could summon, I assured her this would solve her dilemma. I really had no idea what needed to be done, but I wanted to buy some time. I told Beth her immediate job was to list all of the key issues, and I would be back. I marched out as though I had an urgent mission.

As soon as I reached my office, I immediately went to the file cabinet and flipped through a drawer filled with folders until I found my Racz file. I pulled out the PowerPoint show I had made for Shellie Samuels almost nine months earlier. Scanning through it as fast as possible, I refamiliarized myself with the facts. The two timelines I had developed helped immensely to get me back up to speed.

A half hour later, I strolled back into Beth's office, carrying a poster board almost the size of her desk.

Together we worked on it. Beth wrote her key ideas on sticky notes of various sizes and colors. We arranged them, talked it over, and shifted them around, seeking the best order for maximum impact. The whole process took a half hour, and I could see a smile playing on her lips. She said, "This looks good. It's all coming together."

What knocked my socks off was all the additional evidence Beth and the detectives had come up with since I had worked on the case. They had broken loose an avalanche of facts to disprove that Ann Racz had gone on a spontaneous, permanent vacation. Seldom does a case improve with age. Time is generally a prosecutor's enemy, because witnesses forget, disappear, or die. But it worked to Beth's advantage simply because no reasonable person could argue convincingly that Ann could still be alive after sixteen years of invisibility and silence.

Now, with the facts organized into logical and understandable order, Beth had the ingredients for preparation of an excellent PowerPoint presentation. I realized that the planets, the sun, and the stars had to be in perfect alignment for Beth to put an end to this perfect crime.

I hoped that her PowerPoint would materialize for her, but just in case it didn't, I had another idea, and went to work preparing it as a backup.

CHAPTER 33

"TRUST ME, THIS IS A WOMAN THING."

Ronald Bowers:

I rose early Thursday morning, August 16, and drove to San Fernando. Entering the courthouse, I carried the backup poster boards, three feet wide and five feet long, and delivered them to Beth in the third-floor DA's office.

She examined the visual aids with some skepticism. One of them contained two bold red-lettered headings: EVIDENCE ANN IS DEAD and EVIDENCE DEFENDANT KILLED ANN. Under the upper category, I had listed six lines of information, and below the second one, twenty-three lines. To the left of each line, I had inserted a box in which Beth could enter a checkmark as she spoke.

If Beth had misgivings, her assistant, Lewin, indicated he didn't want to use the charts at all, preferring to rely completely on cutting-edge technology, the PowerPoint show. Who needs old-fashioned poster board charts?

I went downstairs for a cup of coffee, then headed for the courtroom. When I took a seat in the gallery, it pleased me to see that Beth had one of my large charts mounted on a tripod, where the jury could see it with only a slight glance away from the PowerPoint screen.

Judge Coen opened the proceedings by saying to jurors, "Good morning. All right, we are on the downhill slide here. As I told you yesterday, the evidence portion of this case has been concluded. This is the opportunity of the lawyers to argue the matter to you. You are admonished, once again, that any statements by the attorneys are not evidence. The people will open the argument. The defense will be able to argue, and the people will close because they have the burden of proof in this case." He then asked Beth, "Are you ready?"

In saying yes, Beth showed none of the turbulence that had been swirling around her. The first rule of a trial attorney is "Don't let the jurors see you sweat."

"Good morning, ladies and gentlemen," she greeted. "I want to thank you for your time and attention." I held my breath, hoping she wouldn't waste her golden window of opportunity with trite, inane verbiage as inexperienced prosecutors often do, hoping to ingratiate themselves with jurors. I tried to transmit a mental message to her: *Beth, please don't squander this chance to make an indelible mark in their minds.*

To my great delight, she moved on without delay by stating that the main issue is "whether or not Ann Racz is alive or dead. If you decide that Ann Racz is alive, then the defendant is obviously not guilty. However, if you find that Ann Racz is dead, based on the overwhelming evidence we presented, then that evidence will show that the defendant must be guilty."

Before they could reach that decision, Beth explained, they had to know who Ann Racz was. She cited Sergeant Salerno's philosophy that investigators have to know the victim.

Beth reminded jurors of the positive qualities numerous witnesses had ascribed to Ann: organized, meticulous planner, immaculate, devoted to her children, unselfish community and school volunteer, faithful church member, completely reliable, along with a plethora of other praiseworthy attributes.

Ann was also a creature of habit, Beth said, who always used a curling iron and took it with her when traveling. And she never went away "unannounced," or without preparing for her children's detailed care.

I thought it great that Beth spent a lot of time showing Ann's dedication to the kids, which could offset lukewarm appraisals from Glenn and Katelin. It might also quash defense hints that Ann would give up custody of them. Beth said, "It is completely unreasonable to believe that Ann Racz would abandon her children."

More than one person found it disturbing that the defense attorney had allowed Ann's children to read the letters to Bob Russell. The intense personal feelings Ann bared in them apparently distressed Glenn and Katelin, and it damaged their opinions of her. Beth tiptoed through this minefield, hoping jurors could see how defenders had turned the kids against the prosecution.

The next level of Beth's argument addressed John's lies and Ann's fear of him. Beth said, "All of the evidence in this case points to the fact that the defendant's stories don't make sense. . . . All of his statements conflict with one another." Time and time again, he had been caught lying.

Ann's terror, said Beth, had been affirmed by testimony from Joann, Pastor Thorp, the church circle of women, Ann's divorce attorney, Emi Ryan, and Kathy Gettman. They said she would never have met with John at restaurants in the days following April 22, nor gone to his house alone. She would not have called him from LAX, while completely ignoring her loved ones.

By this time, I could see signs of adrenaline speeding

through Beth's body and providing wattage to her rhetoric. It made me feel good when she referred to topics on her big chart, and even better when I noticed jurors craning their neck to read it. Without any advance rehearsal, she had seamlessly integrated the chart into her PowerPoint show.

After lunch Beth commenced with the next phase of her argument, shown on the next chart as EVIDENCE ANN IS DEAD. She reminded jurors that abundant evidence had proved Ann's death. Otherwise, she would never have missed holidays with her family, watching her children grow up, funerals, graduations, weddings, the birth of grandchildren, and taking her kids for a new life with Bob Russell. Beth relied partly on testimony from Joann and Glenn, both of whom said that if their mother still lived, she would have been in touch with them. Other substantiation came from proof that Ann had never contacted any family members, used her credit cards or Social Security number, drawn money from her bank accounts, or finalized the divorce.

I knew the defense would do anything within their means to convince jurors Ann was still out there somewhere, living in anonymity. As Beth hammered away on the theme, I flashed back on J. Miller Leavy's story of the defender pointing to the door and stating that the alleged victim might walk in at any moment. Much to my surprise, I heard the screeching sound of the courtroom door opening. Beth stopped dead in her tracks and looked toward it, and jurors' gazes followed hers. My eyes darted over to John Racz, and he stared straight ahead. Just like Leavy had proclaimed, all eyes turned to the door—except the defendant's, because only he knew that the dead victim couldn't possibly enter the court.

Now Beth took the big step forward, tackling the key issue on her chart: EVIDENCE DEFENDANT KILLED ANN.

Homicide detectives often utilize "MOM" factors in their searches for killers. They look for a suspect's motive, opportunity, and means (MOM) to commit the murder. I had deliberately inserted these points in Beth's charts, and she addressed each one of them.

Racz's *motive*, Beth said, stemmed from his obsession with money. He would do anything (his words) to keep her from leaving, and little doubt could exist that he would fight to keep from losing half of their community property. Another motive related to the need to exercise control over his family, which Ann had violated by disobediently moving out and filing for divorce.

One possible *means* to kill her, Beth stated, came from testimony about guns he kept in the house. The other means, which Beth thought more likely, related to what he had learned as a sheriff's deputy—how to apply various types of choke holds, several of which could be lethal.

I realized that the means he used to kill Ann was not the pivotal issue in this case. The defining matter would be his *opportunity* to murder Ann. Beth changed gears to slow motion in explaining that the defendant had plenty of time, after following her on the McDonald's run and before coming back with cold food. Even though Joann had at first estimated her father's absence at about five minutes, other testimony showed a window of opportunity giving him at least ninety minutes, and up to three hours, to render her unconscious, take her to a remote location, kill her, dispose of the body, and return home.

Two major subdivisions of her chart listed DEFENDANT'S DEMEANOR and CONSCIOUSNESS OF GUILT.

Concentrating on the first one, Beth spoke of John's persistent evasiveness with investigators, resistance in cooperating, and his obvious lack of concern about Ann's disappearance. His lies overlapped into this category too. Since the defendant hadn't testified, his defenders were stuck with prior statements easily exposed as false. Beth emphasized that the only possible purpose of so many lies lay in his desire to cover up guilt for murdering Ann.

Consciousness of guilt, Beth asserted, could be seen in

the defendant's multiple inconsistent statements. He had contrived stories about meetings at restaurants to give her money, but kept changing the facts each time he told them to different people. His versions of last seeing and speaking to Ann also bounced all over the map. He had boxed himself in by saying she remained in the area at least four days after April 22. Yet, indisputable evidence showed that Ann had never returned to the condo. No logic could account for that inconsistency.

Racz had said repeatedly that Ann showed up at restaurants wearing the same clothing for three days. Multiple witnesses, though, had attested to Ann's immaculate appearance. With clothing available for Ann at the condo, John's story stretched all limits of credibility. Earlier I wondered why Beth wanted to make such a big deal about Ann wearing the same clothes in succession. She pulled me aside and said, "Ron, trust me, this is a woman thing." Beth understood that every woman on the jury would know that Ann didn't wear the same pink outfit on three consecutive days.

More evidence showing consciousness of guilt appeared in the collect call from LAX. Even Beth had to agree the idea seemed brilliant, and might have worked. To most people, it would appear that Ann, alive and well, had placed the call, then left on a jet plane for an unknown destination, on a permanent, spontaneous vacation. But when diligent work by detectives revealed the two calls made from an adjacent phone to Racz's number, the whole ruse fell apart. And, Beth explained to jurors, the planting of Ann's car at Flyaway would have been ingenious, but the yellow parking receipt proved the vehicle had been parked a whole day before the collect call. So Racz's story—Ann saying she had left her car at Flyaway, taken a shuttle to LAX, and was about to board a plane—didn't work.

After fitting a few more pieces into the puzzle, Beth was interrupted by Judge Coen announcing the day's end. She had been arguing nearly four hours. Closing her notebook as I approached, she told me she was disappointed in not finishing because she had been looking forward to an exciting evening. That meant walking her dog, Jake (she didn't acquire Daisy until after the Racz trial), coming back home, and curling up on the sofa with a book and a big bowl of ice cream. Instead, she would have to spend the time polishing her remaining argument.

I asked how much more she had. Beth opened her notebook and showed me thirty pages in which she wanted to cover all of the inconsistent statements from Racz. I tried to think of a diplomatic way of saying she didn't need to expose every single one. My statesman skills sometimes fail. I suggested that she try to reduce the number by selecting only enough to get her point across to the jury.

On Friday morning, a traffic tangle almost made me late, but I arrived in time to find a seat with an unobstructed view of the jurors. To me, they looked like saturated sponges unable to absorb another drop. Most of them had their notebooks on their laps and none had pencils in hand. Their appearance convinced me that Beth should not try to cover her remaining thirty pages.

Judge Coen announced, "Darryl Mounger is not present. He will not be present for the rest of this proceeding." Rumors circulated that he had been taken ill.

Beth greeted jurors and said, "We are here for round two." Then she spoke of a list of lies told by John Racz, according to witness testimony. "He told Detective Fynan that he talked to the victim two or three times after April twenty-second. We know that's not true. Very hard to talk to the dead." Beth continued with examples of fabrications from the defendant.

To magnify Racz's lack of interest in finding Ann, Beth cited a personal observation. "When I take a walk with my dog,

like I do on a daily basis, I always notice that people put up
signs about their missing pets, usually with photographs. And
I was thinking the other day as I walked Jake, you know what,
people looking for their pets do more than he has ever done
to find his wife."

Offering a parade of examples to illustrate holes in John
Racz's stories, Beth challenged jurors to ask themselves a few
questions. If Ann Racz was still alive two days after she left for
McDonald's, and met John at two restaurants, why didn't she
go to the condo to sleep? Why didn't she drop the VCR off
there? Why? Because she was dead. His ridiculous story about
her wearing the same pink outfit three days in a row was nothing but a cover-up in case anyone ever found her body, clothed
as she was on April 22, the day he killed her. The garbage
about moving the car to shade at the Flyaway? Another alibi
in case someone noticed him parking Ann's vehicle when he
planted it there on April 25.

Beth didn't offer a theory of how Racz returned to his home
after driving the minivan to Flyaway. He may have used public
transportation, but that mystery would remain unsolved.

She did suggest a believable method for choking the life out
of Ann. "He was trained to know how to subdue a person, how
to render someone unconscious, how to kill without leaving any
evidence behind."

I knew that the list of Racz's inconsistent statements numbered at least forty-two. After Beth had talked for fifteen minutes, I surmised that she had not taken my advice to offer only
a few samples. She felt compelled to spell out each and every
one of them. In addition, she recapped his evasive tactics,
bizarre apathy, misdirections, and several mysterious absences
during which neighbors watched the kids. The defendant's
faulty logic came under her spotlight as well.

After an hour, it appeared to me that the jury had zoned out.
Even I was having trouble keeping all of the examples straight.
Just as I tried to digest one, Beth would leap to another one,

Still, as painful as it was to concentrate, I started to realize where she was headed. By the time she started to wind down, she had branded Racz with blazing letters reading "Liar." I felt certain the jury had him pegged. Beth's judgment turned out to be right again.

My chest may have expanded when Beth walked over to the chart, carrying a red felt-tip marker in her hand. She stretched up to the top subheading NOT HEARD FROM OR SEEN IN 16 YEARS, saying, "This is an easy one." She entered a big scarlet check mark in the box. One by one, she read each line aloud, and checked it off. I glanced around and could see that Beth had total control over the entire crowd. Jurors who had appeared ready to pass out a few minutes ago now stared with big eyes, glued to every word.

Beth ended her impassioned speech by saying, "The defendant's story is beyond absurd, given the testimony of every witness in this case. . . . Tell him. Tell him that his sixteen-year charade is over. It ends here. Don't let him get away with murder because that's what you would be doing. The evidence in this case is clear beyond any reasonable doubt that Ann Racz was murdered by the defendant, her husband, on April 22 of 1991. The people of the state of California ask that you seek justice . . . and justice demands that you convict the defendant of first-degree murder of Ann Racz. Thank you."

CHAPTER 34

IMPASSIONED PRONOUNCEMENTS

With an hour to go before lunch, Judge Coen signaled Philip Israels for his turn to make a final argument.

Every attorney tries to find the perfect spot to plant the lectern, without invading an imaginary no-man's-land. In law school, students are taught the impropriety of leaning on, or reaching over, the railing in front of jurors. It is considered poor form to step within two feet of it.

Seeming satisfied with his position, Israels straightened up and shot both hands into the air as if praising the Lord. He said, "Let's slow down for a moment. Let's stop the locomotive. The prosecution has shown you that most of the witnesses believe John Racz is guilty of killing his wife, but they don' have the evidence."

A slight smile could be seen on a few jurors' faces. They had just connected with the defense attorney's sly slap at Beth Silverman's rapid-fire summation.

Israels lashed out again. "This entire case has been a slick production, which is like a television commercial produced to sell you a product. They have a fifty-five-thousand-dollar projector. They have video clips, audio clips. They have got Power-Point presentations. Two of their toughest deputies and tears from their witnesses. They appeal to your sympathies, to your passion, and your prejudices. What they don't have is the evidence. . . . This is not a reality show."

Holding dark-framed glasses in his right hand, Israels waved them to punctuate his commentary. It looked like he might lose his grip and send them flying into a juror's face. His reference to a $55,000 projector irritated Ron Bowers. Since Bowers had purchased the equipment, he knew that each projector cost no more than $3,000.

It also bothered him to see that jurors were furiously writing notes. They had barely lifted a pen or pencil during Beth Silverman's presentation.

Playing the sympathy card, Israels commented, "The Yoshi-yamas, the Ryans, they seem like a very close, nice family. Certainly, we can sympathize with their difficult ordeal of not knowing what happened to Ann." But, he warned, their beliefs—nor any other witness's beliefs—could not substitute for evidence.

For the next fifteen minutes, the defender charged law enforcement with focusing only on John Racz, criticized all of the witnesses for not seeing Ann as a "conflicted woman," suggested that talk about scratches on the defendant's face or hands had been specious, and reproached speculation about a gun possibly being used.

The description of Ann as "conflicted" made Bowers turn to steal a glance at Emi Ryan. Her expression did not register fondness for Philip Israels. The defender's willingness to traverse this slippery slope amazed Bowers. He would have avoided it in front of so many female jurors.

* * *

Attacking the "controlling" characterization of Racz, Israels asked how a man who leaves for work at five in the morning, and gets home after dark, can watch every move his wife makes. Ann's trips without him, attending movies with friends, and participating in community activities did not appear to be a woman under her husband's control. And certainly, the defendant's "control" hadn't prevented her from liaisons with a boyfriend.

Bringing up the defendant's story of walking home from Carl's Jr. after meeting Ann there, and his snatching the calendar from an evidence container to mark out the "Hell Day" entry, Israels criticized them as "stupid mistakes," but he insisted they did not constitute evidence of murder.

Much of Israels's argument centered on what investigators did *not* do. Since the notorious O.J. Simpson trial, this tactic had gained popularity. Charging the police with incompetence had swayed more than one jury. But a "rush to judgment" theory didn't seem very valid, considering that investigators had worked for sixteen years before filing charges.

Israels brought up the woman who claimed she had seen Ann in a vehicle a few days after April 22, and charged the investigators with shrugging off this important sighting. And, he said, the witness who reported that Thomas Deardorff couldn't possibly have seen events at the Racz home was also ignored.

The issue of the answering machine came next, and Israels offered several scenarios to explain it. He said that Racz didn't even have such a device when the collect call was made, and that no evidence came forth to prove that he had gone to LAX to make the calls. Hints that he had installed it just for that one day, then disposed of it, were absurd, the defender said.

To Beth Silverman's arguments about "consciousness of guilt," Israels countered that his client really had a "consciousness of innocence." Trying to show exculpatory evidence in financial transactions at banks, Israels threw numbers and dates around like a handful of gravel, but he didn't appear to hit anything as reflected in jurors' blank expressions.

According to Israels, Racz had no motive to kill Ann. In case jurors wondered about retribution for her love affair, he explained that his client didn't even know of the sex between them until a year later when he read one of the letters.

Was the defendant a violent person? No, said Israels. No evidence even suggested he had ever struck Ann, and when Emi repeatedly slapped him, John kept his hands in his pockets.

Pastor Thorp came under the defense's critique for having made "inconsistent statements." The implication suggested that Thorp had violated privacy ethics, but he handed Silverman and Lewin compliments as "very, very clever, very tough prosecutors" who could "sell ice cubes to Eskimos."

Racz's opportunity to kill Ann on April 22 apparently looked to Israels like the prosecution's Achilles' heel, vulnerable to his arrows. "It's one of the most important issues in the case," he declared. Relying on the original estimate by Joann, in which Racz had been gone only five minutes, and Katelin's early recollection that her father was at home when she arrived, Israels built a scenario of inadequate time for the defendant to commit murder. He bolstered it with Carol Kuwata's testimony estimating Katelin's arrival at about four-thirty. If John left at four, and arrived home prior to four-thirty, he could not have killed Ann.

In the defense version, testimony from neighbors Deardorff and Pedersen either supported the shortened time frame, or were inaccurate due to the passage of sixteen years. Also, Deardorff's view had been obstructed, as revealed by the woman who had walked her dog in the neighborhood. Israels also slammed the investigators for not looking into school records to verify what time the children left classes that day, which might impact the time frames prosecutors presented.

The people's entire case, Israels charged, had no foundation to support it other than innuendo, implication, and inference.

He completed his argument at 3:15 P.M.: "Putting John Racz through this ordeal is wrong. All the evidence in this case is pointed to one—*and one*—conclusion only. John Racz is not guilty. Thank you."

The jurors had listened to hours of rhetoric, discourse, and impassioned pronouncements. They looked tired. Judge Coen decided to call it a day and let them have the weekend to rest before hearing John Lewin's rebuttal on Monday. But at a requested sidebar, Lewin protested. He wanted to start immediately. Coen relented, but only until four o'clock.

If being forced to stay and listen to more speeches disappointed weary jurors, it may have been aggravated when Lewin tried to entertain them. He spent his first few minutes with what appeared to be a comedy routine about his weight and inability to resist stopping for donuts every morning.

With that out of the way, Lewin told jurors how hard it had been to hear Israels criticize Ann Racz, and how he wanted to jump up and scream in her defense.

Accusing Israels of concentrating on "tangential" issues, Lewin said his opponent had made it a complicated case, which "means you won't be able to figure out what occurred." Instead, he argued, it is a simple case.

The prosecution, Lewin said, had purposely delivered a lot of information, especially about the qualities of Ann Racz. "You have one main question in this case—is Ann Racz alive? If so, the defendant's story is true. If not, then the evidence proves he killed her."

One by one, the prosecutor identified the major issues and presented his version of what the testimonial evidence showed.

Regarding the crucial time frame on April 22, Lewin said, "The defendant had all week to figure out what to do with her body. All week! He could have moved her three times. We know that her car doesn't get put there (at the Flyaway) until the twenty-fifth."

Judge Coen had given Lewin until four o'clock, and true

to his word, he interrupted exactly on the hour. He ordered the jurors to return on August 20.

On that Monday morning, John Lewin struck again at the defense, saying their argument made John Racz the victim. "Everybody is out to get John Racz. Everyone. Ms. Silverman. Myself. The detectives. His boss, his neighbors. Even his daughter." Why? asked Lewin, calling it an absurd tactic.

Assuming that jurors may have wondered why the prosecution had used so many witnesses to show Ann Racz's characteristics, Lewin explained it. "To a large degree, Ann almost came back from the dead to help you solve her murder. See, Ann—even though she's dead, and not able to testify—through her habits and customs, you were able to learn what kind of a mother she was. You were able to learn there is no way she abandoned those children. You were able to learn how she felt about Bob Russell. . . . Through her relationship with her family, her children, her boyfriend, her habits of neatness and organization . . . you know right away there's no way this woman took off in the manner the defendant described."

Israels had criticized the investigation, calling it sloppy. Lewin sprang to their defense. "He ignores the thousands of pages of work and the job done by these [detectives]. It was an outstanding investigation. They were dedicated and never gave up."

Ann's letters to Russell, Lewin asserted, were used to poison the children's minds, to beat down the bond between mother and child. And, he said, the defense had brought up the letters, repeatedly, in an attempt to make them into a red herring, a diversion from the truth.

Admitting that he didn't know if Racz drove to LAX to make the collect call himself, or got someone else to do it, Lewin said, "We know that Ann Racz didn't make the call." Although Lewin didn't expand on that point, it raised an interesting possibility.

The defendant had told investigators that he heard traffic noises during the alleged call from Ann. That mistake may have revealed that he didn't know the pay phone used were inside the terminal—perhaps because someone had helped him set up the ruse.

"Joann Racz," Lewin said, "is one of the heroes in this case. Maybe the hero." He added that she loves her father, and asked jurors to imagine how difficult it must have been for her to testify against him. Even though the defense "vilified" her for it, she told the truth.

Jurors may have been puzzled about the huge volume of testimony indicating that John Racz kept detectives away from his two younger children for weeks. Lewin explained that Katelin, in her childish estimate that John had been gone only five minutes on April 22, may have wanted to change that time frame.

Using his own personality, techniques, and emphasis, along with his PowerPoint show, Lewin spent the next two hours re-covering the points Beth Silverman had hammered away at for five hours.

Just before noon, Lewin concluded: "This is not a complicated case. He killed her. Hold him responsible. Let justice happen in this case. It's time. Thank you very much."

After lunch, and hearing the judge's recitation of jury instructions, the dozen triers of fact retired to their room to begin deliberations.

Judge Coen had one more announcement: "The defendant is under strict orders at this time. He must remain in the courtroom or in the hallway at all phases of deliberations. If he wants to go anywhere else, he must ask permission from the bailiff."

The long wait began. When jurors failed to reach a decision that Monday evening, Emi Ryan and the Yoshiyama brothers retreated to the local hotel where they had been staying.

All day Tuesday, the hours slowly ticked by, and still the jurors debated.

On Wednesday morning, August 22, quiet discussions took place along hallway benches, and in the basement cafeteria, rumors and speculations drifted back and forth, until a bailiff came out shortly after ten o'clock to gather the court officers. A buzz of excitement energized people filing in and taking their seats.

Emi and Jerry Ryan had been called by Beth Silverman on Tuesday evening at their hotel. She told them it would be a good idea for them to be in court early Wednesday. Emi's heart pounded. After all these years, would her beloved sister finally have justice?

Joann Racz felt like she couldn't get her breath as she sat close to Katelin and Glenn.

Frank Salerno and Louis Danoff, partners for so long, sat side by side again, hoping for the best.

Judge Coen announced, "We are going to take a verdict momentarily. The policy that I have in my courtroom, if there is any emotional outburst, any display of any kind of emotion, deputies in this court are under strict orders to remove you. If you resist, you will be arrested. There will be no displays of emotion. Can we have the jury and the alternates, please?"

The jury—seven women and five men—came through the deliberation room door and took their respective seats, not making eye contact with anyone.

Coen boomed, "Good morning. Mr. Foreperson, you have reached a verdict. Is that correct?"

A man in the second row said, "Yes, we have, Your Honor."

"Is the verdict signed and dated?"

"Yes, it is."

"Would you please hand both forms to the bailiff?"

To the absolutely silent spectators, the room felt tight, with a diminished supply of oxygen.

After the forms had passed through the judge's hands, and on to the court clerk, she stood and read them aloud.

"'Superior Court of California, County of Los Angeles, *People of the State of California* versus *John Racz* . . .

"'We, the jury in the above entitled action, find the defendant, John Racz, guilty of the crime of murder, in violation of Penal Code 187, subdivision (A), a felony, as charged in the indictment. We find it to be murder in the first degree.'"

Stunned spectators remained silent, many in disbelief. If they had been forced to bet, most of them would have guessed a verdict of not guilty.

After polling the jury, Coen expressed his gratitude to them, ending with, "I thank you from the bottom of my heart." He set September 14 as the date for sentencing.

CHAPTER 35

"SHE SENT ME MANY MESSENGERS."

The Southern California heat wave had retreated very little by Friday morning, September 14, when Judge Coen's courtroom filled early. Court officers took their places; Ann's family, investigators of the case, including Salerno and Danoff, and five jurors having completed their duty joined spectators in the jammed gallery. A television crew and other news media reporters occupied the jury box.

At 9:15 A.M., a bailiff led John Racz in from a side door. His bail had been revoked immediately upon the guilty verdict, and his tan had already started to fade from sitting in jail. Dressed in jail-issued orange coveralls, and manacled, he glanced back at his offspring, then shuffled to a chair at the defense table.

Judge Coen heard legalese from the lawyers. Challenging sufficiency and reliability of evidence, Philip Israels requested a new trial. Beth Silverman argued that no legal grounds existed for such action, and said, "Now it's time for the defendant to face the music."

Coen listened attentively and denied Israels's request. Given the opportunity, neither Israels nor Silverman wished to make further statements. But John Lewin did. He gave a rambling speech about how painful it had been for him to cross-examine Glenn Racz, then expressed hope that John Racz would stand up, be a man, and admit what he had done. "True to form, he comes in here like the victim. He waves at his children. I notice one of his daughters has left . . . court, crying." He ended by saying, "I'm sorry that everybody was put through this."

Israels stood and said, "Based on that statement," his client would like to speak. Judge Coen allowed it, and ordered Racz to remain seated.

John Racz's voice was heard for the first time. "All my life, I tried to be a good husband to Ann, my wife. She's still my wife. And when my wife left, when Ann left in April, she left on her own. I did not kill my wife. I did not kill my wife. After Ann left, I raised the children. Katelin was seven, Glenn was eleven, and Joann was fourteen. I raised my children. I thought Ann was coming home in a few days, maybe a few weeks. Ann didn't come home. And when I parked the car—when—"

Israels leaned over and whispered into Racz's ear. The defendant listened, then continued, "I did not kill my wife. I raised my children the best I could. I'm a good father, and I always was a good husband to Ann. I loved Ann. And I love my children. Your Honor, I did not kill my wife. I did not kill my wife."

In a voice as dry as desert sand, Coen asked, "Anything else, sir?"

Israels said no and thanked the judge.

Joann later described her reaction. "I don't think anything

he said made any sense at all. That was the first time he opened up his mouth. He said, 'I didn't do it,' and he looked around. Not at us, but more at a few jurors who sat in the gallery. And he said he didn't kill his wife, he didn't kill his wife. Well, that's not enough for me. After all that time and stress, that's all you have to say? I would be just like—I'd probably get arrested right there because I'd be jumping out of my seat. I really feel like he really had his last chance to say some important things, and I felt so bad that everyone was looking at him like they hated him, and giving him that silent moment after his talk, and it was just killing me with the embarrassment for him, being in that spot and with his last moment to have for his explanation. And I felt the explanation could have been a little bit better."

Judge Coen turned to Beth Silverman. "You may call whatever people you wish to come to the podium. It is incumbent they address me and not the defendant."

Kathy Gettman rose, stepped up to a lectern, gave her name, and said she was Ann's niece. She spoke of the impact Ann's absence had made and John Racz's reluctance to allow his kids to join in family activities after Ann's disappearance. The tiny memorial plaque in a churchyard substituted for a final resting place, she said. Sniffles and sobs could be heard in the audience. Kathy, too, cried as she told how her mother and grandmother had missed Ann. "I was so happy when Aunty Ann was going to start a new life in April of 1991. . . . She is no longer with us. There will always be an empty spot in so many lives due to the selfish act of this man." Kathy's voice trembled. "There will always be a place in my heart for her."

Patty Keitel, Kathy's sister, spoke next, evoking her memories of Ann as "so pretty" and said she wanted to be just like her. The pain of Ann's loss, Patty sobbed, would remain forever. "In her short life on earth, Ann did so much for other people. Finally we have the opportunity and the obligation to do something for her, to insure that justice is served."

Joji Yoshiyama, Ann's brother, gave a short talk recalling how their mother, before she passed away, always asked, "What happened to Ann? Is she coming back?" He closed by expressing acceptance of whatever sentence the court imposed on Racz, and stating that his brother, Takeo, sitting in the gallery, also wanted to thank the court.

Tears flowed freely in the room. Even court reporter Barbara Reed had trouble keeping her composure.

Emiko Ryan made her way to the lectern, graceful as a queen, with a look of peace on her elegant face. If she felt like crying, she held it back. Articulate and clear, she read the following:

> *My name is Emiko Ryan and I'm Ann Racz's sister. Good morning.*
>
> *Sixteen years ago, at age 42, Ann was gone. Through this act of cowardice, greed, and pride, John Racz killed Ann.*
>
> *Although Ann was leaving John and their marriage, she was trying to be fair with him. She did not take more than she needed from their home when she moved out five days earlier. She wanted custody of their children, but she was willing to share custody. I feel that she was willing to be friends with John, to work together for the sake of their children.*
>
> *In the brown box I found in her Peachland condo, she kept some private papers. After the verdict was read three weeks ago, I found an index card on which she had scribbled a prayer to her Lord. On it, she wrote, "Please give strength and courage to John to forgive me." She wanted to dissolve their marriage, not end John's life.*
>
> *But John acted differently, and for the last sixteen years her children, her family, and her friends were denied their right to be part of her life. And denied Ann to be part of our lives.*
>
> *She was not there when her children graduated from*

grade school, middle school, high school, and college. How proud she would have been.

She was not there when her granddaughter Kayla was born. She would have been tickled pink. She was not there when Glenn got married and did not get to meet her beautiful daughter-in-law, Amber.

She was not there when her brothers [each] celebrated their seventieth birthdays. She would have teased us about getting old. And she was not there when her mother died.

She was the last to leave home from my mom and dad, and now she was the first of us children to join them in heaven.

My mother missed Ann so much. My mother was forty when Ann was born. That was back in 1949, in Hawaii, in an old-fashioned Asian community. Mom admitted to me years later that she was embarrassed for being pregnant at that late age. She also told me that it would be sad because she would probably never live to see Ann graduate from high school or college. Later, she told me that she will probably never live to see Ann get married and have children. Well, Mom lived long enough to see all that happen.

They say that a parent should never have to bury their children. Well, Mom survived and outlived Ann, her youngest child. And the cruelty of it all is that she never got the chance to bury Ann.

In the few months before she died in 2000, at age ninety, Mom went to the hospital four times. Each time she thought she was going to die and each time she looked toward heaven and talked to Ann. One time, she told me to take care of Ann's children and see that they are always okay. Another time, she told me to make sure they bury Ann near her father. And yet another time, she asked to talk to Jerry alone.

Only later did he tell me that she told him to never give up finding what happened to Ann and finding justice for Ann.

Ten days before she died was my birthday. She asked me to get her a birthday card for her to give to me. During that last year she was staying at a family home care. On my birthday, I went to see her and she gave me my card. She had always written profound messages to her children and grandchildren in her cards and letters.

Inside my card, she wrote my name on the top, and signed her name at the bottom. And in the two-inch space between our names, she wrote just one word: Ann.

John could have told us what happened to Ann years ago. He showed no remorse for his cowardly act. He could have given closure to our mother while she was still alive.

In the year before she died, Mom said that before she goes, she is going to curse John for what he did to Ann and not telling us where she is. I told her that as soon as she dies, she will see Ann and she'll know what happened. So I told her when she dies, she should send me a message back.

Well, she did. She sent me many messengers. They are all in the courtroom today.

For sixteen years, John was free and lived his life like the rest of us. I would like to think that he could not have been happy and enjoyed his life knowing that he had done something dreadful. Well, his free days are over. I wish we could add those sixteen years to his sentence. However, he had a fair jury trial and finally Ann can rest in peace.

The only mercy I ask for John is that he lives a long life, which he will spend behind bars, and he can think about how life could have been different.

John has a chance to return to society one day a long time from now. However, he did not give Ann that chance. John had a fair trial with people who supported him. When Ann was fighting for her life, there was no one there to help and support her. I ask that you sentence John to the maximum time in prison which is not as long a sentence as he gave Ann.

We do not know where Ann's body is buried. We hope that John will eventually tell us. However, I'm okay with that. I'm at peace to know that justice has been dealt, and that Ann is in a very good place with our mother and father. And I know that one day I will see her again.

I believe that Ann would want her children, her family and her friends to live life to the fullest. Meanwhile, we have wonderful memories of a sister, aunt, mother, grandmother and friend. I have so many happy and silly memories of Ann.

I remember when she was in kindergarten and her teacher came over to our house to talk to our mother and tell her that Ann talked too much in class.

I remember when I took Ann for a ride in our family car after I got my driver's license at age fifteen and a car hit me from behind. I cried. She comforted me.

I remember when we lived on St. Elmo Street in Los Angeles and she and I went for a walk around the block. A huge dog came bounding toward us. I jumped behind Ann.

I remember when our family lived in Inglewood and Ann borrowed a tandem bike from a friend and made our mom ride and pump behind her. Mom was over sixty years old, and we didn't think she had ever ridden a bike before.

No one, no one, can take away my memories of Ann. We should not let John destroy our beautiful memories. We don't know just how lucky we are that she was part of our lives and she would be loved forever. We had a chance to love her, and she loved us back.

Thank you.

* * *

Judge Coen asked if the people had anything else. Beth said no. John Racz sat at the defense table watching and listening, his face as stoic and dispassionate as ever.

In the manner of a CEO dealing with corporate matters, Coen declared John Racz unsuitable for probation.

Quickly shedding that image, the judge allowed his voice to deepen into a solemn, perhaps angry tone. Looking directly at Racz, and enunciating every word, he said, "This case is a horrible example of greed and control gone awry. You have made many victims besides Mrs. Racz. You are a murderer! How tragic."

In the back row of the gallery, Joann stared at her father. She would later recall the feelings engulfing her. "The judge called him a murderer, and I felt relief that all of this finally happened. If it had to be, I'm relieved that it was sooner than later, because it needed to be done. I don't want Kayla to go through all this. It was weird, though. Hearing [my relatives] come out with their responses. It makes me feel really sad, because I do love my dad. And I don't want him to be put in that spot where everyone's looking at him. Everyone got silent, and everyone's looking at him. Hating him. That was the saddest moment of the whole thing. And they played it on the news. That was the worst part, when they brought my dad out in that orange jumpsuit, and he was handcuffed. He looked back at us for one second. And they showed it on the news. When he did that, I was on the tip of my seat, and crying. My brother and sister were sitting there. I felt almost like I was seeing it in a movie. For him to look at us like that. That was the last time he is ever going to be able to look at us, in public, before being locked up. Without a big glass wall between us. And the last time he's ever going to be able to say anything for people to actually hear."

* * *

Judge Coen continued his sentencing: "For the crime which defendant has been convicted . . . murder in the first degree, it will be the judgment and sentence of this court as follows.

"Probation is denied for the reasons I have stated.

"Defendant is sentenced to state prison for the term prescribed by law, which in this case is twenty-five years to life." Coen declared the proceedings closed.

A bailiff led John Racz through a side door to face the consequences for perhaps the rest of his life.

Lingering in the emptying courtroom, Louis Danoff said, "I've been carrying this thing on my back for so long, and now it's lifted off. It wasn't in vain."

Emi Ryan would later graciously tell her story to an author. But she contacted him a few days afterward to add something else very personal:

> *You asked how it felt all those sixteen years losing Ann and waiting for justice to happen. I didn't want to cry telling you this. I think about Ann all the time, especially when I'm alone. I look up in the sky every night before going to bed and talk to her. I cry, missing her, only when I'm alone. In the shower. When I take a walk. When I'm up late at night in solitude. During those sixteen years, when the case was not too active, I refrained from talking about Ann too much, thinking that others around me believe I should let it go. I didn't want anyone to see me crying, thinking about Ann.*
>
> *I never told this to anyone else.*
>
> *Take Care,*
Emi

EPILOGUE

On the eighteenth of April in 2008, exactly seventeen years after "Moving Day" for Ann Racz, NBC television premiered an episode of *Dateline* about the case, titled "Prime Suspect." Near the hour's end, Glenn Racz made a surprise statement, finally acknowledging belief that his mother had been murdered by his father, John.

Four days later, the anniversary of Ann's disappearance, more than sixty people gathered at the Newhall Presbyterian Church to participate in a memorial service organized by Dee Ann Wood. Guests lingered in the courtyard for a moment of silence next to the remembrance plaque and rosebush in full bloom.

Pastor Glen Thorp, who had left the community seven years earlier, returned to officiate, and led the congregation in singing three hymns, all of which had been sung at the last service attended by Ann in 1991. A doorway to the room where Ann's Elizabeth circle had often met could be seen at one side of the sanctuary. It didn't take much imagination to hear the echoes of her voice expressing fear of being killed and that her body would never be found.

Four speakers paid tribute to Ann. Dee Ann Wood recalled activities she had shared with her dear friend. Joann shared fond memories and her mother's lessons about "peace in life." Glenn Racz said, "I love my mom so much," and he stated that the trial had helped him remember wonderful things about her, especially the inspiration to accept religion in his life. Emi Ryan noted that Ann would always remain young in memory, and never have to suffer the ill effects of aging. Her voice broke while trying to hold back tears.

Afterward, everyone adjourned to an adjacent hall for a buffet luncheon, and the atmosphere turned joyous with lively conversations topped by laughter. Those seated around eight round tables included Beth Silverman, Frank Salerno, Louie Danoff, Sally Fynan, Bob Russell, Glen Thorp, Emi and Jerry Ryan, with daughters Kathy and Patty, Joji and Takeo Yoshi-yama, Glenn Racz, with wife Amber, Joanne Racz, Susan Kato, who was Ann's childhood playmate and bridesmaid, members of Ann's church circle and numerous other friends.

Bob Russell, a quiet, gentle man, slim and youthful in appearance, could be seen chatting softly with Joann and Glenn, followed by handshakes and embraces. Juror Barbara Kaplan had wished for forgiveness by Ann's children, and it appeared to be granted.

The cathartic, emotion-charged, festive event closed the curtain, for many, on nearly two decades of investigation, uncertainty, conflict, trial, and, at last, resolution.

Acknowledgments

By a long shot, the best part of writing nonfiction is the pleasure of meeting so many terrific people while researching the subject. Ranking in very close second place are the amazing coincidences that leave me dumbstruck. Some of them seem to prove the "six degrees of separation" theory. Two remarkable incidents came up in this case.

I sat outside a Starbucks with Joji Yoshiyama, asking him all about Ann and his family history. He spoke of his experiences during World War II as an "internee," then mentioned that his best friend in the Colorado camp was a kid named Eddy Tanaka, who later became the director of Public Welfare in Los Angeles County. It blew me away.

Ed Tanaka and I had been classmates, among only twenty-eight seniors, at Courtland High School, a few miles down the Sacramento River from California's capital city. I e-mailed Ed and told him of meeting Joji. They subsequently got together for lunch, seeing one another for the first time in six decades.

Digging into Beth Silverman's background, I learned that

she had grown up in Westlake Village, the daughter of a prominent physician. At Christmas I visited in-laws who also live in the large community, and asked if any of them knew a Dr. Silverman. Yes. He had delivered several children in the room, including my niece and nephew, twins, who would soon celebrate their fifth birthday. By sheer happenstance, Beth and her father later showed up at their birthday party. I love it!

The list of marvelous new friends I made on this project includes Emi and Jerry Ryan, who welcomed Ron Bowers and me into their beautiful Mesa, Arizona, home. They patiently allowed us to drag them through those painful years, answered all of our questions and provided us with numerous photos depicting the history of Emi's family. Emi is one of my favorite people ever, and Jerry is the perfect mate for her. Joji, also personable and accommodating, came up with even more great photos.

Bowers and I visited the charming Dee Ann Wood in her home. She, too, provided pictures and guided us on a driving tour of the key sites where this story unfolded.

Barbara Kaplan, the juror who believed her service on the panel had been preordained, gave me a fascinating interview. Juror Georgette Adams also volunteered to help me.

Joann Racz, one of the bravest young women it's been my pleasure to meet, cheerfully took me through her bittersweet memories.

I was honored with an invitation to the April 22, 2008, memorial for Ann, and attended the ceremony/luncheon, along with Ron Bowers. Afterward, he and I drove Bob Russell to the Burbank Airport for his return flight home. Bob spoke frankly to us of his relationship with Ann, his fear for many months that John Racz might want to kill him, and his hopes of redemption for Ann's family. He is truly a nice guy, one of the many it was my pleasure to meet during this entire project.

In the courthouse, I had the great fortune of chatting informally with Judge Ronald Coen (not about the case), Louis Danoff, Frank Salerno, Dee Scott, Cheryl Comstock, and

Philip Israels. I also met several of the Elizabeth circle members, including Judy Carter. Plus I got a great big hug from Beth Silverman.

After Emi Ryan delivered her talk at that hearing, which had half the crowd in tears, I saw court reporter Barbara Reed drying her eyes, asking Emi for a copy of the speech. Barbara hadn't been able to transcribe it completely because she'd been sobbing while Emi spoke. I knew right then that I really liked Barbara.

In court records research, I had the generous help of Carol Klimer and Carla Price.

Photographer Gregory Bojorquez snapped that classic portrait of the defendant sitting at the defense table.

As the reader knows, I had a brief chat and handshake with John Racz.

I am often asked if I interview the perpetrators. I have interviewed several (after adjudication), and I've sent letters to most of the killers inviting them to tell their sides of the stories. The great majority write back, saying their appeals attorneys advise them to keep their mouths shut. John Racz did not give me the courtesy of a reply. I suspect he was influenced by a legal advice.

—Don Lasseter, 2008.

Los Angeles district attorney Steve Cooley has provided the leadership, with his able chief deputy John K. Spillane, to tackle difficult "no-body" prosecutions. I have the greatest respect for Assistant DA Curt Hazell for his willingness to take on the toughest of cases, knowing they will be time-consuming and full of risks

I think my admiration of Beth Silverman is clearly manifested in this book. She understands the importance of being well prepared while simultaneously recognizing the usefulness of technology to better present her case to jurors. Although Beth is a fast talker, she possesses the capacity to listen to suggestions and is always interested in improving her legal skills. She has blossomed into one of the elite, highly skilled trial lawyers in the DA's office. I would like to take credit for her success, since I originally hired her to work for the office, but I recognize that her achievement is due to her talent and hard work.

—Ronald Bowers

MORE SHOCKING TRUE CRIME
FROM PINNACLE